CONTENTS

NORTH CAPE	124
ANNE'S LAND	136
CHARLOTTE'S SHORE	146
BAYS AND DUNES	153
HILLS AND HARBOURS	161
LISTINGS	169
Index	202
Photo Credits	208

Library and Archives Canada Cataloguing in Publication

Prince Edward Island colourguide. / edited by Laurie Brinklow. — 4th ed.

Includes index.
ISBN 0-88780-653-8

1. Prince Edward Island—Guidebooks. I. Brinklow, Laurie

FC2607.P733 2005   917.1704'4
C2005-900779-6

Formac Publishing Company Limited
5502 Atlantic Street, Halifax, Nova Scotia
B3H 1G4 • www.formac.ca

Distributed in the United States by:
Casemate
2114 Darby Road, 2nd Floor
Havertown, PA 19083

Distributed in the United Kingdom by:
Portfolio Book Limited
Unit 5, Perivale Industrial Park
Horsenden Lane South, Greenford, UK
UB6 7RL

Printed and bound in China.

Formac Publishing Company Limited acknowledges the support of the Cultural Affairs Section, Nova Scotia Department of Tourism and Culture. We acknowledge the financial support of the Government of Canada through the Book Publishing Industry Development Program (BPIDP) for our publishing activities.

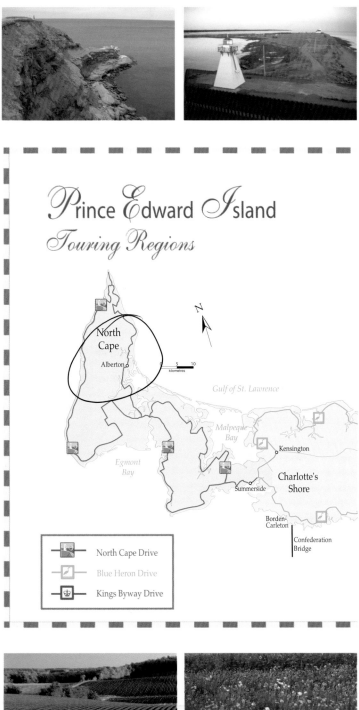

Prince Edward Island
Touring Regions

North Cape

Alberton

Gulf of St. Lawrence

Malpeque Bay

Kensington

Egmont Bay

Summerside

Charlotte's Shore

Borden-Carleton

Confederation Bridge

North Cape Drive

Blue Heron Drive

Kings Byway Drive

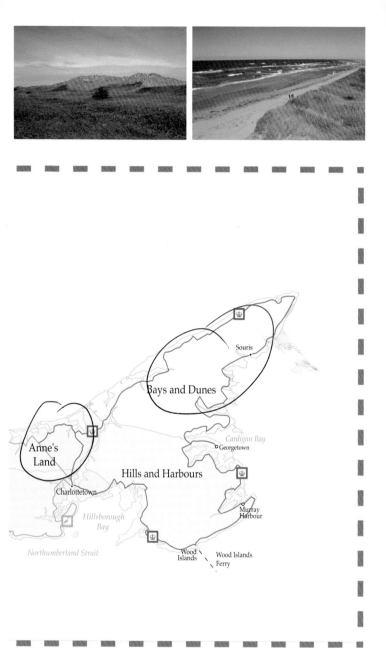

Souris

Bays and Dunes

Cardigan Bay
○ Georgetown

Anne's Land

Hills and Harbours

• Charlottetown

Hillsborough Bay

○ Murray Harbour

Northumberland Strait

Wood Islands

Wood Islands Ferry

Welcome to Prince Edward Island!

This guide has been written to help you prepare a vacation in Canada's smallest province, giving you not only an introduction to the very best that Prince Edward Island has to offer but also detailed information on places to stay, where to eat and many other facilities.

The Island's Best section gives an overview of the landscape and cultural activities. It is followed by the Island Routes section, offering a tour of each of the five regions. The final section of the guide contains listings, with practical information on everything you will want to do in Prince Edward Island: accommodations, restaurants, museums, parks and other attractions.

This book is an independent guide. Its editors and contributors have made their recommendations and suggestions based solely on what they believe to the best, most interesting and most appealing places to visit.

No payments or contributions of any kind are solicited or accepted by the creators or the publishers of this guide.

This book is the work of a team of talented writers, editors and photographers. You can read about them below:

LAURIE BRINKLOW is a writer, editor and book publisher. She is Publications Co-ordinator at the University of Prince Edward Island and publisher of The Acorn Press. She lives in Charlottetown with her two daughters.

KUMARI CAMPBELL lives near Souris. She owns and operates a consulting company which primarily handles tourism marketing. She likes to write about travel and food, writes poetry in her spare time and nurtures the dream of writing fiction.

LOBIE DAUGHTON has published numerous feature articles and essays, on everything from sushi to xenotransplantation. He loves poetry and runs a retreat for writers. Lobie was the recipient of the Quebec-Labrador Foundation "Caring for the Earth Award" in 2000. He has made his home on Prince Edward Island for the past 23 years.

MIKE GAUTHIER is a reporter for *The Guardian* and a sometime avid golfer.

H. SHIRLEY HORNE is an award-winning Charlottetown freelance writer.

JOCELYNE LLOYD is a copy editor for the *Journal-Pioneer* and a freelance writer. A former lifeguard, she spends her summers looking for the perfect beach.

ANNA MACDONALD is publicist at the Confederation Centre of the Arts. She lives in Mount Stewart.

HUGH MACDONALD is a retired high-school teacher; author of a children's book, *Chung Lee Loves Lobsters*; four books of poetry, and a novel, *Murder at*

Mussel Cove. He lives with his family in Brudenell.

WENDY MACGREGOR married into an Island family and has been spending summers in PEI ever since. She winters in Halifax with her husband and three children, but they are all passionate part-time Islanders.

JOY BELL MACKENZIE is an avid cottager and proud Prince Edward Islander. With her husband and two children she has been a cottage renter, and then owner, for 15 years — mostly in the Cavendish area. She lives and works in Charlottetown.

WAYNE MACKINNON is the author of a number of books and articles on Prince Edward Island history and politics.

IAN MACQUARRIE is a retired professor of biology at the University of Prince Edward Island. He is the author of *The Bonshaw Hills* (Institute of Island Studies).

RYAN VICTORIA McADAM-YOUNG is a graduate of the Atlantic Tourism and Hospitality Institute. She has worked for the last five years as a writer and event co-ordinator in Prince Edward Island. In her free time Ryan enjoys creating handcrafts.

DAN McASKILL is a naturalist, birder and writer who lives in Donagh. He is co-author, with Kate MacQuarrie, of *Nature Trails of Prince Edward Island* (Ragweed) and edits *The Island Naturalist*.

ANNE McCALLUM is the media and communications officer at the University of Prince Edward Island. She has worked as a commentary writer for CBC Radio and has written extensively on agriculture and rural topics in Prince Edward Island. She lives in Hazel Grove.

REG PORTER is an historical consultant and former lecturer in art history at the University of Prince Edward Island. He is retired and lives in Belle River.

FAYE POUND lives in Summerside with her husband and twin daughters. She has written extensively on Prince County heritage for the *Journal-Pioneer*, served on the Board of Governors for the PEI Museum and Heritage Foundation, helped establish Wyatt Heritage Properties, and received awards for her work in promoting Island heritage and architectural renovations.

NANCY RUSSELL travels the Island with her sons Callum and Tristan and husband Rob. She has worked as a journalist across Canada with CBC radio and television. She's also the author of several novels for young adults.

JULIE V. WATSON of Charlottetown has had several books published, as well as hundreds of articles in North America and abroad. She specializes in food, travel and entrepreneurship. Her favourite topics are the people and places of Prince Edward Island.

CAMPBELL WEBSTER runs Campbell Webster Entertainment, which represents a number of well-known celebrities and performers. He formerly led cycling tours of the Island, and in 1990 wrote *Cycling the Islands* (Breakwater).

INTRODUCTION

LAURIE BRINKLOW

There's something about "The Island" that makes you feel like you're home. Maybe it's the peaceful landscape, with its rolling hills of red and green, set against the clear blue of the ocean and sky — so sharp, so focused, the colours seldom run together. Maybe it's the ordered countryside, civilized and well-tended, with strict signage laws, Women's Institute annual roadside and beach garbage clean-ups, and laws prohibiting the sale of pop and beer in cans. Maybe it's the way everyone from gas attendants to restaurant servers call you "Dear" — even the 16-year-olds. Or maybe it's because it's an island, a place set apart that conjures up magic and mystery, generally involving a ferry ride or a drive across one of the longest bridges in the world.

Whatever it is, Prince Edward Island is a special place, one with a deep sense of history that comes from a strong attachment to the land. This is understandable, since it's a small island, with only a finite amount of it. And, for the longest time, Prince Edward Islanders couldn't even own land. In 1767, the British Crown parcelled out the Island in 67 lots to about 100 British noblemen, merchants and army officers in a lottery. It took over a century of appeals and arguments — and even the odd bit of rebellion (and joining

the rest of Canada) — to be able to own a piece of it.

For the past few centuries farming, fishing and forestry were the mainstays of the Island economy. As you drive past potato and blueberry fields and grassy meadows dotted with cows, or see fishing boats chugging into harbour, you can still see where your food comes from — not always possible in this global world we live in today. But Islanders, always resourceful, have taken those traditional industries and have built on them: today manufacturing is the Number 1 industry, with growing aerospace, bio-resource and other technology-based industries joining the food-processing sector.

Islanders are lucky to live in a place where we can keep one foot firmly planted in the pastoral and the other in the information age, which is one of the reasons tourists love our Island — more than a million visitors every year. For many, PEI is symbolic of a simpler age: when you don't have to rush to keep pace, where you can slow down and enjoy a real vacation, take long, meandering drives, splash in the warmest water north of the Carolinas, and soak up a landscape that's tranquil and idyllic. Yet you can pick up the pace when you want, with theatre and music, restaurants and cafés, book launches and readings, museums and galleries, golfing and sailing — activities sure to please the most discerning of travellers.

You may be coming to the Island for a relaxing time on the beach, to check out our historic lighthouses and churches, to play a few rounds of golf, or to try out the hiking and biking. You may be coming to experience some of our history and culture, such as the Birthplace of Confederation or to see where *Anne of Green Gables* came from. Or maybe it's the landscape you want to see: these photographs are really just a teaser! Whatever your reason, we invite you to take a step back, take a deep breath and enjoy the Island and its people.

The chapters in this *Colourguide* have been written by people who are experts in the subjects they cover — and all good writers, too. The five tours, as named by Tourism

PEI, are all presented by writers who live in or near that particular area. They were asked to pretend that you are a favourite relative or best friend coming for a visit. Where would they take you? And what would they tell you? You might be surprised that for such a small place, there are so many things to see and do.

Finally, a guide book needs to have the basic information you need to get around. We've divided the Listings section into practical categories, including some of our writers' recommended places to stay, eat and visit, and some of their favourite things to do. Included are names, addresses, telephone numbers, websites, hours of operation and other helpful information you might need to know to make your stay on Prince Edward Island a memorable one. With any luck, it won't be your last!

LAND AND SEA

IAN MACQUARRIE

ORBY HEAD

Islands are different. Lack of physical contact with the mainland allows life to go its own way, to develop separate patterns and to foster uncommon relationships. With both plants and people, there is an island way of surviving.

Not that mainlands aren't important. Indeed, Prince Edward Island was once firmly joined to the continent; rising waters in Northumberland Strait effected a divorce comparatively recently, perhaps only 5,000 years ago, and signs of the old union are still quite evident. A few millennia earlier, glaciers thoroughly scoured the land, resetting the ecological clock. Much before that, erosion of ancient mountains provided material for the sedimentary bedrock on which the Island stands. These widely spaced historical occurrences have left a legacy of markers for the modern explorer.

GEOLOGY, GEOGRAPHY, BASIC ECOLOGY

The Island rests upon part of a great plain of sedimentary rocks, formed in Permocarboniferous times and now mostly submerged by the Gulf of St. Lawrence. Prince Edward Island and the Magdalen Islands (with parts of

Nova Scotia and New Brunswick) are still above the tides, and bear witness to the character of this bedrock. The typical red colour of the bedrock is from its oxidized

GRAND RIVER
ESTUARY

iron (rust) content. Informally, these rocks are called "redbeds," which are younger than the granite, slate and quartzite so evident in neighbouring provinces. Redbeds are soft, easily broken and eroded or smoothed by water and ice action. Fossils are uncommon. Rocky outcrops are highly visible along the coastline, but inland a thin mantle of glacial debris (till) now hides most of this foundation.

VICTORIA HARBOUR

The arrangement of bedrock controls general land form; the orientation of rivers, hills and valleys is as old as the rocks themselves. However, much more recently glaciers reorganized the landscape. The advance of the ice brought granite boulders from the mainland. These erratic visitors are common in the western part of the province. The glacier's huge weight crushed and scoured the terrain, smoothing the hills and actually pushing the land itself down. As the ice melted and retreated, beginning about 14,000 years ago, relationships between land and sea were quite changeable. Shell-encrusted beach terraces in western Prince Edward Island are now well above sea level; the land rebounded when released from its burden. Later, to the east, forests were drowned as the sea came surging back.

As glaciers retreated, plants and animals occupied the newly exposed ground. Some, following the ice closely, were able to reach the Island before the land bridge was inundated. Others never made it, or were forced to wait for thousands of years and catch a ride with humans. The Island flora and fauna contain no unique species, but the diversity and abundance are different from our neighbouring provinces. Later, the arrival of European settlers resulted in many rapid additions and deletions to the lists. Thus, disturbances hundreds to thousands of years ago brought about change that is still occurring; Island ecology still hasn't settled down.

At present, this is a small, crescent-shaped island, in area about 5,600 km^2, or one-tenth the size of Nova Scotia.

FARM NEAR NEW LONDON

TOP: BURLINGTON
RIGHT: DARNLEY
BASIN

The distance from tip to tip is about 230 km, with a highly variable width due to a much-indented coastline. No part of the Island is more than a few hours' walk from salt water, and this closeness to the sea profoundly affects all life. The sea is slowly claiming the land; coastal erosion may capture one metre per year (more in some places). The broad estuaries are drowned river valleys; rivers were longer when the sea level was lower. These productive estuaries, fertilized from the land and warmed by the sun, are important in the lives of many species, including humans. Fishing and farming have been Island mainstays since settlement began.

The tidal range in this part of the Gulf is not great; high and low lines on a wharf are often only a couple of metres apart. However, the waters, particularly on the Strait shore, shoal so gently that even a short tide drop may expose a kilometre of sand bars. While the soft bedrock provides poor holding ground for marine algae (seaweeds), the bars and mud flats are good habitat for shellfish. There is no

CAVENDISH CLIFFS

shortage of sand for beaches, often backed by dunes on the north and eastern shores. Seaward drainage may be blocked by the dunes, providing more rich coastal wetlands and ponds.

SUNSET, BRACKLEY BEACH

Inland, the topography is undulating and gentle: even the hills in central and eastern Prince Edward Island are seldom over a hundred metres high. The red soil looks deceptively fertile; it is really only a thin, fragile skin stretched over glacial rubble, with bedrock never far below the surface. The land is easily worked, but it requires lime and fertilizer for good crops. Farming has, perhaps only temporarily, shaped the surface and particularly the appearance of this land. The trees remain at the fringes, ever ready to return.

FLORA

While the Island, like its neighbours, belongs to the Acadian forest region, its isolation and profound degree of disturbance by European settlement result in a different array of species. As the glacial ice retreated, tundra-like vegetation followed closely; this, in turn, was displaced by spruce and pine, with the Acadian beech/sugar maple/yellow birch complex following later still. Indeed, many of the slower-migrating plants never got here at all. The aboriginal inhabitants would have known an excellent forest, with fine trees in both hardwood and softwood stands. This was the forest encountered by the Europeans, and they proceeded with great passion to cut, burn or clear almost all of it.

TRAIL AT GREEN GABLES

Forests today cover almost 50 per cent of the Island, but the composition is a shadow of the original; it is regrowth, with only scattered old trees remaining. Disease has decimated the beech. The mighty pines are mostly gone, as is the red oak, the Island's provincial tree. Many early settlers cleared,

TOP: PURPLE LOOSESTRIFE AT WEST POINT
RIGHT: LADY SLIPPER

burned and then moved on; the land grew up into a new forest, dominated by white spruce, alder and, after a time, white birch. Short-lived species such as poplar and cherry are much more common now. It is good wildlife habitat, but contributes little to the provincial economy.

The settlers brought with them, by accident or design, many Eurasian plants; hundreds of these became successful in their new home. Almost one-third of the present vascular flora can be traced to such recent introductions. Many of our most troublesome weeds first crossed the Atlantic with the immigrants, and remained here after the more restless humans moved on to New England or western Canada. Daisy and hawk-weed are found now with the earlier-arrived goldenrod and wild strawberry; this multicultural mix is pleasing to the eye if not to the farmer's pocketbook.

Changing agricultural patterns also led to the contraction or expansion of species range. Lupins, troublesome weeds in pastures, were once strictly controlled by farmers. Now they riot for miles along roadsides; a weed has become a photo opportunity, its picture infesting the tourist literature. On the other hand, the opportunistic purple loosestrife of the marshes is widely condemned, although the rhetoric greatly exceeds any significant control measures. There are fashions in wild plants, as well as in their garden relatives, and yesterday's enemy may become tomorrow's friend.

WILDFLOWER MEADOW

FAUNA

Animal presence, or absence, has been controlled by the same factors: glaciation, land bridge and human settlement with addition and deletion. Some common mainland animals never got here; the porcupine and white-tail deer are conspicuous by their absence. Domestication of the native red fox brought about a short-lived bonanza for fur ranchers early in this century. Other non-native mammals such as the raccoon and skunk were then brought in by optimistic ranchers. The market for such fur was not as

ANCIENT APPLE TREE AT MACNEILL HOMESTEAD, CAVENDISH

17

TOP: ABANDONED FARM
MIDDLE: SEAL PUP
BOTTOM: RED FOX

strong as expected. Consequently, the animals were released and they happily spread over the entire Island.

When they became nuisances, larger animals such as the bobcat and black bear were easily exterminated, as was the beaver (since reintroduced). The latest addition is the coyote, first noted in the 1980s and now at home everywhere, including suburbia. The still-common red fox, once the Island's main mammalian predator, is now readjusting its life to this new rival, as are livestock farmers and pet-owners.

Relatively few amphibians and reptiles arrived before rising water cut off the land route. Only three species of snakes are present — inconspicuous ones at that — while there are no turtles or tortoises at all. On the other hand, most of the expected mice, voles, chipmunks and squirrels, minks and weasels are fortunately present; they seem to cope with modern Prince Edward Island with little difficulty.

SETTLEMENT

The first recorded comment on the Island came from Jacques Cartier, in 1534. He wrote of its beauty, of its tall trees and of the potential for good farms. He also saw aboriginal people in canoes, who obviously had much earlier priority in discovery.

Archaeological digs have established the presence of humans at least 10,000

years ago. Shell mounds and tools are evidence that this Island provided a home for native populations for millennia. Their hunting economy would leave little mark on the landscape.

This was to change as the French arrived. Settlement began in the early decades of the 18th century, with the establishment of the first permanent Acadian communities. They were coast-dwellers; for a time their habit of using marshlands left much of the upland undisturbed. However, as the population grew, forest clearing, particularly burning, began in earnest. By 1755 perhaps 4,000 people were present, but the legacy from the old country included war, and the victory of the British led to the expulsion of the Acadians in 1758. A few escaped deportation and rebuilt their culture, but Île Saint-Jean became St. John's Island.

The British dealt with their new acquisition in a curious way. It was roughly surveyed and divided into 67 parcels of 20,000 acres each, more or less, which were then awarded to worthy supplicants through a lottery. Most of

TOP: YOUNG TURNIPS AT ORWELL CORNER
MIDDLE: PIPING PLOVER

GREAT BLUE HERON AT FRENCH RIVER

FARM ON THE NORTH SHORE

the winners became absentee landlords; their struggles with tenants (and each other) dominated the political life of the Island until after Confederation. Thus was born the "Land Question" — who may own land and under what conditions — which remains an emotional issue today.

Now non-resident land ownership is discouraged. Exactly how many acres a farmer may own has been the subject of innumerable enquiries, commissions, regulations ... not to mention sermons and letters to the editor. Some issues seem immortal.

In the 19th century, successive waves of land-hungry immigrants, mainly from the British Isles, reached the shores of Prince Edward Island. Irish and Scots put aside homeland differences in a new struggle. The forest was now the enemy, to be destroyed by any means. Thousands of small farms and hundreds of rural communities were established, many being quickly abandoned once the realities of agriculture in this climate became clear. A century ago the Island supported about 100,000 people, primarily on about 15,000 farms or in other rural trades. Today, the number of farms has shrunk to about 2,000; the present population of just under 140,000 is decidedly urban-oriented. While agriculture remains an important part of the economy, tourism is now becoming the major industry. Landscape beauty is more important than food production, and perhaps that's the way it should be.

CHARLOTTETOWN FROM VICTORIA PARK

FEATURES

CONFEDERATION

WAYNE MACKINNON

PROVINCE HOUSE, CHARLOTTETOWN

To hear Islanders tell it, you'd think it was they who invented Canada. For years, the province has touted itself as "the Cradle of Confederation." Province House, the seat of the Island's legislature, where the Fathers of Confederation first met in 1864, is a national historic shrine, as is the street where the delegates walked from their ships to attend that celebrated Charlottetown Conference.

As proud as Islanders are of their role as Canada's birthplace, when they joined the rest of Canada in 1873 the Governor General was moved to remark that they were "quite under the impression that it is the Dominion that has been annexed to Prince Edward Island."

Truth is, the only reason Prince Edward Island became the Birthplace, or Cradle, of Confederation was that the Island delegates refused to attend any conference unless it was held on the Island. And when the people of Prince Edward Island finally decided to join the rest of Canada, their reasons were motivated more by pragmatism than by patriotism to their newly adopted country.

Established as a separate colony in 1769, the Island had long struggled against external domination. Its inhabitants fought to gain control of their own land against a system of absentee proprietorship. The need to gain autonomy was reflected in the long and sometimes bitter struggle for self-government. Islanders became solidly and strongly united behind the desire to win independence for themselves and their little country.

By the 1850s, Islanders had achieved a remarkable degree of progress on their "million-acre farm." The land was being steadily cleared and settled, and the neat pattern of farms and fields defined the nature of rural communities and the gently rolling countryside. Shipbuilding brought prosperity, and there was a flourishing local manufacturing industry. With a growing population and expanding economy came great optimism. Such was the level of confidence by Islanders in their independent status and outlook that they hosted a U.S. Congressional delegation in the 1860s to discuss free trade between Prince Edward Island and the United States.

Islanders had also developed a strong sense of their own identity. The constant tension with Great Britain over the land issue and the struggle for responsible government instilled a deep attachment to local institutions, and quickly led to their "coming of age." The farm, the school, the church and the local government became the centre of their world in "that little end of all creation."

This was not fertile ground for discussions of a union with neighbouring colonies, let alone with Upper and Lower Canada. When the idea of a Maritime Union was promoted in the early 1860s, largely by the British-appointed governors of the region, there was little support. The Island government grudgingly appointed delegates to attend a conference to discuss Maritime Union in 1864, but insisted the conference take place in Charlottetown. At the same time, the Canadian government was considering a broader union of all the British North American colonies. Led by John A. Macdonald, it inquired whether it could send delegates to discuss its proposals.

LIGHTHOUSE AT CHARLOTTETOWN HARBOUR

And so came about the Charlottetown Conference of 1864. For Islanders, the timing could not have been worse. The first circus in 21 years had come to Charlottetown, and there was no room for all the delegates in the capital's few small hotels. Only one member of the government was on hand to greet the Canadian delegates when their ship arrived in Charlottetown Harbour. Summoning as much dignity as was possible under the circum-stances, he rowed out in a small oyster boat to welcome them.

But ever the gracious hosts, Islanders treated the Fathers of Confederation to a round of meetings, banquets and balls. George Brown, one of the Canadian delegates, said, "The ice became completely broken, the tongues of the delegates wagged merrily and the banns of matrimony between all the provinces of British North America formally proclaimed."

The idea of uniting the three Maritime provinces under a single government, which

(continued on page 26)

ONCE UPON AN ISLAND TIME

WAYNE MACKINNON

PROVINCIAL CLOCK

If Prince Edward Islanders were concerned about the loss of their distinctive identity following Confederation, they were not prepared for an assault on one of the symbols of that identity: their own time.

The Island prized its independence. Its geographical separateness gave the Island its own sense of place. And it had its own local time, measured as "twelve minutes and twenty-nine seconds fast of the local time of the meridian which passes through the Provincial Clock on the Law Courts Building in Charlottetown." With their own sense of time and place, Islanders considered themselves in complete harmony with the universe.

Islanders were therefore thunderstruck with the heretical proposal to adopt a new system called Standard Time. The concept of Standard Time was first introduced at a conference in Washington in 1884, where agreement was reached to arbitrarily divide the world into uniform time zones. A document circulated throughout Canada advocated the notion that time "is in no way influenced by matter, locality, distance or space," and went on to assert boldly that it was "essentially non-local." The view that time was "non-local" struck at the heart of one of Islanders' most cherished beliefs.

The campaign to introduce Standard Time was unrelenting and unremitting. When Canada adopted it in 1884, Dominion Government offices on the Island switched to Atlantic Standard Time, twelve minutes and twenty-nine seconds ahead of Island Time. The Island's railway switched to Eastern Standard Time to conform with the Dominion railway schedule. That was forty-seven minutes and thirty-one seconds behind Island Time. The result was confusion and annoyance. For example, to travel to Charlottetown to conduct business with the Dominion government, one would get up on Island Time, catch the train on Eastern Standard Time and make an appointment on Atlantic Standard Time.

The railways' switch to Eastern Standard Time was particularly galling. Islanders bitterly recalled that one of the conditions under which it was forced into Confederation involved giving up control over their own railway and they were unwilling to tolerate the further ignominy of the railway operating on "Upper Canadian" time.

Seizing on the confusion, proponents of Standard Time introduced a bill, An Act to Alter the Present Method of Reckoning Time, on April Fool's Day of 1889. Proponents made it clear the Island had little choice in the matter. Pointing out that since Standard Time was generally adopted throughout North America, "No deviation of the rule will be permitted in this Island."

Opposition to this affront on the Island's right to self-determination was swift. A Mr. Sinclair rose in the legislature and denounced the bill. "I believe that Standard Time was adopted on the Dominion railways for the accommodation of strangers," he thundered. A Mr. Bell said the Dominion government had erred when it adopted Standard Time in the first place, and that Prince Edward Island should not further compound the mistake. Their remarks were greeted with loud applause from the public gallery.

Nonetheless, the bill passed, and the Island lost its

own time. A local paper reported on the adoption of Standard Time. "The minutes and the seconds are now the same everywhere," it lamented.

One dark night in May of 1889, three officials climbed the narrow stairs of the Law Courts Building and wrenched the hands of the Provincial Clock ahead by twelve minutes and twenty-nine seconds. The Island has never been the same since.

KENSINGTON RAILWAY STATION

FANNINGBANK, THE LIEUTENANT-GOVERNOR'S RESIDENCE

was not widely supported in any case, quickly died. The Canadian proposals, which would establish a federal union under which local governments would retain some measure of control over their own affairs, were generally favoured by all delegates, including those from Prince Edward Island.

Although the Island delegation continued to participate in subsequent discussions, they had little interest in joining. They feared their individuality and identity would be lost forever and the interests of their small province subsumed by the larger union.

Confederation was also seen to be politically and economically disastrous to Prince Edward Island. The Island delegates were concerned that under the terms of union they would have little representation in a federal parliament and the role of their own legislature would be significantly reduced. Opponents said there would be little left for politicians to do but "legislate on the running about of dogs."

The result was predictable: Islanders and their government rejected Confederation outright. They were generally indifferent about the founding of the new nation on July 1, 1867, and regarded their neighbouring provinces which had joined the union with a mixture of smugness, piety and pity.

CONFEDERATION BRIDGE AT SUNSET

The Island's decision was a cause of consternation in both Canada and Great Britain. Eventually, the Canadian government, in a move to woo the Island into Confederation, came up with what it called "better terms." Following half-hearted discussions on the part of the Island government, the offer was rejected, and Prime Minister Macdonald felt he and his ministers had been "humbugged."

Finally, it was the spectre of economic ruin which brought the Island back to the table. In 1871, the Island government undertook construction of a railway with the promise of new prosperity. The contractors were to be paid by the mile and as a result the lines snaked their way across the province, pushing the project beyond the Island's limited financial capacity.

The Island government, finding it difficult to raise funds from lenders, was forced to reconsider. Representatives of the Island government went to Ottawa to see if the "better terms" offer was still on the table. Agreement was finally reached and put to the people in an election.

By now Islanders had generally recognized they had no choice. After extracting a few concessions Prince Edward Island became Canada's smallest province on July 1, 1873.

Over the years Islanders have sought to reconcile their traditions of independence and self-reliance with their subordinate and dependent role within Confederation. It has not always been easy. Shortly after Confederation the Island economy went into decline. The shipbuilding industry, based on the construction of wooden vessels, all but disappeared. Thousands of Islanders left their homeland to go to the Boston States and other destinations.

CONFEDERATION CENTRE OF THE ARTS

Today, the railway is gone, the Confederation Bridge is open, and the Island's cultural traditions have faced the great challenge of mass communications. Yet Islanders remain committed to their way of life. In 1973, on the hundredth anniversary of joining Confederation, a semi-satirical group was called into existence for the year to protest what it called the distortion of the Island's resistance to Confederation and to remind Islanders of their history of independent-mindedness. It was named the Brothers and Sisters of Cornelius Howatt, after one of the two politicians who voted against Confederation.

For a small geographical and political unit to maintain its distinct identity inside a vast country is a testament to the Island's strong traditions. As Lucy Maud Montgomery wrote in her autobiography, Islanders "may suspect that [the Island] isn't quite perfect, any more than any other spot on this planet, but you will not catch us admitting it."

HORSE AND CARRIAGE, DOWNTOWN CHARLOTTETOWN

THE REAL LUCY MAUD MONTGOMERY

ANNA MACDONALD

For most people, Prince Edward Island conjures up images of white sand beaches, red roads and *Anne of Green Gables*, the fictional red-headed orphan created by Island-born writer L.M. Montgomery. Anne's familiar face with its red braids and freckles forms the centre of a thriving industry here, appearing everywhere from gift shops to licence plates. But how well do people, Islanders and visitors alike, know Lucy Maud Montgomery, author of *Anne of Green Gables*?

L.M. Montgomery was born in Clifton (now New London), Prince Edward Island, on November 30, 1874, to Hugh John Montgomery and Clara Woolner Macneill. Shortly after Montgomery's birth, her mother developed tuberculosis. Clara became so ill that Hugh John moved her and their baby daughter to Cavendish to stay with Clara's parents, Alexander and Lucy Woolner Macneill. In 1876, Clara died, leaving behind her husband and 21-month-old Maud. With the death of his wife and the

failure of his business in Clifton, Hugh John left his daughter with the Macneills and moved to Saskatchewan, where he eventually settled in Prince Albert and married Mary Ann McRae.

At the time of their daughter's death, Alexander and Lucy Woolner Macneill were in their mid-50s and had already raised six children. To be faced at this point in their lives with bringing up another child, especially one as lively, emotional and intelligent as Montgomery, must have been daunting for them. For emotional sustenance, Montgomery turned to nature, books, her imagination and especially to writing.

ABOVE AND BELOW: LUCY MAUD MONTGOMERY'S BIRTHPLACE IN NEW LONDON

Montgomery did not lose touch with other members of her parents' families, particularly her paternal grandfather, Senator Donald Montgomery, and her Uncle John and Aunt Annie (her mother's sister) Campbell in Park Corner. There, she found the warm family atmosphere that was lacking in her Cavendish home. Her Grandfather

Montgomery, who lived close to the Campbells, enjoyed her company, and her young Campbell cousins kept her well-entertained. She developed a love for Park Corner that was to last a lifetime.

In 1880, at the age of

L.M. MONTGOMERY MUSEUM, PARK CORNER

six, she began attending school in Cavendish. In 1890, at age 15, she decided she wanted to live with her father in Prince Albert. While there, she wrote a poem and sent it to *The Patriot*, a newspaper in Charlottetown. To her great joy, *The Patriot* printed it.

She stayed in Prince Albert for a year, but homesickness and an unhappy relationship with her stepmother brought her back to Cavendish. She returned to school in 1892-93 to prepare for entrance exams to Prince of Wales College in Charlottetown, where she studied for a teacher's licence. She completed the two-year course in one year, finishing with honours.

In 1894, Montgomery began her teaching career in Bideford, a small community over 70 kilometres west of Cavendish. After teaching there for a year, she spent a year (1895-96) at Dalhousie University in Halifax, where she received her first payments for her writing by publishing poems and short stories in Canadian and American newspapers and magazines. She returned to Prince Edward Island in the spring of 1896 and in the fall took a teaching post in Belmont. She stayed there until July of 1897, continuing to write and becoming secretly — and soon unhappily — engaged to her second cousin, Edwin Simpson.

She then obtained what was to be her last teaching post in Lower Bedeque, a community close to Summerside, and while still engaged to Simpson fell in love with a young farmer, Herman Leard, with whose parents she boarded. Although she loved Leard passionately, she did not pursue this romance because she knew she could never marry him. In June 1899, Herman Leard died of complications brought on by influenza.

PARLOUR AT PARK CORNER

While Montgomery was teaching in Lower Bedeque, Grandfather Macneill died suddenly on March 6, 1898. She returned to Cavendish to care for her grandmother, broke her engagement to Simpson, became assistant post-mistress and wrote when she could. With the exception of a nine-month stay in Halifax in 1901-02 when she worked as a proofreader for the *Daily Echo*, she remained in Cavendish for the next 13 years. In 1906, she became engaged — again secretly — to Reverend Ewan Macdonald, then the Presbyterian minister in Cavendish. When her grandmother died in 1911 she married him.

GARDEN AT GREEN GABLES

The years Montgomery spent in Cavendish with her grandmother were very productive. She sent off scores of poems, stories and serials to various Canadian, British and American magazines. In the spring of 1905, she wrote her first novel, *Anne of Green Gables*, published in 1908 by the Page Company of Boston after several other publishing companies had rejected it. Following its immediate success, she wrote three more bestsellers: *Anne of Avonlea* (1909); *Kilmeny of the Orchard* (1910); and *The Story Girl* (1911).

After Montgomery and Macdonald married in July 1911, they moved to Leaskdale, Ontario. Montgomery never lived on Prince Edward Island again. She kept in touch but returned to the Island only for visits.

Maud Montgomery Macdonald settled into life in Leaskdale. She raised two sons, Chester Cameron (born 1912) and Stuart (born 1915). Another son, Hugh, was stillborn in 1914. She led a busy life, but no matter how busy she was, she found time to write, maintaining a voluminous private correspondence, answering every fan letter personally, and making detailed entries in her

RESTORED SCHOOLHOUSE, LOWER BEDEQUE

(continued on page 35)

ANNE OF THE ISLAND

WAYNE MACKINNON

Imagine exploring one of the world's great islands with one of the world's most popular authors — someone who knows and loves the province well, and who will show you her favourite haunts.

Your guide is Lucy Maud Montgomery, author of the world-famous book *Anne of Green Gables*. Set in

"ANNE" AT GREEN GABLES

Cavendish, Prince Edward Island, this classic story was largely inspired by her deep attachment to the natural beauty which surrounded her. "Were it not for those Cavendish years, I do not think *Anne of Green Gables* would ever have been written," she recalled.

Chronologically, your first stop is in New London (on the Blue Heron Drive, at the intersection of Routes 6 and 20) where Maud was born on November 30, 1874. This house, now open to the public, remains relatively unchanged and contains many treasured personal effects from Maud's life, including her wedding ensemble and personal scrapbooks.

POST OFFICE AT GREEN GABLES

When Maud was 21 months old, her mother died. As a result, she was sent to live with her maternal grandparents, Alexander and Lucy Macneill, in Cavendish. Quiet gardens surround the stone cellar where their farmhouse once stood (just east of the intersection of Routes 6 and 13.) This was the site of Maud's home from 1876 to 1911.

It was here that she wrote *Anne of Green Gables*. "I wrote it in the evenings after my regular day's work was done, wrote most of it at the window of the little gable room that had been mine for years."

The tranquil heritage property has been passed down from father to son over four generations. John Macneill, a great-grandson of Alexander Macneill, and his family still live on the farm, and visitors are welcome to view the stone cellar and enjoy the grounds much as Maud must have done.

Close by, beside the Cavendish Church, a house similar to the original Macneill homestead has been relocated and restored as a postal museum.

One of the must visits for Anne enthusiasts is the Green Gables homestead in Cavendish. Located just west of the intersection of Routes 6 and 13, Green Gables House was the setting for Maud's story of Anne. Her grandfather Macneill's cousins lived here and she spent many happy hours in their home. In 1937, Parks Canada restored the house, furnishing it as it would have been in Anne's day. The grounds and outbuildings have been recreated and depict the Victorian setting described in the novel. The nearby Balsam Hollow and Haunted Wood trails reflect some of Maud's most precious woodland haunts.

L.M. MONTGOMERY BIRTHPLACE, NEW LONDON

After receiving her teacher's qualifications, Maud accepted a teaching position in Bideford. The young 19-year-old teacher boarded at the Anglican parsonage in Bideford, which is now open to the public (on Route 166.) Her room has been faithfully recreated and the museum also includes the actual cupboard that inspired the liniment cake story. In her *Journals*, the young Maud recounted her days in Bideford, with skating on the ponds, enjoying community socials, and her experiences as a first-time teacher.

Following her first year in Bideford, Maud accepted a teaching position in nearby Belmont, overlooking Malpeque Bay. "I boarded in a very cold farmhouse," recalled the young teacher and struggling writer. "In the evening after a day of strenuous school work, I would be too tired to write. So I religiously arose an hour earlier in the mornings for that purpose. The fire would not yet be on, of course, and the house would be very cold. But I would put on a heavy coat, sit on my feet to keep them from freezing, and with fingers so cramped I could scarcely hold the pen, I would write my 'stint' for the day...."

After a year's further study, Maud accepted a teaching position at a school in Lower Bedeque (located on Route 112 on the south side of the road). It was here in Lower Bedeque that it is said she first fell in love, but a future with the local farmer was not to be. The school house has been restored, and visitors are welcome.

In March 1898, her grandfather Macneill died and she returned to Cavendish to care for her aging grandmother. She spent the next 13 years there and, in 1908, *Anne of Green Gables* was finally published.

The one place on Prince Edward Island that Maud loved best was her Uncle John Campbell's house at Park Corner on Route 20. The house, still owned by descendants, contains many artifacts relating to Maud's life, including rare

first editions of her books. She spent summer holidays there as a girl, went there to live when her grandmother died, and was married in the parlour in 1911.

Maud described Park Corner as "a big white beautiful house smothered in orchards that was the wonder castle of my childhood. Here, in other days, there was a trio of merry cousins to rush out and drag me in with greetings and laughter. The very walls of that house must have been permeated by the essence of good times."

Many of Maud's stories were inspired by the house at Park Corner. "If I ever could build a house I would change nothing," she said. "It would be exactly like this old home." The enchanted bookcase described in *Anne of Green Gables* may be found at the museum. The pond on the Campbell farm became her "Lake of Shining Waters."

At the Montgomery Manor, also in Park Corner, the china dog Magog, of Gog and Magog fame, is on proud display, along with other artifacts in the parlour of the heritage homestead built by Senator Montgomery, Maud's grandfather. Still owned by the Montgomery family, the house is open to the public during the summer months.

Lucy Maud Montgomery died in 1942. She lay in state at Green Gables and was buried in the Cavendish Cemetery in a plot on the crest of a hill she had selected herself because "it overlooks the spots I always loved, the pond, the shore, the sand dunes, the harbour." The cemetery is at the intersection of Routes 6 and 13.

You can view the author's original manuscripts, scrapbooks and other personal items at the Confederation Centre Art Gallery and Museum in Charlottetown.

Kindred Spirits is a unique quarterly publication developed on Prince Edward Island by Montgomery's descendants. L.M. Montgomery and Anne enthusiasts may receive more information by calling 1-800-665-2663 or writing to: Kindred Spirits, Avonlea, PEI, C0B 1M0 Canada. As Anne herself said, "Kindred spirits are not so scarce as I used to think. It's splendid to find out there are so many of them in the world."

And, every year, the L.M. Montgomery Festival is held near Cavendish, bringing together people from around the world to recognize and celebrate the creator of Anne of the Island with music and stories, fun and friendship and, of course, ice cream. For information, go to www.lmmontgomeryfestival.com.

Montgomery's life and career has led to the establishment of the L.M. Montgomery Institute at the University of Prince Edward Island. The Institute, with an international scope, is a centre for research on Montgomery's life, her work and her Island. It hosts events and projects to bring together those who wish to learn more about the many facets of Prince Edward Island's most illustrious writer.

LUCY MAUD MONTGOMERY'S WEDDING DRESS AT HER BIRTHPLACE IN NEW LONDON

journals. She always looked forward to her trips home.

In 1919, Maud discovered that her husband was afflicted with religious melancholia, a serious mental illness. This illness returned periodically and sent him into bouts of depression and insomnia. For the rest of their lives she did everything she could to keep his illness a secret and to help him through each debilitating episode. All the while, she continued to write, publishing six more novels based on Anne and creating other popular heroines, including Emily (*Emily of New Moon*, *Emily Climbs*, *Emily's Quest*). She also published two novels she called "adult": *The Blue Castle* and *A Tangled Web*.

In 1926, the Macdonalds moved to Norval, Ontario, where they remained until Macdonald retired from the ministry in 1935. They then went to Toronto where they bought a house Montgomery aptly named "Journey's End." There Maud Montgomery Macdonald lived until her death on April 24, 1942. She was buried in the Cavendish cemetery, close to the fields, woods and sea she had known and loved since childhood. Her husband died in November of 1943 and was buried beside her.

A prolific author, Montgomery wrote some 500 short stories, 500 poems and 20 novels, 19 of which were set on Prince Edward Island. She also left behind an invaluable legacy of journals, letters and scrapbooks in which she recorded her thoughts on virtually every topic from gardening and cats to religious philosophy and current events. Her fictional and non-fictional works are now prized as social records of late 19th- and early 20th-century Canadian life. Her novels have been published in over 20 languages, including Japanese, Polish, Swedish, Norwegian and French.

Perhaps the best way to get to know Montgomery is through her own words. Several decades after her death, her son, Dr. Stuart Macdonald, placed her journals at the University of Guelph. In 1985, Drs. Elizabeth Waterston and Mary Rubio published *The Selected Journals of L.M. Montgomery, Volume 1: 1889–1910* (Toronto, Oxford University Press). Four more volumes have since been published (1987, 1992, 1998, and 2004).

Particularly in her journals, Montgomery reveals the depths of her emotional, sensitive nature. Like the heroines

GREEN GABLES

of her books, the emotions she felt — whether painful or joyful — affected her very deeply. She suffered greatly over unhappy events that affected her personally and the world in general. Her journal entries reflect the anguish she felt over certain events in her life, but they also disclose her sense of humour, her intense love of beauty and nature, her deep attachment to Prince Edward Island, her intelligent and creative mind, and her passionate need to write.

Despite her international fame, biographical information about Montgomery has been slow in coming. There have been a few biographies published over the years among the most recent is *Writing a Life: L.M. Montgomery*, by Waterston and Rubio (ECW Press, Toronto, 1995). This excellent book follows Montgomery from her birth to her death.

The fame Montgomery achieved during her lifetime and posthumously did not earn her high praise from academics nor from all reviewers and critics. Until recently, academics tended to dismiss her as a writer of little importance who wrote charming stories mainly for girls and women. But this evaluation is changing. In the

BEDROOM AT PARK CORNER

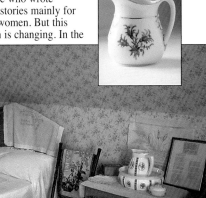

past 20 years, Canadian and international scholars have begun to study Montgomery as a novelist, journal and letter-writer, autobiographer, poet and short story writer. Articles on various aspects of her life and works have appeared in numerous scholarly publications.

Montgomery has also received press in popular media such as magazines, newsletters, videos, television (the popular *Road to Avonlea* series), movies and newspapers. On Prince Edward Island, a publication devoted entirely to the author, *Kindred Spirits*, has been published quarterly since 1990 by her cousin George Campbell.

PARK CORNER

In 1993, the L.M. Montgomery Institute was established at the University of Prince Edward Island to celebrate Montgomery, her works and her Island home. In June 1994, the Institute hosted the first-ever international symposium on Montgomery. International conferences are now held biennially at the university. The Institute also hosts an electronic discussion list about Montgomery, with subscribers from around the world. It co-produced an award-winning CD-ROM entitled *The Bend in the Road: An Invitation to the World and Work of L.M. Montgomery*. One wonders what Montgomery would have done with the luxuries of e-mail and word processing.

GARDEN AT GREEN GABLES

Prince Edward Island touched something very deep within L.M. Montgomery. In turn, she brought Prince Edward Island to readers around the world through her vivid descriptions of the landscape. Each year, thousands of people are drawn to the Island because of her. They come to walk the beaches, admire the red roads and sandstone cliffs, look at the green fields filled with wildflowers, and find for themselves the Prince Edward Island that Montgomery knew and loved.

COTTAGE LIFE

WENDY MACGREGOR AND JOY BELL MACKENZIE

Cottage life in Prince Edward Island offers a perfect summer escape, whether one is looking for a quiet hideaway or a launch pad into playland. Bring the whole family, come and go as you please, barbecue fresh fish or read a book on your deck as the sun goes down over the gulf. These are only some of the benefits of renting a cottage for your vacation in Prince Edward Island — and there are plenty of cottages to choose from.

First, consider the area in which you want to stay. The wide, white sand dunes at Cavendish Beach are well-known to many families and, of course, Cavendish is also

the home of Anne of Green Gables. Here, the cottages that are close to the water and well-maintained with full services are generally booked a year in advance, so don't leave this until the last minute. That said, it is always worth checking at the beginning of the season to see if there have been cancellations at any of the most popular settings.

If the Cavendish area of the PEI National Park is your destination of choice, but you cannot find anything appropriate, do try the neighbouring areas of North and South Rustico, Stanley Bridge and New London. All these locations are close to the north shore and boast many attractions — from music to antiquing to

nature trails and biking. The Acadian flavour of the
Rusticos appeals to many.

FISHING BOATS IN HARBOUR

At the eastern end of the national park, Brackley Beach
and Stanhope have fewer cottages on the water, but many
that are a short walk from the beach. There is also deep-sea
fishing off Covehead Wharf and scenic boat tours. There is
nothing better than a feed of fried clams right on the dock.
There are interpretive tours in the National Park and two
self-guided trails — Long Pond Loop and Bubbling
Springs/Farmlands Trail. From the park it is a short trip
into Charlottetown for those much-sought-after souvenirs.

Travelling west from Cavendish toward Summerside,
cottages are available in the nearby Hebrides cottage
development or at Clinton or New London. French River's
dramatic views take visitors a little off the beaten path. The
Darnley and Seaview areas offer beautiful white sand
beaches that are not in the National Park. A lot more
privacy comes with a little more distance from the
amusements, and many travellers are attracted to the rustic
cottages right on the sand at Malpeque, home of the
famous oysters and Penderosa Beach.

For a quiet getaway steeped in protected dunelands and
marshes, consider the serenity of Greenwich and St.
Peter's, 40 kilometres east of Charlottetown, or even

FRENCH RIVER

further east to the "singing sands" of Fortune Bay and Souris. This area is renowned for its unspoiled scenic beauty, and the TransCanada Trail runs right through it. Here you will find the spectacular Greenwich Beach, the newest addition to PEI National Park, and the top-rated Links at Crowbush Cove golf course.

There are inns and bed-and-breakfasts along the route, and private cottages at Lakeside, Red Head, Greenwich and Fortune. Restaurants are neither frequent nor lavish, but there are more every year. If you plan ahead, you could book a room and enjoy gourmet dining at the Inn at St. Peters, a few kilometres before the entrance to Greenwich, or at the Inn at Bay Fortune, former home of George C. Scott and Colleen Dewhurst.

On the south shore, Victoria is another charmingly picturesque destination. This flourishing artistic community boasts delightful galleries, rental cottages, B&Bs, good food and local theatre. The south shore tends to have warm shallow water and red sand beaches, perfect for playing, clamming or leisurely walks at low tide on the hard-packed flats. Check tide times though, because the small tidal pools at low tide give way to high tides where the water actually reaches the bank — then it's time for a raft!

Visitors to Prince Edward Island often have a preference for either the north or south shores, but both have their merits. Coming from Charlottetown, toward Victoria, you will also find many cottages for rent in nearby Augustine Cove, Rice and Rocky Points, and further west past Borden-Carleton at Chelton Beach and in the Bedeque area.

On the eastern shore at Brudenell River Resort, you can relax in cabins on the premises or take golf lessons at the Island Golf Academy — fun and learning for the whole family. The nearby town of Montague offers amenities, cottages on the Brudenell River and a lovely restaurant called Windows on the Water Café.

At the west end of the Island, private cottages and B&Bs are available at Tyne Valley and Alberton. A new inn

and restaurant have been built at Northport and, at West Point, a lighthouse is outfitted as an inn and restaurant. The resort at Mill River offers challenging golf and a fun park for children. It is a great family destination in winter because of its skating rink, tubing hill and cross-country skiing facilities.

In trying to choose between PEI's many wonderful cottage options, you need to establish whether your personal priority is the beach, swimming, golf, amusement parks, fishing, cuisine or some other interest. Stay close to the attractions you plan to visit. Ask about the rating for the cottage: the Canada Select system awards stars based the facilities that are offered. This will give you an objective standard by which to compare cottages.

VICTORIA WHARF

Be aware of cottage operators' cancellation policies. Many cottages have their own websites giving prospective renters sneak previews. Because business is competitive, and the season is so short, prices are generally consistent. You will pay a little more to be in Cavendish, or to be right on the water. And if you come in the shoulder- or off-season, you can generally get a better rate.

Remember, one of the great things about PEI is that even if your kids force you to book by the beach when you want to be by the golf course, nothing is ever all that far away.

ABOVE: ARTIST'S STUDIO, VICTORIA

COTTAGE AT MONT-CARMEL

41

THE ISLAND FOR KIDS

NANCY RUSSELL

AVONLEA — VILLAGE OF ANNE OF GREEN GABLES

My kids like to call this "Our Island" — with capital letters, of course. Being quite young they can't be bothered with actually saying Prince Edward Island, which is a mouthful. As far as they're concerned, it is their Island, which they're more than happy to share. And share we do, every summer, with dozens of relatives and friends who are eager to visit when the sun is warm and the ocean waters even warmer. Where are they in the middle of February, I wonder?

As someone who spent her formative years in Manitoba, I marvel that my children are growing up with the beach at their doorstep and a neighbourhood seal swimming in the harbour water outside our fence. The beaches of Prince Edward Island are one of our greatest sources of entertainment. One summer, I watched my children and some visitors from Ontario and England spend a couple of hours building a makeshift dam to hold back the tide. Some of the rocks are still in place, a lovely memory of that summer day.

EXPLORING TIDAL POOLS

Island beaches are ideal for young children to scour for pieces of polished glass, crab shells, driftwood and other treasures. For older kids, the beaches are a place to bodysurf in the waves or snuggle in the sand for that first-ever summer romance. One word of caution: beware the rip-currents on the Island's north shore. Stick to beaches with lifeguards, particularly when the surf is up.

DEEP SEA FISHING

Should we tire of the beach, my kids and I have a list of "must-visit" places every summer. We love to fish for trout at Ben's Lake, about half an hour east of Charlottetown. The deep-sea fishing expeditions are also a big hit with kids. My friends from England, and their kids, aged ten and eight, took great pride in bringing home a bag of fresh halibut and cod cheeks for us to fry up after their two-hour fishing trip out of North Rustico harbour. There are also great kayaking adventures at several locations around the Island. The tandem kayaks are great for taking younger children along.

My eldest son likes "old-fashioned" things. At Orwell Corner Historic Village and the Agricultural Museum, halfway between Charlottetown and Wood Islands, kids can see how a farm was run in the late 1800s. The nearby Macphail Woods has an interpretive centre perfect for kids who love nature, as well as some great nature trails and a tearoom for after. And if you're around Orwell in the evening, there are plenty of ceilidhs during the summer. You can hear fiddle music and local tunes, usually performed by up-and-coming young musicians. But don't forget the mosquito spray.

If it's music you like, then take your children to hear the bagpipes played beautifully at the College of Piping in Summerside.

AVONLEA — VILLAGE OF ANNE OF GREEN GABLES

The history that resounds in the pipes is also found at Woodleigh Replicas in Burlington. There are castles smaller in size than a three-year-old, or big enough for an adult to explore, the towering point of Nelson's Column from Trafalgar Square, the Queen's jewels and, every kid's highlight, a dungeon complete with a spooky skeleton. Everyone stops to pose with their head and hands in the stocks in the village square. You can always pick out the Islanders. They're the ones who, like my husband, walk around marvelling at how small everything is now that they're grown up.

If you're out at Woodleigh, Cabot Beach Provincial Park in Malpeque is just a short drive away. Be sure to take the local roads to experience driving on authentic PEI clay, unless it's spring or fall and impassable. A visit to the car wash aside, it's worth it! At Cabot Beach, there are fishing boats for tiny landlubbers to climb on, as well as some of the original set of the television series *Emily of New Moon*, which was filmed for several years on Prince Edward Island.

Cavendish is, of course, a mecca for kids. You have to put aside your adult restraint and relish in the sheer silliness of the Fantazmagoric Museum and Ripley's Believe It or Not. Rainbow Valley has a boat ride through a magical lagoon and a rollercoaster that looks like something from the 1960s. The toddler to eight crowd loves it, and it's the standard motivational bribe at the end of every school year on PEI. Sandspit has more heart-pounding rides to appeal to a slightly older crowd than Rainbow Valley.

For the more historically minded, Avonlea Village warrants a stop, with its re-creation of a rural community in the late 1800s. How can you go wrong with making ice-cream and drinking raspberry cordial, never mind lively entertainment and a visit to Lucy Maud's classroom? Fans of *Anne of Green Gables* recommend a tour of all the local Montgomery sites and for those who have read all the books, it's a pilgrimage worth making. For those who prefer Arthur the Aardvark, the beaches of Cavendish are blissfully white of sand and soft on the foot.

My children are disappointed that PEI no longer has any trains. The former railway tracks have been turned into trails, which are great for mountain bikes. I often see families touring from one small community to another, particularly from Mount Stewart to St. Peters. We don't have trains, but we

RAINBOW VALLEY

do have the Elmira Railway Museum and its newest feature, a working miniature train. If you're planning a trek to the eastern end of the province, drop by Elmira and then head to Basin Head. You didn't hear it from me, but ... Islanders love to jump into the water from the bridge at Basin Head. There is a fisheries museum and, at East Point, a wonderful lighthouse.

My children and I are determined to someday visit all the lighthouses on the Island. A few favourites so far are East Point (past Souris) and West Point (on the way to Tignish), where we climbed to the top and had to shield our eyes from the working light. You can even stay overnight in the West Point Lighthouse. Just past Tignish is North Cape, where the wind farm and wind turbine test site will surely impress. My kids also like the blockhouse, which keeps watch over Charlottetown Harbour.

You will see a lot of wildlife on Prince Edward Island, if you look hard enough. The largest mammal is a coyote

BASIN HEAD

CAST OF *SOMEWHERE IN THE WORLD*, CONFEDERATION CENTRE OF THE ARTS

— rarely seen. Foxes, on the other hand, are regular visitors to our neighbourhood, even climbing into our backyard. The crows and foxes will regularly pillage for golf balls at local courses. The great blue herons stand like sentinels at dusk, searching for fish. Another local favourite is the piping plover. We love to catch a glimpse of the lithe bird, but we always heed the "keep away" signs on the local beaches when the tiny plover eggs are hatching.

The Island has one drive-in movie theatre, near Brackley Beach. Charlottetown and Summerside have multiplex movie theatres, which are particularly crowded on rainy days during the summer. The malls carry the latest trends for teens who like to shop, and even bargain brand names at the Factory Outlet stores in North River, on the outskirts of Charlottetown. If you want a true authentic

Island adventure, go dig through the bins at Froggies, a second-hand clothing nirvana in Charlottetown. For more highbrow entertainment, the Confederation Centre of the Arts has a great library and programs for kids. Check out the family musical entertainment performed weekdays at noontime in the Centre's outdoor amphitheatre by the Charlottetown Festival's Young Company. For the historically minded kids, there is a great new program about Confederation performed daily at Province House. The Parks Canada film is interesting enough that my seven-year-old sat through it with no squirming at all.

Kids seem to get a kick out of the Harbour Hippo, an amphibious vehicle that takes visitors on a land and water

HARNESS RACING AT SUMMERSIDE

tour of Charlottetown. And, speaking of water, the new Capital Area Recreation Inc. (CARI) aquatics facility in Charlottetown features diving boards, a rope swing, and a water slide with an impressive G-force rating — at least when the parents use it.

Every summer, we play a few rounds of mini-golf and make a few visits to the local go-kart track, both popular pastimes for visitors. My eldest son also loves to visit the Charlottetown Driving Park to watch the horses race. It's harness racing with standardbred horses pulling sulkies, or bikes as they're called. Think chariot racing, as one friend described it to her kids. There are also lovely local harness tracks — my favourite is Pinette, featuring a community race night you will never forget.

If you're here during the summer, keep an eye out for local community festivals. It is these small, community-focused events that are really the heart and soul of what

ELIOT RIVER DREAM PARK

makes this Island a great place for kids. The biggest are the Lobster Carnival in Summerside and Old Home Week in Charlottetown. Many Islanders look forward to taking their kids to one of several powwows held every summer across the Island.

Prince Edward Island has great food for children. Every kid has to climb on the giant cow at Cows for a photo opportunity, eating ice cream, of course. The Wowie Cowie flavour is a family fave. Frosty Treat in Kensington and the Richmond Dairy Bar, up west, as we say, have wonderful ice cream and "fries with the works" (not the time for a lesson in nutrition)! Then there's the seafood. One of our friends was trying to introduce his

eight-year-old son to mussels during a visit to the Island and offered to pay him a loonie per mussel. After $27, my friend pleaded bankruptcy! My kids don't eat much of their annual feed of lobster, but we sure get some great photos. And they're great fans of Island potatoes, with lots of sour cream.

You can work off all those calories by taking the kids for a walk on the boardwalks in Charlottetown or Summerside. Kids will also love climbing and swinging on the Eliot River Dream Park, a community-designed wooden playground for all ages in Cornwall, on the outskirts of Charlottetown.

When you're arriving or leaving the Island, be sure to make the most of the coming and going. You haven't really visited the Island unless you've tried to keep a toddler entertained in the ferry line-up. There's a wonderful wooden re-creation of a fishing village where kids can play, near the Wood Islands lighthouse, close to where the ferry docks. You can get great photos of the Confederation Bridge down on the rocks just past Gateway Village in Borden-Carleton. And minivans give you a fantastic view going over the bridge.

For years, a favourite Prince Edward Island tourism slogan has been "Come Play on Our Island." With your pick of beaches for a sandbox, the Gulf of St. Lawrence for a swimming pool, and more adventures than the latest episode of Rugrats or Scooby-Doo, Prince Edward Island is a place all kids will love. So come play on our Island — and bring the kids.

LOBSTER SUPPERS

JULIE V. WATSON

LOADING TRAPS AT ABRAMS VILLAGE

The lobster has long been recognized as part of the tradition of Prince Edward Island, and nowhere is it enjoyed more than at the community suppers that have become an integral part of every summer.

Community suppers began many decades ago as a joint celebration honouring the arrival of the lobster season and warm weather. Held in community halls, church basements and even on lawns, members of the community would traditionally offer lobster, chowder, potato salad, and probably some slaw, with pie, squares and strawberry shortcake for dessert. Homemade bread and pickles rounded out the feast.

The logic behind the menu was simple — it consisted of whatever was available. Local fishers would donate the lobsters. Potatoes for the salad and the chowder would come from someone's cold storage, as would the cabbage and carrots for the coleslaw. Strawberries were usually a good bet, as the season usually coincided with the lobster harvest. Biscuits, bread, pies and squares were made by local women and donated, along with jars of their own pickles.

These suppers were quickly recognized by "townies" and locals alike as being both delicious and a great bargain. Tourists, having already displayed superior intelligence by choosing Prince Edward Island as a vacation destination, were quick to sniff out these terrific experiences. The word quickly spread.

Verifying the fact that they, too, are intelligent beings, quick to seize an opportunity, fundraisers extended these events from one-day affairs to a full season of suppers. The labour would be supplied by the people of the community, and all the profits would go into the coffers of the church or organization holding the event. Just as the profits were important for the good of the community, so were the

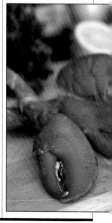

opportunities for employment. That is why so many of the suppers are found in rural villages. Many a student has paid for his or her education by serving up lobster dinners.

As time passed, more and more lobster suppers were added until most of them became

LOBSTER POUND, SUMMERSIDE

privately owned businesses. Each has a distinctive personality, and one supper can't be said to be better than the rest. Islanders, after all, do know how to cook their lobster. Some suppers have down-home entertainment or sing-alongs, and some are licensed for alcoholic beverages; these all help determine a personal favourite. No matter which you choose, the atmosphere will be casual, even homey. You could be seated next to someone from the other side of the village, or from the other side of the world.

So successful have the suppers become that tour buses now make them a regular stop. The informal celebration of the province's premier seafood harvest has become part of the Island experience that summer visitors seldom miss. Few other establishments offer up such an accurate representation of a down-home celebration in yesteryear's style.

Today, more than 35 years after the first formalized suppers began, menus have changed just a little. Another Island seafood, the Island blue mussel, is often added to the typical fare of chowder, lobster, salads, homemade rolls and desserts. Grown on the Island, the mussel is plump and delicious — and often offered up for repeats. Some locations offer a garden salad instead of coleslaw, or perhaps a baked potato instead of the salad. But the important ingredient — the traditional lobster of Prince Edward Island — is always there.

Delicious lobster, served hot or cold according to your preference, is the star of the meal. For some years,

MACKINNON'S LOBSTER POUND, CHARLOTTETOWN

several establishments offered all-you-can-eat lobster for a set price, but these are pretty much a thing of the past. Instead, you've got the option of buying a second or even a third or fourth lobster, if so desired. Second helpings are often offered of other items such as chowder, mussels, rolls, salads and even desserts. Some establishments offer all you can eat of these items, or a salad bar.

In recognition that some people, admittedly very few, actually don't like lobster, there are always alternatives. Ham, scallops, steak, pork chops, salmon or sole are examples. Children's menus are always available. The suppers are still prepared and served by locals, most of them trained by professionals to offer the best service possible. Staff are friendly, and generally impart a sincere Island welcome.

Credited with starting it all, St. Ann's Church Lobster Supper, located between Stanley Bridge and New Glasgow off Route 224, is still very popular. Held in the church hall, it gained fame not only for the superb food, but also because the parish priest entertained with the organ, leading a singsong of old and new favourites. There is no guarantee of such entertainment today. After all, a priest has to save some voice for the Sunday sermon. But you can count on a delightful time with dinner music and a satisfyingly full feeling to send you on your way.

New Glasgow Lobster Suppers are another great favourite. Evening after evening, tour bus after tour bus rolls in. Amazingly, its two dining rooms accommodate everyone without ever seeming to be over-crowded. On the contrary, the crowds add a feeling of gaiety to the occasion. New Glasgow's policy of unlimited rolls, chowder, mussels, salad, dessert and beverages ensures that they are busy. Not to mention the fact that they have a legion of excellent cooks in the kitchen. Situated on the banks of a lovely river in a small village, this supper is one of the best.

You can also get lobster in the village. The Prince Edward Island Preserve Company, just down the road, will serve it up for lunch as long as you phone ahead. While there, check out the beautiful New Glasgow Country Gardens.

Cardigan Lobster Suppers, served at the historic Old Store heritage building in a small village near Montague, took the tradition to the eastern end of the province. It's a grand spot, with two decks and the dining room overlooking the Cardigan marina and harbour. The five-course supper is a little different because it comes with hot veggies and a baked potato.

Fisherman's Wharf in North Rustico is a good place for abundant food. With a gigantic 60-foot salad bar, lobster

ST. ANN'S CHURCH LOBSTER SUPPER, STANLEY BRIDGE

PEI PRESERVE COMPANY, NEW GLASGOW

MacKinnon's Lobster Pound, Charlottetown

right from its own holding tanks, and a general party atmosphere with lots of chatter to accompany your meal, you'll have an experience like no other.

"Up west," as Islanders like to say, the Centre Expo-Festival Centre in Abrams Village serves up a touch of Acadian culture with their lobster suppers. At West Point lighthouse you can enjoy your supper on a patio beside the sea or in the dining room. The folks at West Point have even been known to arrange a lobster boil on the beach (with prior notice). It's a wonderful experience to sit with a bonfire crackling, sucking out every morsel of tender lobster meat as the sun sets over the sea. West Point is a magical sort of place, a country inn located in an operating light-house, which carries on the community tradition.

Festivals are held during the summer and fall, and many feature a lobster supper, particularly the Northumberland Fisheries Festival in Murray River, the Tyne Valley Oyster Festival and the Summerside Lobster Carnival. The folks at the Visitor Information Centres can help you track down what is available during your visit.

Then, of course, there are the diehard lobster lovers who simply want a "scoff" without the trimmings. In this case, it's do as the Islanders do, which is to head down to a wharf, such as those at Rustico, Stanley Bridge, Covehead, Charlottetown, Wood Islands or Victoria. Here, the seafood outlets offer fresh-from-the-sea lobster — either cooked on the spot or ready for your own pot. Find a picnic table overlooking the sea, or head back to your cottage or cabin, for you have the makings of a feast fit for royalty.

The wharf at Rustico

Fun, indeed, but it doesn't quite compare to experiencing the suppers. The advice we Islanders offer is to check them out, call to see when they are the least busy, and make a reservation. Whichever lobster supper you choose, go with an empty stomach and a desire for good food, good fun and a rare ambience.

BEST BEACHES

JOCELYNE LLOYD

With over 500 kilometres of coastline, Prince Edward Island offers seemingly endless opportunities for every beach lover. Whether you want to relax under your umbrella, walk for miles along the water's edge, splash around with the kids or hunt for interesting rocks and marine life, PEI has a beach for you.

SURFING THE WAVES ON THE NORTH SHORE

All supervised beaches, and those falling under the jurisdictions of the provincial and national parks systems, are marked on Tourism PEI's highway maps. Many of these beaches have changing facilities, picnic areas and playgrounds. For those looking for more secluded areas to swim and sunbathe, there is often a beach to be found at the end of a dead-end road or near a lighthouse — but residents appreciate it when you respect "No Trespassing" and "Private Property" signs.

The Island's most famous beaches — the white sand beaches that stretch for miles bordered by grassy dunes — are found on the north shore in Prince Edward Island National Park. You have to buy a pass to enter the park

ABOVE: BRACKLEY BEACH
MIDDLE: CAVENDISH
BOTTOM: GREENWICH NATIONAL PARK

and its beaches, but you can save money by buying family and season passes, or by purchasing an early bird pass by late June. Cavendish is the most popular beach for tourists as it's close to shopping, golf, Green Gables House and many other attractions. In recent years Brackley, Stanhope and Dalvay beaches have become increasingly popular.

Stanhope Beach is good for small children as it is supervised and has a small playground, picnic facilities and a canteen. Foxes and hares are becoming tamer by the season, resulting in more frequent sightings, but Park officials prefer that you not feed them. An unsupervised part of the National Park, and therefore a much less crowded area, is Robinson's Island. You can find this by coming through the gates at Brackley Beach, and taking the first left past the entrance to the parking lot.

Rip currents are common on the north shore, so it is important to always swim with a friend and stay close to the shore, especially on unsupervised beaches. If a rip current pulls you away from the shore, you

can usually get out of it by staying calm and swimming parallel to the beach.

The recently developed Greenwich adjunct to the PEI National Park boasts pristine white-sand beaches and magnificent dunes. Three walking trails criss-cross the peninsula, letting you experience the dunes, marshes and wildlife close up. Walking from the parking lot all the way around to the supervised area of the beach is also a beautiful route. The St. Peters Bay side offers shallower, warmer water, ideal for snorkellers, or you may prefer a nice, secluded spot tucked near a dune on the north side of the peninsula. The whole walk can take hours though, and you'll need to carry water with you on hot days.

Other beaches that offer white sand and magnificent dunes, but do not have an admission charge, are Panmure Island Provincial Park near Montague at the eastern end of PEI, and Cabot Beach Provincial Park near Malpeque in the northwest. Both these parks have overnight camping facilities. Blooming Point Beach is one of the more beautiful beaches on the Island, and it is rumoured that there has been a "clothing optional" area further down the beach. Access to Blooming Point is via a narrow road, and it can be difficult to get in and out on a sunny Saturday or Sunday.

A unique beach offering something for nearly everyone is Basin Head. Near the northeast tip of the Island, Basin Head has a surfguard station, picnic area, canteen and ice cream stand, washroom and changing facilities, and is at the end of a short boardwalk from gift shops and the Basin Head Fisheries Museum. You can leap into the rushing river, letting it carry you to the beach, dive off the footbridge, swim in a more shallow area or walk for miles along the "singing sands." The polished sands of this beach squeak when you walk on them.

The south shore is the preferred destination for some. The water is considerably warmer, and parents with small children like these beaches

TOP: WEST POINT BEACH AND LIGHTHOUSE

GREENWICH

because they tend to be shallower. Snails, minnows, hermit crabs and the like abound in the tidal pools. You do need to check the tide schedule in the daily papers though, or you could end up walking halfway to Nova Scotia before the water is deep enough for swimming. Another down side to south shore beaches is the seaweed, which is smelly when the tide is out and sometimes a considerable barrier to clear water when the tide is in. Others find the red sands of the south shore to be not as appealing as the white sands of the Gulf of St. Lawrence.

Tea Hill Beach is a terrific spot to bring the kids for a picnic, followed by a swim. About a 10-minute drive east of Charlottetown, Tea

LOW TIDE, VICTORIA BEACH

Hill has a decent-sized playground and picnic tables nestled under pine trees. Besides being pretty, the trees have the added bonus of keeping the blazing afternoon sun at bay. The water is bathwater warm by the end of June and when the tide is in gets deep (but not too deep) quickly.

Other family-friendly south shore beaches are Chelton Beach Provincial Park near the Confederation Bridge and Argyle Shore Provincial Park halfway between the bridge and Charlottetown. Victoria-by-the-Sea on the Argyle Shore is a lovely little village for poking around in, and offers a relaxing picnic spot and beach as well.

Cedar Dunes Provincial Park, at the western end of the province, is ideal for a long walk along the beach. More open waters here have created white sands and dunes reminiscent of the north shore. The West Point lighthouse has a magnificent view.

Although dangerous for swimming, the waters of the Gulf of St. Lawrence and the Northumberland Strait converging over Canada's longest natural rock reef at North Cape is fun to watch. At low tide, stroll along the reef and look for marine life, shore birds and seals. You may even be lucky enough to witness Irish moss harvesters using horses to haul what they have gleaned from the beach.

Although agricultural run-off and private property make many of the Island's river beaches unusable or inaccessible, there are a couple of inviting places to swim, walk and canoe. At the western end of the province, Mill River and Green Park provincial parks have large campgrounds with river beach facilities. The Rodd Mill River Resort also runs a marina where you can rent canoes,

WATERSKIING AT SOURIS BEACH

kayaks and pedal boats for an afternoon of fun on the river. In the east, the Brudenell River Provincial Park is another river beach with a marina nearby or, for a quiet day at the river, try Pinette Provincial Park just past Point Prim when coming from Charlottetown.

The best months for swimming at the beach are July and August, when the air and water temperature are both warm enough. It's also good to know that later in the summer there are fewer jellyfish. These jellyfish aren't as toxic as some varieties — their stings feel like being slapped with a wet towel, and rubbing a handful of sand on sore skin will usually lessen the sting — but sometimes the pure proliferation of them keeps people out of the water.

If you can stand the air temperature when you exit the water, September can be a wonderful time for swimming too. There are fewer people at the beach and the water is often as warm as it was in August. Supervised beaches usually employ lifeguards from Canada Day weekend to Labour Day.

If your day at the beach does not include swimming, but just a leisurely stroll or an exploration of tidal pools, you can set out as soon as the snow melts and the dirt roads have firmed up, right until the first big snowstorm in the fall or winter. And even then, if you're properly dressed, walking on a winter beach strewn with ice floes can be the perfect sunny winter afternoon adventure.

CAVENDISH BEACH

BIRDING

DAN MCASKILL

The diversity of habitats in short distances combined with a wide variety of birds makes birding on Prince Edward Island a wonderful experience. Some of the many species that make birding on Prince Edward Island a pleasure throughout the seasons are the northern gannet, great cormorant, brant, Barrow's goldeneye, bald eagle, peregrine falcon, piping plover, whimbrel, lesser black-backed gull, Iceland gull, Caspian tern, black guillemot, barred owl, brown creeper, Cape May warbler, black-throated blue warbler, Blackburnian warbler and Nelson's sharp-tailed sparrow. From late may to early autumn, birders can record over 100 species in a single day in mid-winter. A day's outing can yield 40 species or more.

Over 353 species of birds have been recorded on the Island. Four of the hottest woodland birding sites are the Macphail Woods (Orwell), the Brookvale Nordic Ski trails in the spring and summer, the Valleyfield Demonstration Woodlot (near Montague) and the New Harmony Demonstration Woodlot (near Souris). The softwood, mixed wood, hardwood and shrub areas in these woodlots host a variety of breeding birds. A birder can often find mourning warblers, black-throated blue warblers and Blackburnian warblers, and hear the songs of the winter wren and brown creeper at these sites. In early spring and autumn, hundreds of warblers pass through the woodlands in various parts of the Island, particularly at migration points such as East Point, North Cape and Cape Bear.

JUVENILE BLACK-BACKED GULL

Three species of owls are widespread on the Island, namely great horned, barred and northern saw-whet owls. Late spring to early summer birders wishing a night excursion can usually hear their calls on near-windless nights in areas with fairly extensive woodlands. With really good luck, long-eared, short-eared, screech or boreal owls might be heard, and sightings of snowy owls are common some winters.

BARRED OWL

ENDANGERED DUNES
ON THE NORTH
SHORE

The salt marshes adjacent to Covehead Harbour in the PEI National Park and the Souris Causeway are excellent for shorebirding during the spring migration period and from late July to early October. You might even encounter rarities such as the western sandpiper or a stilt sandpiper. During spring and summer birding trips along sand spits or near the entrance to barachois ponds, you may encounter the protective fencing for the piping plover. This is the Island's only nesting endangered species and it is struggling to survive. Please move quickly away from the sites if you discover them. Guided viewing opportunities for piping plovers are sometimes available through naturalists in the PEI National Park. At Covehead Harbour, you can safely view one of the breeding areas from the bridge or parking lot. In addition, the Covehead salt marsh is great for viewing Nelson's sharp-tailed sparrows and willets.

PIPING PLOVER

Coastal and wetland birding opportunities abound on the Island. From spring through autumn, one can often see northern gannets, great cormorants, common eiders, black, surf and white-winged scoters and long-tailed ducks from coastal viewing points such as East Point, North Cape, Cape Tryon, West Point and Cape Bear. These are also great spots during windy days for viewing a variety of pelagic birds such as razorbills, common murres, shearwaters and phalaropes through a telescope. In northeastern Prince Edward Island in particular, there have been autumn sightings of black-headed, lesser black-backed, Iceland and glaucous gulls. The Pigot Trail at Mount Stewart and the Bubbling Springs Trail in the PEI National Park offer good trails for freshwater marsh birds.

BALD EAGLES

The principal birding events on the Island are co-ordinated by the Natural History Society. The Bain Bird Count is held on the last Saturday in May and there are four Christmas bird counts. The Neil Bennett Autumn Birding Classic fundraiser welcomes visiting birders. Contact the Society at P.O. Box 2346, Charlottetown, PEI, C1A 8C1, or visit its website.

A birding centre is located at Murray River at the Eagle's View Golf Course and Interpretive Centre.

Copies of the *Field Checklist of Birds* are available on-line at www.peiplay.com or at www.isn.net/~nhspei and at

GREAT BLUE HERON

Visitor Information Centres. There is a listserv for birds through the University of Prince Edward Island and the details for subscribing to it are on the Natural History Society's website. The checklists feature sighting frequency by season and the breeding status of each species. Some of the Island's birding hot spots are featured in Jeffrey Domm's *Formac Pocket Guide to Prince Edward Island Birds* and Geoff Hogan's *Familiar Birds of Prince Edward Island*.

GOLF

MIKE GAUTHIER

GOLF LESSON AT THE CANADIAN GOLF ACADEMY

From the scratch player to the high handicapper, there's no disputing Prince Edward Island has something to offer every golfer. There's nothing like getting my clubs out that first fine Saturday in spring, with fresh breezes blowing off the Gulf, and enjoying life outdoors amidst scenery usually found on postcards. Depending on the kindness of the spring, I've been known to tee off as early as mid-May. Rustico Resort is renowned for its early starting time, which is sometimes as early as late April. Golfing in the fall has become more popular, as courses are less crowded and the weather remains beautiful into much of September and October.

With the Island's numerous links and all the amenities, golfers of every skill level can find a place to either hone their game or simply unwind with a friendly, yet challenging, round. With prices ranging from less than $20 for 9-hole courses to upwards of $80 for high-end 18-hole championship courses, it's also affordable. Another attraction is that all the courses are close to major centres, as well as to each other.

The Island is most famous for its hospitality, its agriculture and *Anne of Green Gables*, but over the last number of years PEI has also become known internationally for golf. A concentrated effort has been made to get the word out across Canada and throughout the Eastern Seaboard that the Island is a fantastic golf destination. Case in point: *Golf Digest* ranked PEI as the world's 26th best golf destination while *SCOREGolf* magazine thinks the Island is the best golf locale in Canada, and has thought that way for quite some time.

This country's golfing public agrees. In the annual golfers' choice awards conducted by *SCOREGolf* magazine, The Links at Crowbush Cove garnered a silver in the category of best course. It was one of the 14 medals won by the Island in 2003 by what is recognized as the most reputable publication for the sport in Canada.

From a provincial perspective, the Island's government-owned courses are more than holding their own. Dundarave has been awarded a four-and-a-half star rating by *Golf Digest*. The red-sandstone 18-hole championship golf course was designed by architects Dr. Michael Hurdzan and Dana Fry and opened in July 1999. *SCOREGolf* magazine rated Dundarave, which is part of the Brudenell River Resort, in the top six best golf resorts in Canada.

ON THE LINKS AT DUNDARAVE

The three provincial golf courses have also hosted their share of professional and amateur championships. The Canadian Professional Golf Tour used Brudenell as a regular stop for a number of years. In 1996, Mill River hosted the first du Maurier Team Challenge, a format that had the top Canadians from the LPGA tour paired with the du Maurier Series in a team skins format. Crowbush was the site of the 1997 Canadian Amateur Golf Championship and the 1998 Export "A" Skins Game. Names like Mike Weir, Fred Couples and John Daly drew the golfing, and non-golfing, public to the course hoping to get a glimpse of golfing greatness.

A suggestion for anyone not familiar with the Island: you may want to hit Kings County first, because that's

where three of the most majestic courses in Canada are located. They are Brudenell River, the Links at Crowbush Cove and Dundarave. There are also 9-hole courses in that part of the province, including Beaver Valley in Martinvale, Belfast Highland Greens in Belfast and Rollo Bay Greens in Souris. Other 9-hole courses on the Island include St. Felix near Alberton, Red Sands between Cavendish and Summerside, and Countryview on the West River near Charlottetown. There are many other 18-hole courses, including Glasgow Hills, Green Gables and Rustico Resort on the North Shore; Belvedere, Fox Meadow, Avondale and Stanhope near Charlottetown; Forest Hills (a 9-hole course), Glen Afton and Clyde River in Central Queens County; and Mill River and Summerside in Prince County.

BRUDENELL RIVER

Teaching the game has become a specialty service on the Island, at the Canadian Golf Academy in Brudenell. Widely known as one of the top teaching facilities in the country, its director is Anne Chouinard, whose prize pupil is none other than Charlottetown's own Lorie Kane, a winner on the LPGA Tour. The 9-hole, par-30 academy course overlooks the Brudenell River. Relatively new courses have also sprung up across PEI: Anderson's Creek and the Eagles Glenn, two 18-hole championship layouts on the north shore and in the Cavendish area; and Eagle's View, a 9-hole course nestled in Murray River. Eagle's View has carved out its own little niche, featuring an interpretive centre that focuses on the region's history. The centre is built around MacLure's Pond, the Island's largest body of fresh water.

GREEN GABLES

That brings the total number of courses belonging to Golf PEI to 25 — not bad considering that when the organization began in 1989 only six were part of the fold. My personal favourite is Brudenell, partly because of its layout, and partly because it's forgiving and challenging at the same time. Like every course, Brudenell has its own signature holes, such as the par-3 10th hole, which can be very difficult if the wind is blowing the right (or wrong) way. The following hole, a par-5 with a pond lying directly in front of the green, is conceivably reachable in two, as

FOX MEADOW, STRATFORD

long as you don't let the water get in the way. It's for these reasons that this course can either be kind to the average player or torture to the country's best professionals, depending, of course, on where the tees and pins are placed. Viewed as one of the Top 50 golf courses in Canada, Brudenell is one that definitely has it all — spectacular scenery to complement the course's layout,

which includes six par 3s, six par 4s, and six par 5s. It's the type of course that you will enjoy playing, no matter what your score. With rolling fairways that hug the shorelines and treelines, the walkabout is a joy in itself even when my score isn't what I want it to be.

As a sign of the times, there are many courses that accept tee-time

bookings online through their websites. In the spring of 2002, the six golf courses in the Cavendish area launched an online reservation system, considered a first for Canada. Now, golfers can book their tee times in real time at many of the Island golf courses.

THE LINKS AT CROWBUSH COVE

Economically speaking, the sport plays a major role in the Island's financial well-being. Overall, the golf industry is estimated to create upwards of $85 million in annual economic spinoffs in PEI. With several of the Island's top resorts offering golf vacation packages, it can be a good-value vacation with activities to keep all members of the family, golfers or otherwise, occupied.

CYCLING

CAMPBELL WEBSTER

CYCLING THE CONFEDERATION TRAIL AT MOUNT STEWART

While PEI feels uncluttered, natural and rural, it is in fact the most densely populated province in Canada. This is often an appealing paradox for cyclists. Once you leave a town or community, another one begins, as the back-to-back road signs can attest. Cyclists like choices, and as you slip through the warm salt-air of PEI you are consistently presented with new towns, new people to visit, new harbours and new beaches. Couple this with PEI's highly sociable people and you will understand why my good friend and sometime cycling companion, Erskine Smith, once observed, "The thing about PEI is, no matter where you are, you are always somewhere."

The conversion of 350 kilometres of rail beds to walking and cycling trails has further added to your options. These trails also have the gentle quality of never being too steep, a result of the gradual incline required for trains.

PEI is ideally suited to the day ride or multiple-day continuous touring. The day ride is a personal favourite. When I find time to cycle in the summer and early fall, I typically take out my map of PEI and pick out a circular route that is between 60 and 80 kilometres long. While I have favourite routes, even after years of cycling I often find new round trips that include roads and communities that I have yet to visit. The day-ride approach is recommended to tourists who want to include cycling as part of

TANDEM RIDERS IN
CHARLOTTETOWN

their vacation, but don't plan to spend their entire time on a bicycle.

You can usually tell from just looking at the Tourism PEI map and consulting the very detailed *Visitors' Guide* (both available from Visitor Information Centres and the Department of Tourism at no charge) what will be an interesting ride. To set out on a day ride, simply pick your circular route, choose a starting point, and drive to that point. (I have never had trouble finding a parking spot anywhere when heading out on a day ride.) Lock your car and begin your trip.

One favourite day route of mine starts at the West Point lighthouse and heads north on Route 14 towards Skinners Pond. The first 20 kilometres of this ride affords the cyclist a rare continuous cliff-edge ride along the ocean, passing numerous harbours and historic churches set against the bluffs of the Northumberland Strait. There is ample

CONFEDERATION
TRAIL

WEST POINT LIGHTHOUSE

opportunity to stop and go swimming, as well as a variety of communities to visit along the way. When you get to Campbellton, you head east towards Alberton and the north shore (it is only about a one-hour ride from the south shore to the north shore on this part of the Island). You can get to Alberton via Route 145 or Route 150 or by taking Route 145 and hooking up with the Confederation Trail. Once in Alberton, there are a number of routes back to West Point. Taking an alternate route is often a positive experience for cyclists on PEI.

The second route, and one that I usually ride alone, provides long stretches of interior roads that offer distant horizons and extensive views of woods and farmlands. This route begins at the corner of Routes 2 and 8 in Summerfield. There is a small church on the corner. Follow Route 8 south towards Bedeque and enjoy the view. The Village Store in Bedeque is a great place to stop for lunch and chat with community members who use this store as an informal meeting place. From Bedeque, there's a variety of ways to return to Summerfield — simply pick one from your map. All the return routes are interesting and have very little car traffic on them.

LANDSCAPE NEAR BURLINGTON

The same approach can be applied to picking multiple-day continuous rides. The advantage of planning a bike

tour on PEI is that virtually all of the roads and all of the Confederation Trail are rewarding rides. With the exception of the highways (Routes 1–4, 6, 7, 13, 15 and 16), almost all of the roads have light traffic. So when planning multiple-day rides, you can construct your own routes based on what you'd like to see and do — go to the beach, deep-sea fishing, the theatre or a lobster supper.

Three of the most important concerns of the cyclist are the topography of their cycling destination, the traffic and the quality of the roads. PEI is unique in all these areas and it is important to take these factors into consideration before you begin. If you were playing a word association game and the word "Island" came up you might, being a devout cyclist, respond with the word "flat." While it is true that you won't find any snow-capped mountain ranges on the Island, you mustn't expect it to be one long countertop. It is generally quite flat along the shores, but also considerably more windy. Most inland routes have some hills, and although very few Island hills should take you more than 10 minutes to cycle, they tend to come in rapid succession. If the most feared words of the cyclist are "Lunch is just over that

TRAILSIDE CAFÉ

ROAD NEAR IRISH TOWN

71

mountain," then the most-often-heard words of the Island cyclist are, "Lunch is just over those hills — all five of them." They are not backbreakers, but do not be deceived by their quality or you may be deceived by their quantity. If you want to avoid steep hills completely, stick to the Confederation Trail, although you will likely find the best routes are a blend of the trail and the roads.

PEI has the distinction of having the greatest number of roads per square mile of any Canadian province. For this reason, you can usually get from any given point A to any given point B in a number of ways. This is ideal for cyclists who want to avoid busy routes and still cycle to the most popular areas. If you are setting out to one of these popular destinations, you might try the following method in selecting quieter roads: on your Visitor's Map select the direct route to your destination. These routes, particularly in Queens County, will have a fair amount of traffic. Then choose the route you will take; you should have no trouble finding a secondary road or part of the Confederation Trail beside, or near, the main route. These secondary roads are usually quite narrow and have little or no shoulder, but this is usually not a problem owing to the extremely light traffic. Generally, you will find the most traffic in Queens County, some traffic in Kings County, and very little in Prince County. In early spring and fall, almost anywhere on the Island is lightly travelled with the exception of Routes 1 and 2.

Keeping these tour-planning facts in mind, and opening yourself to the rich amount of choice and community that is PEI, you are bound to have an excellent cycling vacation on the Island.

CYCLISTS AT WEST POINT

WALKING AND HIKING TRAILS

DAN MCASKILL

With the many hues of green from the crops and the deciduous and coniferous forests, interspersed with the vivid reds of our soils, the vistas on the Island are often breathtaking. A simple turn in a trail can bring you to fields of wildflowers rippling in the breeze, shaded forest glades alive with the calls of birds or ponds dappled with autumn leaves. There is something here for everyone — from those who enjoy the boardwalk and waterfront trails of Charlottetown to those who wish to see the Island much as it was when Europeans first visited these shores.

BRIDGE OVER THE MIDGELL RIVER

SHORT HIKES

For walking enthusiasts, the Island features more than 60 short trails scattered throughout the province. The vast majority are designed for a brief exposure to our natural habitats and range from one to three kilometres long. The gentle topography of the Island means that the majority of these trails can be walked by most people, with usually only short slopes of a grade up to 15 percent.

Should you be visiting Charlotte-town and wish a short walk or series of hikes, there is a boardwalk along the waterfront that follows the harbour

CHARLOTTETOWN BOARDWALK

edge and goes past some of the historic homes, such as Beaconsfield. This trail takes you to a trail system through the woodlands and grasslands of Victoria Park. Another trail system, called Routes for Nature and Health, extends from the University of Prince Edward Island to the inlets and rivers on the northwestern edge of Charlottetown. For part of its length it runs beside the Ellen's Creek Wildlife Management Area, where thousands of waterfowl may be seen in autumn. This trail can be accessed from Charlottetown's core by taking the Confederation Trail to the east of the University, and then crossing the campus to the eastern entry point for the trail. In addition to these trails, the Royalty Oaks Natural Area trail on the eastern side of Charlottetown offers an interpretive walk through a four-hectare hardwood woodlot that features some very large specimens of our provincial tree, the red oak.

The six demonstration woodlot trails in the provincial forest, which are marked on Tourism PEI's map of the Island, offer an opportunity to look at various forest management choices. There are two trails in each county, located at New Harmony (near Souris), Valleyfield (near Montague), Auburn (25 kilometres northeast of Charlottetown), Brookvale, Wellington (near Summerside), and Foxley River (near Portage). Each woodlot features self-guided trails with interpretive brochures and signage describing various practical forest management options available to private landowners.These options focus on forest stewardship for timber, wildlife or other forest values. At the other end of the forest-management spectrum, the three trails at Macphail Woods near Orwell focus on nature interpretation and forest management treatments geared to ecological forestry. While at Macphail Woods, a visit to the nature centre or the Sir Andrew Macphail House will add to the experience. This site is

WATERSHED AT HILLSBOROUGH RIVER

near the TransCanada Highway, about 32 kilometres east of Charlottetown.

For those who wish to experience some of the Island's oldest remaining forests, the trail at Townshend Woodlot north of Souris on the Souris Line Road (Route 305) offers the opportunity to see a remnant portion of the Acadian hardwood forest that dates back to the mid-1800s. In southeastern Prince Edward Island, the Eagle's View Golf Course and Interpretive Centre's trails bring you through a stand of magnificent red and white pine along the side of MacLures Pond. This site features two trails and an interpretive centre exploring the culture and natural history of this region. Both these sites form part of the Island's natural areas system, designed to conserve representative biological reserves in the province.

The Pigot Trail features a freshwater marsh located 20 kilometres east of Charlottetown in Mount Stewart. This trail can be accessed off the Confederation Trail just south of the Hillsborough River Eco-Centre or via Main Street. The trails at the Harvey Moore Wildlife Management Area (Route 4 south of Montague) meander around ponds that are teeming with waterfowl, especially during the migration season. An interpretive trail circles Mooneys Pond on Route 22 about 10 kilometres south of Mount Stewart. This is a semi-natural area for rearing Atlantic salmon, and an interpretive centre on the site allows one to explore the life history of this species.

Prince Edward Island National Park occupies the central north shore of the province. Here you can venture along wooded pathways, across marshlands and ponds, through old fields, and across dunes to the beach. The area has many attractions, and some may golf, shop for crafts or go to an amusement park while others hike. The trails in Cavendish offer the walkers and hikers of the group a variety of choices. There are the Balsam Hollow and Haunted Woods trails at Anne of Green Gables House (note: there is a small additional access charge at this site), or the longer, double-loop Homestead Trail through coastal marsh, old fields and woodlands. On the eastern side of the National Park in Dalvay and Stanhope, the Bubbling Springs, Farmlands, Reeds and Rushes, and Woodlands Trails will bring you through wooded old fields, past barachois

FAMILY PICNIC ON ST. PETERS BAY

ponds and through dunes. Lying still further east and separate from the main park, the Greenwich adjunct to the PEI National Park is located on the north side of St. Peters Bay. This magnificent area features one short and two longer interpretive trails.

BOARDWALK AT GREENWICH

The 4.5-kilometre Greenwich Dunes Trail travels through old fields, woodlands, a pond via a floating boardwalk, dunes and the shore, leading the walker to a spectacular viewpoint over the Greenwich sand dunes. Steps and short steep slopes make this trail inaccessible to those in wheelchairs. The 1.3-kilometre Havre St. Pierre Trail explores the Acadian period of our history, while a slightly longer trail takes visitors through archeological sites dating back 10,000 years.

In the western part of the Island, the Fairy Trails at Cedar Dunes Provincial Park offer an opportunity to explore lowland forests of spruce, balsam fir and cedar. The adjacent sand beach allows you to cool off after the hike. The Black Marsh Nature Trail in the extreme northwestern tip of the province wanders along coastal cliffs and via a boardwalk through a bog near the Atlantic Wind Test Site. Seals can often be seen in the coastal waters. On Route 2 near Coleman Corner, the Trout River Trail winds along the historic river after which it is named. North of Summerside, tucked in the northwest corner of Malpeque Bay, lies the Path of Our Forefathers Trail with its two loops (3 kilometres and 7 kilometres). These trails allow the hiker to explore the Mi'kmaq culture and their use of plants amidst the Lennox Island landscape.

CEDAR DUNES PROVINCIAL PARK

In the south-central area, the Strathgartney Nature Trail located just east of Bonshaw runs through the woodlands overlooking the historic West River. To the north of this site, the Nordic Ski Trails in the Brookvale Provincial Forest have over 10 kilometres of walking trails. In addition, this is a great woodland birding site.

A stop at the local Visitor Information Centre or PEI National Park offices will provide brochures for some of the better trails. A Trail and Nature Map is available from the Island Nature Trust and other outlets. Some of the trails in the PEI National Park in Charlottetown and at other sites such as Lennox Island are designed for mobility-challenged individuals.

CONFEDERATION TRAIL, HILLSBOROUGH

EXCURSIONS

Confederation Trail

The pre-eminent trail system on Prince Edward Island for those desiring true excursion hiking or cycling is the Confederation Trail. This low-slope trail runs 357 kilometres along the abandoned railway beds that transect the Island, and grows longer every year. The main Confederation Trail now spans the Island tip to tip, a distance of 279 kilometres. It takes you through woodlands, rich fields, along some of our magnificent harbours and bays and through many of the communities that played a key role in the development of Canada's smallest province. The compacted stone-dust surface provides excellent footing.

WOOD ISLANDS PROVINCIAL PARK

Besides the main line, branch lines provide hiking routes from Emerald to Borden-Carleton (18.5 kilometres), Royalty Junction to Charlottetown (9 kilometres), Mount

Stewart to Georgetown (39.5 kilometres), Montague Junction to Montague (10 kilometres) and Harmony Junction to Souris (8.2 kilometres), and a section of trail in the southeast runs from Murray River to Murray Harbour. The latter section is now being expanded to connect these areas to Wood Islands. Agriculture was not the only thing that moulded this landscape over the centuries. The need for shipping access points along the train route led to frequent stops in many small communities. Today this has

yielded a trail system on which hikers have many options — from a few kilometres to as much as one can cover. Communities are scattered along the trail and offer resting places and shopping sites. In some of these communities, shorter trails allow one to explore various landscapes and cultures.

SCENIC TRAIL BESIDE THE HILLSBOROUGH RIVER

Two of the Confederation Trail segments follow historically important waterways. The route eastward from Charlottetown follows the Hillsborough, a Canadian Heritage River. Here, hundreds of sailing ships were built along the tidal estuary that stretches over 30 kilometres upriver from Charlottetown. The Mi'kmaq, French, Scottish and Irish all used this water corridor to access the Island. In the east, the branch lines between Georgetown, Cardigan and Montague join the major communities along the Three Rivers, which was designated a heritage river in 2004.

FIELDS AT ST. ANN

In the northeast the termination point of the trail is in Elmira. Here one of the branch museums of the Prince Edward Island Museum and Heritage Foundation celebrates the Island's railroad history. From Elmira, roadways allow the hiker to continue the excursion to the eastern terminus of the Island at East Point.

The western section of Confederation Trail extends from Charlottetown to Tignish (actually mile "0"). This 180-kilometre section of trail leads through the central uplands region, providing spectacular views, particularly during the autumn when the hardwood and mixed forest provides a dazzling display of colour. From Kensington westward, the topography is relatively flat. Amidst the agricultural landscape, small woodlots, wetlands and streams abound. The wetter soils in this area yield some different plants for those exploring the trailside botany.

For further information and maps, contact Island Trails, Box 265, Charlottetown, PEI, CIA 7K4, ask for a Confederation Trail brochure at a Visitor Information Centre, or visit InfoPEI at www.peiplay.com

Provincial Forests

In 2000, the provincial government designated a system of 22 provincial forest areas and 187 satellite provincial forests scattered throughout the Island. These properties have over 270 kilometres of forest roads that are accessible to the public. The forest road and highway junctions are marked by a green diamond-shaped sign on which there's a gold image of an acorn with a leaf/conifer on top of the acorn.

SCENIC HERITAGE ROADS

A campaign by concerned Islanders and the Island Nature Trust led to the creation of a protected system of Scenic Heritage Roads in 1987. This allows visitors and Islanders alike to carefully drive or walk on sections of tree-canopied and open roads that have outstanding beauty. These narrow, low-maintenance roads are designated on the PEI highway map and a brochure highlighting them is available at the Island Nature Trust.

NEAR IRISH TOWN

ARCHITECTURAL TREASURES

REG PORTER

ST. SIMON AND ST. JUDE	**ST. SIMON AND ST. JUDE, TIGNISH** The Church of St. Simon and St. Jude at Tignish was built by its first resident pastor, Peter McIntyre, an energetic man who, in 1860, the year of the church's completion would become the Island's third Roman Catholic bishop. McIntyre obtained a design from the New York architect Patrick Keilly, an Irish follower of Augustus Welby Pugin, one of the greatest of 19th-century proponents of the Gothic style as suitable for Christian worship. The church is immense and built entirely out of locally made brick,
 **PIPE ORGAN AT ST. SIMON AND ST. JUDE**	most of which still covers the building. The interior, once decorated to resemble stone blocks, was repainted in 1888 by a Montreal painter and decorator, Frans-Xavier Meloche. He and his students painted life-size statues of the twelve apostles on the walls between the large stained glass windows in the aisles. The chancel has two huge murals representing the Assumption of the Virgin into heaven and the Transfiguration. **CHURCH OF THE IMMACULATE CONCEPTION, PALMER ROAD** This little-known wooden church was built between 1891 and 1893. Its architect was Frans-Xavier Meloche.

The church is in the Gothic style and covered entirely in elaborate designs of shaped wooden shingles, typical of building practices of the time. The three altars, built by Island craftsman Bernard Creamer, have survived in perfect condition and give visitors an accurate impression of the original appearance of the structure. The elaborate wooden trusses that support the vault and the patterned wood create a rich interior.

One extraordinary addition to the building is a complete stained glass cycle designed by P. John Burden and executed by Blaine Hrabi, both Island artists, to replace the original clear glass of the church's many windows. Begun in 1985, the windows are striking, especially the great rose window in the façade of the church, which combines traditional Christian symbolism with exceptionally fine contemporary design.

McLEAN HOUSE, SOUTHWEST LOT 16

The Queen Anne Revival Style (c. 1885–1900) is characterized by a large central core topped with a hipped roof decorated with classical motifs of an earlier age, and a tall corner tower with a high conical roof. The McLean House at Southwest Lot 16 is one of the finest examples of this style on the Island.

The house was designed around 1912 for J. G. McLean by Percy Tanton, a self-taught Summerside architect. An unusual feature of this Queen Anne house is the fact that the great corner tower was left open, providing two large balconies overlooking the splendid vista of Grand River with the tall profile of the gothic church of St. Patrick's in the distance. The effect this creates is far more harmonious than in most surviving houses of the period on the Island.

CHURCH OF THE IMMACULATE CONCEPTION, FAÇADE AND ROSE WINDOW

McLEAN HOUSE

**ABOVE AND BELOW:
YEO HOUSE**

YEO HOUSE, GREEN PARK PROVINCIAL PARK, PORT HILL

James Yeo was an entrepreneur and shipbuilder from North Cornwall near Bideford, England, who had settled in the area of Port Hill by the early 1820s. A rough and driven man, he eventually founded a mercantile and shipbuilding empire in the area of Port Hill. In 1866 he decided to build a new home overlooking his shipyard.

This house, the culmination of an earlier Romantic trend of centre gable decorated with elaborate barge

boards along the eaves, has been restored to its original condition by the Prince Edward Island Museum and Heritage Foundation.

The interior has formal parlours, a dining room and a study flanking a centre hall which runs the length of the main house into the kitchen wing.

It is at this isolated site, more than any other, that visitors may feel a powerful affinity with the past.

ST. MARY'S CHURCH, INDIAN RIVER

In 1896 the old church at Indian River was struck by lightning and burned to the ground. By October 1902, the present structure, designed by Charlottetown architect William Critchlow Harris, was consecrated. An imposing structure on high ground, it can be seen for miles.

ST. MARY'S CHURCH

In recent years, the fate of this church was in doubt because there was no longer a congregation to support a parish. Its renewed life is due to the efforts of passionately dedicated local individuals who raised funds, with Island-wide support, for its restoration

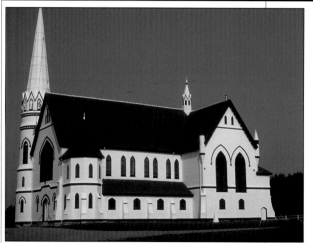

ST. MARY'S CHURCH

and repair. Now concerts of various kinds are held there every summer and the fame of this exceptionally well-designed church is spreading.

The exterior of the church is typical of the shingle style developed in the United States before the turn of the century: shingles literally wrap around everything, even the smallest turrets. The chancel and altar are particularly fine, representing Harris's design at its best.

THE FARMERS' BANK, ANGLO RUSTICO

The Farmers' Bank in Rustico was built in the 1860s by Father Georges-Antoine Belcourt, a priest with years of missionary experience in western Canada who was sent to take over the administration of this mostly French-speaking parish.

It is constructed out of local sandstone which was quarried and shaped by local masons. The marks of their chisels on the stones remain as testimony to their individuality and skill. The style chosen for this building was English Georgian, at that time the supreme style of the reigning establishment. The function of this bank was far from the ordinary concept of banks in the country. Prefiguring the co-operative movement in Prince Edward Island, the bank served as an organization for local farmers, providing security in the form of low-interest loans in times of need. The bank even printed its own paper currency, now incredibly rare and known only through a few surviving examples. It served the local population from 1864 to 1894. Today this structure has undergone a major restoration and houses the local historical museum.

THE FARMERS' BANK

STRATHGARTNEY HOMESTEAD, STRATHGARTNEY

In 1875, Robert Bruce Stewart, the largest landed proprietor in Prince Edward Island and master of Strathgartney, was forced to sell most of his 67,000 acres of land to the Island government. This was the end of a long and bitter struggle against British absentee landlords that had been going on for a century.

Although the house has undergone many changes over the years, including the addition of a larger "new house" to

STRATHGARTNEY

the original homestead, the feeling of a grand home surrounded by unbounded acres of timber and agricultural land is still to be encountered in this spot. The oldest part of the house is the smaller centre gable structure, which retains much of its character as a building of the pre-Confederation period. The larger, later addition looks over the remains of a terraced garden, which, to gauge from its remnants and stray perennials, must have been of extraordinary beauty.

Nearby is Strathgartney Provincial Park where visitors may explore one of the last great stretches of upland forest left on the Island.

THE ATWELL STONE HOUSE, CLYDE RIVER

During the 1830s and 1840s a fair number of local red sandstone houses were built in the style popular at that time, consisting of a central plan with one or two bays and a centre gable or dormer above the front door. Today only a handful of these precious houses remain as witnesses to the determination of British settlers to build in the style and materials they knew best at home. By the 1850s, such houses were no longer built because the framed timber house was cheaper and better adapted to PEI's climate. At the same time, the Island's brick-making industry began to overshadow sandstone in popularity.

The Atwell house, built in 1842, always attracts a great deal of attention because of its peculiar hooded gable, the only one of its kind in the province.

The exterior of the house is well-preserved and demonstrates clearly the style of most of these stone houses. Windows and doors were framed in a similar manner. The rest of the wall area was carefully filled in with rubble construction. The contrast between the smoothly finished major blocks and this rubble infill creates a dramatic texture that is particularly visible when the sun shines obliquely on any of its wall surfaces.

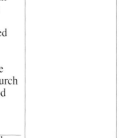

ALL SAINTS CHURCH

ALL SAINTS CHURCH, CARDIGAN

This picturesquely situated church, built in 1874, is in the neo-Gothic style. It was later enlarged by the addition of a transept.

The high altar of this church is of particular interest. It was built by William Lewis, a native of Dumfries in Scotland. Lewis was a stonemason whose work is to be found in cemeteries all across the Island. The architectural framework for the altar is carved out of a grey-green Nova Scotia sandstone. All the panels of the altar table and arches are filled with a white marble with pale grey veining, upon which are carved various sacred symbols. The design can be called primitive, but its execution is flawless and the general effect is magnificent.

The building is bright and cheerful and is one of the best surviving examples of a pre-Vatican II Council church where all the statues of saints and two fine carved-wood side altars have been preserved.

THE BEATON/LEARD HOUSE, SOURIS

This small elegant neo-classical house was built around 1854 by Donald Beaton, an important fish merchant and politician. He chose the centre-plan Georgian country villa style, popular on the Island in the early years of the last century, with a centre hall and staircase leading to pairs of rooms on either side.

In the 1950s the house came into the possession of the Leard family, and they renovated it very sympathetically in a New England Colonial Revival style. Although the original details of the house were all replaced with new cladding, the earlier style and proportions were entirely compatible with the new shell.

This building demonstrates, perhaps more than any other structure on the Island, the persistence of the neo-classical styles on the Island, even though the period between 1850 and the First World War was marked by a tremendous flowering of all the late Victorian eclectic styles that imitated Gothic, Italian Renaissance, a non-existent Queen Anne, Romanesque and, finally, a return to the classical values of another age.

POINT PRIM LIGHTHOUSE

POINT PRIM LIGHTHOUSE, POINT PRIM

To the east of Charlottetown is a long splinter of hard sandstone that forms a spearhead-like peninsula of land, which the French and Acadian settlers of the 18th century called Pointe Prime. From earliest times, the point and the dangerous rocky shallows in its vicinity proved a hazard to navigation. In 1845 a decision was made to build a permanent structure to aid navigation through these treacherous waters.

POINT PRIM LIGHTHOUSE INTERIOR

Isaac Smith, a Yorkshireman who immigrated to the Island in 1817 at the age of 22, built the lieutenant governor's residence (1834), an insane asylum and the Central Academy, which was to become Prince of Wales College. Smith built Point Prim Lighthouse while he was in the middle of constructing the Colonial Building, now called Province House, in Charlottetown.

This circular sixty-foot shingled tower was built of brick over a massive timber core which can still be seen by visitors. The polygonal lantern is the original, and although it is now run by electricity, all original elements remain.

THE MACPHAIL HOUSE, ORWELL CORNER

Sir Andrew Macphail (1864–1938), a pathologist at McGill University in Montreal, was a writer, doctor, organizer of the Canadian Field Ambulance in the First World War and an agriculturalist. Through his research on lobster canning, he became the saviour of the Island lobster industry which, at the time, was suffering from spoiled stock resulting from improper sanitary conditions during packing.

Sir Andrew, who liked to spend his summers at the family farm at Orwell, loved the good things of life. Around 1911 he had a baronial dining hall built on the site of the kitchen wing so he could entertain his friends, a veritable Who's Who of the day.

Today the Macphail estate is owned by a foundation dedicated to keeping alive the memory of Sir Andrew and his times. The house has become a tea room and conference centre, and the remains of the extensive estate feature a nature trail and experimental woodlot.

MACPHAIL HOUSE

THE CHURCH OF CHRIST'S PAGODA-LIKE ROOF

THE CHURCH OF CHRIST, MONTAGUE

Travellers entering Montague are often surprised by a small, very attractive, brick church with a tower capped by an enigmatic pagoda-like roof. The Church of Christ was built of locally made brick in 1876, probably to the designs of a very energetic and talented builder named John McLellan (1820–1887). In 1856, a Rev. George Bowler in Roxbury, Mass., had published a richly illustrated book called *Chapel and Church Architecture*. John McLellan owned a copy of this book and he seems to have combined two of Bowler's designs into one! The first was in the Italianate style with the typical round-headed window, which gave its shape to the building. But the pagoda-like tower roof came from an entirely different design. The two have been combined to produce this extraordinarily attractive structure. Recent additions have been discreetly built so as not to distract from the church's soaring profile.

FESTIVALS AND CELEBRATIONS

JULIE V. WATSON

The dictionary describes a festival as a regularly occurring occasion of feasting or special ceremonies; a series or season of cultural events; conviviality and revelry. The folks in Prince Edward Island took those words to heart eons ago, beginning traditions that see a great spirit of celebration throughout the year. Quite simply put, Prince Edward Island has great festivals with themes to tickle any fancy. Indeed, these special community-based events represent the gems in a crown for Prince Edward Island.

Prince Edward Islanders have demonstrated their love of celebrations and festivities since the days when the Fathers of Confederation arrived in 1864 for the Charlottetown Conference, which led to the founding of our nation. While meetings and great debates were going on among politicians, Island citizens gathered from far and

MIDWAY DURING OLD HOME WEEK IN CHARLOTTETOWN

CEILIDH AT BRUDENELL

wide to have some fun. It didn't take long for those visiting dignitaries to realize they were missing out. Grand balls, parties onboard ships and in the governor's mansion, and spectacular dinners were quickly organized to celebrate their coming together in fine Island style.

The celebrations have changed in nature. Things are more casual today. We tend to party on shore instead of on

PEI INTERNATIONAL SHELLFISH FESTIVAL

ships, but Islanders still celebrate both our heritage and all that is great in this more modern time.

The Charlottetown Festival sets the tone of summer entertainment in the capital city, with free outdoor performances whose young performers gain a loyal following, as well as mainstage productions. Its venue, the Confederation Centre of the Arts in the heart of downtown Charlottetown, is home to the original stage show *Anne of Green Gables—The Musical*™ , and offers a variety of on-stage performances.

Festivities around the city are topped by the Festival of Lights held on July 1, Canada Day, an event that bills itself as Canada's biggest birthday bash east of Ottawa. The city rocks with nightly concerts, international buskers, a food fair, carnival and midway, all topped by a fireworks display over Charlottetown Harbour.

At the other end of the summer season the city waterfront is the place to be. A huge tent rocks with the PEI International Shellfish Festival held in mid-September. This celebration of PEI shellfish includes oysters, lobster,

mussels and clams — those same delicacies enjoyed by the "Fathers" so many years ago. Great fiddlers with toe-tapping-style Maritime entertainment in a kitchen party atmosphere, the PEI/Eastern Canadian Oyster Shucking Championships, the PEI/International Chowder Championships and much more make for a simply great weekend.

This is just a sampling of dozens of PEI festivals. You can be sure Islanders celebrate their heritage, and just about anything else, given the opportunity. The prime season runs from May through September. Summer events range from professional productions that last the season to small one- or two-day affairs, which many consider to be tiny jewels in the calendar year.

There is no doubt that music is the backbone for many of the Island's best gatherings. While traditional offerings are the heart and soul of our festivals and events, they represent just a portion of what is available. From classical to Celtic, from production song-and-dance numbers to humourous one-man acts, our festivals are renowned for their on-stage performance.

Bluegrass and old-time band enthusiasts can get a double whammy with back-to-back toe-tapping weekend festivals held in Rollo Bay and Abrams Village each July.

Organizers of the Indian River Festival decided to add a little romance to their fine music series, which invites lovers of chamber music, jazz and choral concerts to surrender their senses to the breathtaking acoustics of the

sA SCENE FROM *MURDER IN THE CATHEDRAL* PERFORMED IN ST. MARY'S CHURCH AS PART OF THE INDIAN RIVER FESTIVAL

CONFEDERATION CENTRE OF THE ARTS

RE-ENACTORS AT THREE RIVERS

MEMBERS OF THE COLLEGE OF PIPING AND DRUMMING

century-old St. Mary's Church in Indian River. In the summer, enjoy gourmet coffee and treats on the lawn, but also check out this festival of "music you can hear with your heart" year-round, including a very fine Christmas concert.

As much as they love music, Prince Edward Islanders also love to celebrate their roots, and do so through Acadian, Irish and Celtic festivals, concerts and games. These gatherings focus on things traditional—after all, descendants can trace their families back to the pioneers who arrived from across the Atlantic as early as the 1600s.

HIGHLAND GAMES

The College of Piping in Summerside is home to a Celtic Festival, which kicks off with competitions and celebrations of the Highland arts of piping, dancing, drumming and all things Scottish at the Summerside Highland Gathering. In August, the Caledonia Club of PEI hosts an annual Highland Games at Lord Selkirk Provincial Park in Eldon, adding traditional athletic competitions and a kilted golf tournament to the usual concert, piping and dancing. Or for a true "over 'ome" setting, the castles and gardens of Woodleigh Replicas provide an appropriate backdrop during the Woodleigh Highland Games.

Acadian flavour reigns at the Festival Port-LaJoie de Charlottetown, which kicks off Acadian and Francophone celebrations in May with three days of music and a super kitchen party. North Rustico's Festival Rendez-vous Rustico is an Acadian celebration of traditional music, dance, food and games, which happens in late July. Then there's the

SAILING IN
CHARLOTTETOWN
HARBOUR

Centre Expo-Festival Centre in Abrams Village, which celebrates Acadian music, warm hospitality and traditional dishes (yes, lobster is one of them) during July and August.

The newest Acadian Festival, Fête Roma, held in late September, includes re-enactments at a newly restored historic site. This rural event celebrating 1730s life in PEI's "Roma at Three Rivers" site in Eastern Prince Edward Island is a refreshing change for the history buff. It's a good idea to go early, as the narrow clay roads that take you back into the woods can get clogged with visitors.

The Fiddlers and Followers weekend in Cavendish adds barbecues, lobster parties and old-fashioned picnics to their music festival held in Rainbow Valley. The Irish Festival in Charlottetown celebrates traditional Irish music and dance, bringing together some of the best East Coast talent. Emerald Junction promotes Irish heritage and community spirit with an Irish Festival in late July. For an alternative sound, there's the annual Cymbria Music Fest in Rustico, which combines camping revelry and Maritime bands for a fun September weekend.

Islanders celebrate their harvests and fine foods, particularly seafood, with great gusto. The Tyne Valley Oyster Festival is a down-home rural party complete with a parade and, as one jolly fellow said, "great grub."

The Summerside Lobster Carnival has been going on since the 1950s. Along with lobster, of course, it features great harness racing, dinners, talent shows, street sales, a fiddling contest and a spelling bee, along with a traditional midway and entertainment. There is also a Cornfest in Cornwall, a Wild Blueberry Festival in St. Peters, a Potato Blossom Festival in O'Leary and wine festivals in Charlottetown. And, in Tignish, they celebrate Irish Moss!

FIDDLER AT
RICHMOND

Lovers of things that move—cars, boats and motorcycles—are not left out. July is highlighted by the annual PEI Street Rod Association Show, one of the oldest and largest outdoor car shows in Eastern Canada with street rods, antiques, special interest and classic cars. British Car Days Across the Bridge is a smaller affair, but is attracting more enthusiasts each year.

The Island Rally, now 20 years young, lures hundreds of motorcyclists to the Brackley Beach area each Labour Day weekend for a family-oriented gathering that includes motorcycle games.

The Souris Regatta Festival of the Sea adds

GOLD CUP AND SAUCER RACE, CHARLOTTETOWN

ACADIAN FLAG, MONT-CARMEL

such things as wood-carving competitions, and fear factor and greasy pole events to the traditional boat races, beauty pageant and live entertainment.

For a real Maritime experience, the Northumberland Provincial Fisheries Festival in Murray River has activities ranging from provincial dory races to dances to a poultry show. For a similar experience, there's also the West Point Lighthouse Festival and Boat Races.

And then there are the celebrations that focus on the agricultural lifestyle enjoyed by so many Islanders. Many of them have new events that make for great spectator enjoyment. Noting the loyal following garnered by traditional horse pulls, some folks decided to add their own twist to the competitions, which prove both noisy and exciting. They like to "pull" with just about anything mechanized—tractors, three- and four-wheelers and lawnmowers. Whether four-footed or four-wheeled, the demonstrations of horsepower are great fun.

Horse shows with draft horses, English and Western riding and now miniature horses are ever popular. The tiny equines in particular are attracting a growing audience that delights in their antics.

Of course, the agricultural exhibitions still include livestock, home arts and crafts, and many more traditional components. You'll find woodsmen's competitions, meals, midways, antique engines, exhibits and displays, trade shows, all manner of competitions and just plain old-fashioned good neighbourly visiting going on.

Old Home Week in Charlottetown draws folks back to the Island from far and wide to take in the PEI Provincial Exhibition. The longest and largest of the exhibitions, it has 15 cards of top-notch harness racing held over 10 days in August. It also includes a huge parade through Charlottetown with floats and bands luring folks streetside. In fact, the capital shuts down for this popular forerunner to the Gold Cup and Saucer Race. Gold Cup Night fairly vibrates with excitement as one of the region's most prestigious harness races brings the best horses to the gate.

Other great exhibitions to take in include the Crapaud Exhibition in late July, Alberton's Prince County Exhibition in mid-summer, and L'Exposition Agricole et le Festival Acadien in Abrams Village in late August.

While there are lots of traditional festivals, the fun extends to things that might be considered beyond the norm. Capture PEI, for example, attracts writers and photographers; the Gay and Lesbian Pride Festival is fun-filled and colourful; and the Studio Tour Weekend celebrates Island crafts.

THEATRE

CAMPBELL WEBSTER

While all things tourism in PEI may not lead back to *Anne of Green Gables*, a great deal of it does. The influence of the Anne novels is considerable and has had the happy effect of introducing a vibrant summer theatre scene, both Anne-related and otherwise. PEI is unique among the Maritime provinces in having a play as a pillar of its tourist industry, and attending *Anne of Green Gables — The Musical*™ is a common part of many PEI vacations.

And rightly so, because as a play Anne succeeds on many levels and has few detractors. But its popularity has always presented Island theatre professionals with a peculiar challenge: how to inspire tourists to see theatre other than Anne.

One answer may once again simply be *Anne*. A new play, also based on the *Anne* books, gives Anne-lovers a chance to see a new musical about the courtship of Anne of Green Gables. Entitled *Anne and Gilbert, the Island Love Story*, this definitive Island romance graces the historic Victoria Playhouse in the near-magical setting of Victoria-by-the-Sea.

GONDOLIERS

***ANNE OF GREEN GABLES — THE MUSICAL*™**

VICTORIA PLAYHOUSE, VICTORIA

Over the years, concerted efforts of a variety of groups to build regular theatre audiences has produced some great amateur and professional theatre, whose quality often exceeds what you would expect of a small community.

The oldest of these other theatres is the Victoria Playhouse, now in its third decade. In addition to *Anne and Gilbert* it runs a full season of live theatre, a Monday-night concert series and regular storytelling shows by artistic director Erskine Smith. You might begin your Victoria theatre experience with dinner at the fantastic Landmark Café, run by the Island's number one extrovert, Eugene Sauvé, giving you the makings of a memorable Island evening.

Many smaller venues across the Island feature storytellers, a re-emerging Island tradition that takes you deep into the heart of Island history and culture. Storytellers have built a devoted following by telling stories from across the Island, often presenting them with traditional musical accompaniment provided by local musicians. Some of the more popular storytellers are David Weale, the group Hedgerow, with Alan Buchanan and Allan Rankin and Erskine Smith. They turn up at various venues including the Barn Theatre in Stanley Bridge, the Jubilee Theatre in Summerside, the Victoria Playhouse and small theatres and tiny community halls (often former one-room schools) that dot the Island.

The Indian River Festival has become increasingly popular in recent years. The Festival is set in the majestic St. Mary's Church, which was designed by famed Island architect William Critchlow Harris, who had a gift for architectural acoustic design. Programming is a range of classical, jazz, theatrical and popular shows from across Canada and around the world. This impressive lineup features new shows a few times each week, and includes such diverse acts as South Africa Sings and the Belfast Pipe and Drum Band to classical and popular concerts under artistic director Robert Kortgaard. The new line-up is announced in the spring.

The Arts Guild in Charlottetown is a popular and active theatre space. Its programming is eclectic, ranging from the energetic productions of aspiring young performers to

A PERFORMANCE OF *MURDER IN THE CATHEDRAL* AS PART OF THE INDIAN RIVER FESTIVAL

HARBOURFRONT JUBILEE THEATRE, SUMMERSIDE

95

plays by the finest Island writers, such as Governor General's Award–winning playwright Kent Stetson. It is also often the site of performances by the Island's sketch comedy groups. The best and most memorable production in recent years has been *Sketch 22*, the visceral and hilarious attack on all things Prince Edward Island and beyond. The comedic writing skills of its principals — Rob MacDonald, Matt Rainnie and Graham Putnam — stand up to the best in Canadian sketch comedy.

To get off the beaten track check out the Festivals and Events page of the Prince Edward Island government website at www.gov.pe.ca, the monthly Arts & Entertainment publication *The Buzz* and the local newspapers. There you will find a very complete listing of almost every public performance at community centres and theatres, churches and museums. There are real finds in these listings, such as the Basin Head Fisheries Museum speaker series or the weekly ceilidhs at Malpeque Community Centre. In recent years more and more of these smaller shows are appearing, proving that Island culture may start with *Anne*, but it does not end there.

ANNE OF GREEN GABLES —THE MUSICAL™

CRAFTS

RYAN VICTORIA MCADAM-YOUNG

Making crafts is part of the rural tradition on PEI. As the tourism industry grows, more Islanders are turning this tradition into a commercial enterprise.

Many of the Island's artisans have gained an international reputation. The craft shops and outlets mentioned here are a few favourites from each region. With a road map and a bit of luck, you'll probably find a little gem of a shop not listed here.

ISLAND CRAFTS ON DISPLAY

CRAFT SHOP IN RUSTICO

HILLS & HARBOURS

If you reach PEI via the Wood Islands ferry, the Hills and Harbours region will give you your first taste of Island craft-hunting. Travelling east along the Kings Byway Scenic Drive will lead you through Little Sands, home of Rossignol Wines and some wonderful works of folk art. Murray Harbour boasts shops such as the Village Emporium and Miss Elly's Genteel Gifts & Stuff, a Victorian-style shop that allows visitors to peruse the shelves of Island-made items and catch a weaving demonstration. More weaving takes place down the road in Murray River at Moon Shadow Mementos. You might also want to visit this quaint little village's Old General Store, which combines past and present with an array of crafts in an old-fashioned setting.

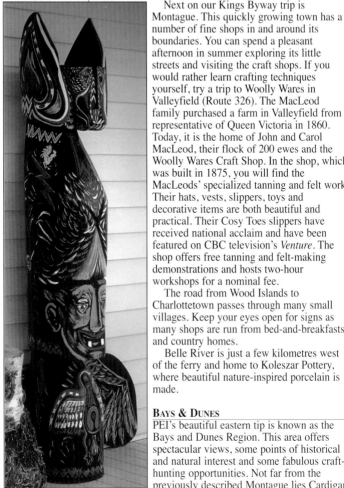

MI'KMAQ CRAFT

Next on our Kings Byway trip is Montague. This quickly growing town has a number of fine shops in and around its boundaries. You can spend a pleasant afternoon in summer exploring its little streets and visiting the craft shops. If you would rather learn crafting techniques yourself, try a trip to Woolly Wares in Valleyfield (Route 326). The MacLeod family purchased a farm in Valleyfield from a representative of Queen Victoria in 1860. Today, it is the home of John and Carol MacLeod, their flock of 200 ewes and the Woolly Wares Craft Shop. In the shop, which was built in 1875, you will find the MacLeods' specialized tanning and felt work. Their hats, vests, slippers, toys and decorative items are both beautiful and practical. Their Cosy Toes slippers have received national acclaim and have been featured on CBC television's *Venture*. The shop offers free tanning and felt-making demonstrations and hosts two-hour workshops for a nominal fee.

The road from Wood Islands to Charlottetown passes through many small villages. Keep your eyes open for signs as many shops are run from bed-and-breakfasts and country homes.

Belle River is just a few kilometres west of the ferry and home to Koleszar Pottery, where beautiful nature-inspired porcelain is made.

BAYS & DUNES

PEI's beautiful eastern tip is known as the Bays and Dunes Region. This area offers spectacular views, some points of historical and natural interest and some fabulous craft-hunting opportunities. Not far from the previously described Montague lies Cardigan. Hugging tightly to the shore, this charming village is home to one of PEI's most exciting artisan organizations, the Cardigan Craft Centre. While you visit you can find spinners, weavers, potters and woodworkers turning raw materials into stunning works of art.

Continuing east along the Kings Byway Scenic Drive, you will pass through Rollo Bay, home of the "Road To Rollo Bay" concert series. Look for signs for in-home craft shops, as craftspeople will advertise their wares with front-yard signs that simply say "Quilts For Sale" or "Woodworking."

Next on the map is Souris, location of the Magdalen Islands ferry terminal and commercial centre of eastern King's County. Here you will find Log Cabin Arts & Crafts and Naturally Yours. Both of these stores offer a broad range of locally made items, from dried flowers to books and paintings.

Continuing on the Kings Byway we come to East Point, which as the name suggests, is PEI's most eastern tip. The East Point Lighthouse Craft Shop has a wide array of regional books and crafts.

Rounding the tip of the Island and heading west, you will pass through St. Peters Bay, Morell and Mount Stewart, each of which has its own craft shop offerings. If you are interested in quilting and rug hooking, make sure you stop at the Red Stone Gallery & Island Craft Centre in North Lake.

ANNE'S LAND

On PEI's central north shore the Blue Heron Scenic Drive is filled to the brim with restaurants, family attractions, outdoor adventures and craft shops. A map will come in handy when you take a few detours off the beaten track to hunt for the attractions that are of particular interest to you.

PETER JANSONS AT THE DUNES STUDIO

The eastern part of this region is home to the Dunes Studio Gallery in Brackley Beach. The gallery is one of the Island's best-known and distinctive handcraft studios. It doesn't look like it from the road, but its low front profile sweeps up to the back, where a mostly glass wall provides views down rolling fields to the sea. You will find here the crafts and artwork of 70 contributing artists, including that of award-winning designer and craftsman, and Dunes owner, Peter Jansons. The pottery shop is open for viewing. The displays include hand-made pottery, wood, metal and glassware, paintings, sculptures and gold jewellery, as well as furniture, crafts and artwork brought back from Peter's winter trips to Bali and Indonesia. Plan to spend an afternoon at the gallery to really enjoy all that it has to offer. The café is worth a visit as are the beautiful water gardens that have been pictured in *Canadian Gardener* and *Gardening Life*.

DUNES STUDIO GALLERY

WOODWORKER JACQUES GAUDREAU

MEMORIES GIFT SHOP, NEW LONDON

VILLAGE POTTERY, NEW LONDON

Travelling west along the Blue Heron Drive will take you to the Rustico area. Here you will find Gaudreau's Fine Woodworking. At New Glasgow's Toy Factory along Route 258 you can watch as they make a variety of wooden toys.

Back on the Blue Heron Drive you can travel west to Cavendish, Stanley Bridge and New London where there is a plethora of craft and gift shops. Cavendish is sure to keep the most exuberant craft hunter busy for several hours, if not several days! Memories Gift Shop and Village Pottery in New London and Stanley Bridge Studios in Stanley Bridge are long-time favourites.

People looking for an off-the-beaten-path experience in this region can visit Trout River Pottery in Millvale.

CHARLOTTE'S SHORE

If you arrive on PEI via the Confederation Bridge you will find yourself in the Charlotte's Shore Region. Craft-hunting opportunities begin as soon as you leave the bridge and come to Gateway Village, home to more than 20 restaurants and stores, many of which are craft shops.

Travelling east along the Blue Heron Scenic Drive will take you through one of the Island's most beautiful areas, where rolling hills meet the waves. One of the prettiest seaside villages is Victoria-by-the-Sea, where you can visit several craft shops and sample handmade chocolate.

Charlottetown and its outlying areas have an abundance of galleries, studios and shops. The Charlottetown Farmers' Market is a good place to start. The market, full of both foods and crafts, is a favourite gathering place for local artists, musicians and crafts people. Located on Belvedere Avenue, it is open Saturdays from 9 a.m. to 2 p.m. and also on Wednesdays in July, August and September.

INUIT ART GALLERY, CHARLOTTETOWN

In the downtown, the Island Craft Shop on Victoria Row is a showcase for work by the juried members of the PEI Crafts Council. Queen Street's Home Accents shows how decorative artists turn interesting materials into wonderful home decorating objects. Moonsnail Soapworks and Aromatherapy on Water Street is a store and production studio where you can view the soap-making process and purchase some deliciously scented handmade items. Next door is the Reading Well Bookstore, which

VICTORIA ROW

also houses Ten Thousand Villages crafts.

While in the area, a quick trip across the Hillsborough River will take you to Hazelbrook, home of Happy Red's Train

DENISE REISER'S *LEGEND OF THE MI'KMAQ* AT THE GATEWAY VILLAGE INTERPRETIVE CENTRE

Station, Folk Art Store and Dairy Bar. This is one of the Island's most whimsical shops and a fun place to get some ice cream.

On the other side of Charlottetown, nestled in the woods near Breadalbane, is the Stanley Pottery Studio and Shop. In this peaceful rural location you will find Malcolm Stanley and family members creating nature-inspired hand-painted pottery. Malcolm has been creating his art on the Island since 1975, and his work graces private collections all over the world. The studio has been featured in publications such as *A Day in the Life of Canada*, *A Craftsman's Way* and *National Geographic*.

BASKETS AT LENNOX ISLAND

NORTH CAPE DRIVE

Summerside is a thriving artistic community and the commercial centre of the North Cape Coastal Region. While in this seaside city, you'll want to visit Spinnaker's Landing. This waterfront attraction is a great place to browse through craft shops and take in some free Maritime entertainment. Water Street is home to the Cinnamon Tree and the College of Piping's Celtic Gift and Highland Supply Outlet.

Lennox Island, which lies northwest of Summerside, is home to PEI's largest First Nations community. The Cultural Centre features educational exhibits about the

Mi'kmaq people, and offers local handcrafts at Indian Art & Craft of North America and Micmac Legends, Canada's only maker of earthenware Mi'kmaq figurines.

Next we travel southwest of Summerside to PEI's Acadian Shore. Here, another cultural craft experience awaits you in La Région Evangéline. The Abrams Village Handcraft Co-op has some of the best traditional and contemporary Acadian crafts that the Island has to offer. If you have a little more time, you might want to check out Boutique à Point in Wellington for handmade children's and ladies' clothing, and the Acadian Museum in Miscouche.

ACADIAN FLAG HOOKED RUG

Continuing on Route 2, or the Western Road as it's known locally, you will reach the westernmost tip of the Island. This area is one of PEI's least travelled and is known for its spectacular sunsets. At West Point you will find a lighthouse that has been converted by the community into a museum, restaurant, inn and shop that sells locally made crafts. Next, make your way north to Bloomfield, home of The Old Mill Craft Company. Here you can find traditionally made blankets, along with sheepskin and knit goods. Adjacent is MacAusland's Woollen Mills, making blankets of 100 percent virgin wool.

Near Alberton, you'll find Back Road Folk Art in Lauretta. Artist Kerras Jeffery will introduce you to his folk-art friends in his workshop and studio.

Tignish is the last stop on our Island-wide craft-hunting tour. Holiday Island Production's Tignish Treasures Gift Shop produces clay miniature replicas of historic buildings, ornaments and souvenirs. The staff will gladly take you behind the scenes to see how these products are made.

LIGHTHOUSES

WAYNE MACKINNON

SOURIS LIGHTHOUSE

Carrying out their centuries-old vigils of the sea, lighthouses hold a unique fascination for people. They occupy a treasured place, particularly on an island.

Prince Edward Island's earliest lighthouse was built at Point Prim in 1846. It is still among the Island's most interesting, one of the few round brick lighthouses in Canada. Soaring to a height of over 18 metres, it is easily visible from the Charlottetown waterfront and along the south shore.

The first colonial lighthouses were octagonal in shape, in contrast to the square towers with sloping sides built after 1873. And they were built to last. Exposed to some of the most extreme weather conditions on Prince Edward Island, the fact that these structures remain basically unchanged is testament to traditional craftsmanship.

The lights themselves, known as lanterns, were originally fuelled with cod-liver oil and the light was projected by an elaborate arrangement of mirrors. Later on higher intensities were achieved with lenses, a significant improvement over the reflector arrangements which had to be protected from the sun to prevent fires. With electricity came the present mercury-vapour lights.

Lightkeepers faced a demanding and unremitting task. Fuel had to be carried up the three or four flights of stairs to the top of the tower, and the clockwork mechanisms had to be wound. Dwellings were often attached to the lighthouses, which meant constant vigilance of the light could be carried out with relative ease.

Lighthouses were vulnerable to the elements. During a heavy gale in 1879, the New London lighthouse was literally lifted from its position and carried 200 metres westward, destroying the lantern. Hazards of a different kind encroached on the Panmure Island lighthouse. In

VICTORIA
LIGHTHOUSE

1861 a fence was erected to prevent pigs from rooting away the sandstone foundation.

The East Point lighthouse occupies a unique footnote to Canadian history: it has been relocated twice. In 1882, when the British warship *Phoenix* was wrecked, the disaster was blamed partly on the lighthouse being located too far from the cliffs. It was jacked up and moved closer, and a fog horn was installed. By 1908, however, erosion was threatening the foundation, so it was jacked up again and moved 60 metres inland to its present location.

West Point, the tallest of the square wooden towers, is 17.5 metres high. Painted in broad horizontal bands of black and white, the tower itself supplements the light as an aid to navigation. Interpretive displays in the tower recall the life and times of its keepers — there were only two in all the 87 years the light was manually operated. West Point also offers accommodation and a restaurant — the only inn in Canada to operate in a functioning lighthouse. Several other lighthouses across the island are now operated by community groups and are open to the public.

Automation has brought the era of lightkeepers to an end. The structures remain, however, solitary and serene — symbols of steadfastness in a world of infinite change.

RUSTICO HARBOUR
AT DUSK

MUSEUMS

FAYE POUND

Islanders have a deep attachment to their province. They go out in the world across the water, and when they come back it's as though they're baseball players rounding third base and heading for home.

This strong sense of pride in place makes the telling of the Island story important to Islanders. And nowhere is this better told than in the Island's museums. The Island has more than its fair share of those special places where story is told in photographs, maps and artifacts — as well as through the people, the keepers of these stories.

L.M. Montgomery put the Island on the world map with her international bestseller, *Anne of Green Gables*. Her popularity has led many a history buff or local volunteer organization to celebrate her accomplishments by establishing museums across the province. The PEI National Park in Cavendish has even centred its operations around Green Gables House, which served as inspiration for her novel. Other museums include the Lucy Maud Montgomery Birthplace museum in New London, the Anne of Green Gables Museum at Silver Bush in Park Corner and, across the road, the Lucy Maud Montgomery Heritage Museum in her grandfather Senator Montgomery's old homestead. All provide fabulous opportunities for experiencing an up-close-and-personal glimpse into some of the Island's typical Victorian interiors — and a look into the old rural order of

ANNE OF GREEN GABLES MUSEUM, PARK CORNER

Montgomery's PEI, before electricity and pavement changed it all.

Heading west from Park Corner you will come upon the Keir Memorial Museum in Malpeque, which is housed in an old Presbyterian Church. Here the local people have poured their hearts into gathering artifacts that interpret life along the north shore, from the time of the Mi'kmaq through the Acadian era to the settlement of the Scots and Irish in the late 1700s, to farming and fishing before the 1950s. William Pound's 1887 horse-drawn hearse, Dr. William Keir's collection of 19th-century medical instruments and a display of MacNutt's country store are some highlights in the story of early Malpeque life. Hand-forged oyster tongs and wooden hand rakes from the mid-1880s interpret "men's work," while an entire wing is dedicated to the womanly arts of butter-making, mat-hooking, spinning and weaving. Volunteers teach the old crafts with a hands-on approach using vintage spinning wheels and looms.

KENSINGTON TRAIN STATION

Train enthusiasts will enjoy the Kensington Train Station, which provides a tour of the Island's railroad heritage. The early 20th-century stone station is the site Montgomery had in mind when she wrote the scene where Matthew Cuthbert meets Anne at the train station.

It's a short drive to Summerside and its cultural treasures, including the Wyatt Heritage Properties, the culture and heritage division of the City of Summerside and the J. E. Wyatt House, a restored Confederation era house left to posterity by his daughter. Across the street is the MacNaught History Centre and Archives, perfect for delving into a bit of research on genealogy or local history. Their Master Name Index provides genealogists with a broad research tool on microfilm, providing an excellent way to search hundreds of thousands of entries organized by name. Transcripts of all PEI cemeteries are on hand, as well as the church records of Prince County and a collection of fine art interpreting Summerside history. For $3 you can buy the booklet *Heritage Walking Tour*, a self-guided walking guide to city architecture featuring 40 properties.

The International Fox Museum is only a short walk away and takes you into the glory days of the "Fox Years,"

THE EPTEK ART AND CULTURE CENTRE

THE GREEN PARK SHIPBUILDING MUSEUM

when this area was a world headquarters for the industry.The museum is housed in "The Homestead," the splendid 1853 house of R. T. Holman, one of the founding merchants of the city. The Holman Garden is one of oldest gardens in North America. A walk down to the harbour leads to the Eptek Art and Culture Centre with its ever-changing exhibits. Eptek, a Mi'kmaq word for "hot place," presents exhibitions on fine art, history, visual arts and crafts, and programming to interpret local and Canadian cultural heritage. A bookstore supplies some of the best titles of Island interest, and a small research holding of microfilm of local papers from the 1860s to 1950, census and business directories are also on hand. The south hall has local heritage on display in maps and photographs.

The drive west on Route 2 takes the traveller to the crossroads of Miscouche and the Acadian Museum, which tells the vibrant heritage of our Acadian community. A well-stocked genealogy room helps visitors find their ancestors. Exhibits explain the culture and lifestyle of the Island's first European settlers from 1720 to the present.

A drive around Malpeque Bay (the Mi'kmaq word for "great big bay") to Green Park Shipbuilding Museum and Historic Yeo House ends in a magical experience: ascending the stair to the cupola or "Widow's Walk" to look over the surrounding fields and the bay where James Yeo, Sr., launched his ships for England. Understanding the importance of shipbuilding gives a broad understanding of the pattern of settlement and the development of the province in coastal trading times.

The Bideford Parsonage Museum up the coast gives another view inside a community museum that interprets the golden age of sail and documents the times when L.M. Montgomery lived in the house and taught at the local school. A few minutes' drive away is the Ellerslie Shellfish Museum, which tells the story of the Malpeque oyster. Lennox Island is home to much of the Island's Mi'kmaq population, and the Lennox Island Mi'kmaq Cultural

Centre houses displays about Mi'kmaq heritage. The "Walk of Our Forefathers" takes you through the woods along three to ten kilometres of trail with interpretive murals explaining the culture of our First Nations people.

The Alberton Museum is one of the province's finest community museums, a place for the traveller to gain a well-rounded understanding of life in Prince Edward Island. It is possible to lose oneself in time travel in their extensive photograph collection of local farming and fishing, military history and community life. The old courthouse has a comprehensive collection of compiled genealogies, scrapbooks and local church records. Nowhere is there more hands-on help and information with a personal touch.

Wind power enthusiasts will find there is much to learn at the North Cape Interpretive Centre. Established in 2001, eight gigantic white windmills form the first commercial "wind farm" in Atlantic Canada and produce three percent of PEI's energy. The centre has an extensive display on the technology of wind power, a marine aquarium and a section devoted to local heritage. documents explaining the geology of the area, its fishery, and the Acadian and Irish population who work on some of the most dangerous fishing grounds in the province. The North Cape lighthouse provides a fabulous view of the sunset or the meeting of the tides off the long rock reef.

Down the coast is Miminegash, the centre of the Irish moss harvest. This plentiful seaweed (*Chrondrus crispus*) became a financially viable crop during the Second World War, when research developed new uses for the moss and its carrageenan as a gelling/stabilizing agent in the production of ice cream, toothpaste, cosmetics and medicine. In 1942 about 750 tons were shipped, resulting in a new harvest the locals called "easy money" — though its harvesting is back-breaking labour. Along the coastal drive, huge horses haul Irish moss off the beaches, and boats come and go with their loads of lobster traps.

In O'Leary is the Prince Edward Island Potato Museum, home to "the world's largest potato." The museum celebrates the monumental contribution the lowly potato has made to the Island. For lighthouse enthusiasts, the West Point Lighthouse houses a charming exhibit on the history of all the lighthouses on PEI. They serve up some of the finest in local seafood, and provide accommodations in what used to be the bedroom of the light-keeper, located directly below the lantern room.

Charlottetown is a beautiful city at the edge of a splendid harbour, with some good walks for stretching your legs while appreciating the 19th-

St. Dunstan's Basilica, Charlottetown

century architecture. Throughout the summer months, the Confederation Players tour the downtown in their lavish 1860s costumes. Well-informed of Charlottetown's buildings and their historical significance, these young people are master interpreters of "olden times" — and are especially good at inspiring children toward a love of history. Their street theatre serves up the story of the town during the Charlottetown Conference in 1864 in an engaging way, full of the colour of the day when a visiting circus stole local attention away from the first meeting to establish a Dominion of Canada. Actors take the roles of the Fathers of Confederation — Sir John A. Macdonald, George Etienne Cartier and W.H. Pope, to name a few — as well as local folk, some opposed to Confederation, others lamenting the land troubles of Islanders or interpreting Mi'kmaq heritage. Actors stage vignettes in front of Province House and engage in impromptu debates on street corners for the amusement and education of all.

Founders' Hall tells the story of the Confederation of Canada in a hi-tech way that is sure to engage children. A walk up Great George Street to Province House National Historic Site offers up the real thing. Confederation Centre Library is next door, and it's the best stop for books on local heritage. The Public Archives on the fourth floor of the Coles Building is open for those interested in a more scholarly dig.

BEACONSFIELD HISTORIC HOUSE

Beaconsfield Historic House is a beautifully restored 1877 shipbuilder's mansion on the Charlottetown Harbour. A climb to the cupola will take you back in time, and Beaconsfield's well-stocked bookstore is open for browsing. A leisurely walk around the boardwalk through Victoria Park passes Fanningbank, the historic residence of

the Lieutenant-Governor, which offers daily summer tours. Across Charlottetown Harbour is the Fort Amherst-Port LaJoye Historic Site at Rocky Point.

TOP AND BOTTOM: ORWELL CORNER HISTORIC VILLAGE

The drive east across the Hillsborough Bridge takes the traveller through some of the prettiest countryside, particularly if one dallies along the shore roads to Orwell Corner Historic Village. The clock stopped round about 1890 in this country village of 19th-century buildings. The Prince Edward Island Museum and Heritage Foundation began restoring the abandoned buildings in the 1970s and recently opened a new agricultural museum. A three-minute drive leads to the 1850 Sir Andrew Macphail Homestead, the 12-room house in which his classic book, *The Master's Wife*, is set.

Skirting the coast, one can make a wonderful lighthouse tour with stops at Point Prim, Cape Bear, Wood Islands and Panmure Island. These lighthouses have exhibits outlining local history and tours of their interiors. The Point Prim lighthouse, the Island's first, was built of local brick in 1845 to a design by the English architect, Isaac Smith, who immigrated to the Island at the age of 22. It's a steep climb to the lantern room in a polygonal cupola 25 metres above sea level where the mercury-vapour light penetrates 27 kilometres across the Northumberland Strait on a clear night. Run by two local Women's Institutes, tours explain the evolution of lighthouse technology from the days of seal oil–burning in the 1840s to electricity and automation in 1969.

The picturesque town of Montague is home to the Garden of the Gulf Museum, a lovely sandstone building by the river. The museum's director, Donna Collings, is helpful and knowledgeable when it comes to interpreting the Island's past. A highlight of their collection is a volunteer militia coat of Captain John MacDonald of Tracadie, one of the oldest garments in existence on PEI, dated by its buttons that read "Island of St. John," the Island's name before 1799. An extensive photograph collection of Montague and area from 1867 to 1967 is the cornerstone of their offering. For the hunter of genealogy in Kings County, there is no better place to begin than here. Local historians give the best directions, so there's no need to reinvent the wheel or become frustrated.

No trip to Kings County is complete without a visit to Basin Head Fisheries Museum. Their interpretive displays

TOP: ELMIRA STATION
RIGHT: KIDS OF ALL AGES ENJOY THE MINIATURE TRAIN AT ELMIRA STATION

provide details on the different methods of lobster fishing and canning. Basin Head is a part of the provincial museum system. From the bridge that spans the "Run" it's easy to imagine the lobster boats plying this fast stretch of water to an artificial harbour dredged in the early 20th century.

The East Point Lighthouse is close by, as is the Elmira Railway Museum on what is now the Confederation Trail. This is a restored 1912 wooden station, the end of the line for the "friendly little railroad" that connected the Island with a meandering iron rail. A stop at one of the wharves at North Lake, Naufrage or Red Head is a good idea to round out one's understanding of the Island's fishery.

The Rustico Harbour Fisheries Museum on the wharf in North Rustico is centred around understanding fishing in the good old days. Their exhibit is colourful and has a down-home appeal with a sense of humour. The wooden building on the wharf has the smell of the sea—a perfect backdrop to perusing the exhibits and photos relating the story of the local fishery. A wonderful little film brings to life the oral tradition of fishermen about the back-breaking days of lobster fishing with wind and manpower while showing how large gas and diesel engines and hydraulic gear changed everything. A quote from an old fisherman, Long Vincent Gallant of Rustico, said it all: "You had to be rugged, boy, then. You had to take it. Couldn't go in the cabin like you can today. You had to take everything that nature chucked at you. But times were good. Lots of fish!"

To understand Prince Edward Islanders, it's important to stand on the beaches and wharves with the Island's sun and salt breeze—but it's equally helpful to mix it in with a tour of the Island's museums. Only then will the visitor truly be carried into the heritage and culture of Prince Edward Island.

THE RUSTICO HARBOUR FISHERIES MUSEUM

ISLAND ROUTES

CHARLOTTETOWN WALKING TOUR

REG PORTER

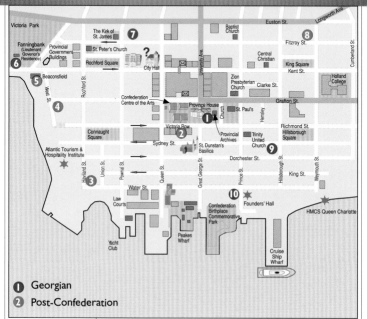

① Georgian
② Post-Confederation

England gained an immense empire in North America after the conquest of France on the Plains of Abraham. This empire was so large that, to the educated mind of the 1760s, the only similar empire was that of Rome. It is not surprising, then, that the classically educated minds of 18th-century planners thought as the Romans did. Charlottetown was laid out as the capital of the colony of St. John's Island in the style of a Roman settlement.

HISTORIC GREAT GEORGE STREET

Everywhere a grid system prevails, and, at the centre, there is a large square containing all the features that citizens require: a church for the health of the soul, a market for the health of the body, and a legislative building and courthouse for the good of an ordered society. Charlottetown had them all — and more. At diagonals flanking the central square were four green areas, or parks, reserved for the enjoyment of the citizens; they still exist today. In fact, if Samuel Holland, the surveyor of 1764–65, and his successors visited the city today, they

would know where to find most places they needed, and they would certainly know all the street names. On this walking tour of the city you will find it has miraculously survived as a perfect 18th-century space, rational and logical: the streets are named after the great noble patrons of the time, the city after Queen Charlotte, and the main street leading to the central square, Great George, after King George III.

THE INNS ON GREAT GEORGE

This tour introduces two periods of architectural heritage: Georgian buildings, indicated in red on the map, and post-confederation buildings, indicated in blue. Description of the Georgian buildings follows; for the post-confederation buildings turn to page 119.

GEORGIAN CHARLOTTETOWN

1 — PROVINCE HOUSE, QUEENS SQUARE
In Queens Square is a magnificent Nova Scotia freestone building best known for that momentous meeting of 1864. Today, Province House is where the provincial legislature sits. It also contains rooms restored by Parks Canada, open to the public, that show how this structure was furnished at the time of Confederation. Constructed between 1843 and 1847, it was called the Colonial Building. It would continue to be so until 1873 when Prince Edward Island joined Confederation.

PROVINCE HOUSE

It is built in the Georgian Palladian style, reminiscent of many English country houses built in the 18th and early 19th centuries. When work began in 1843, the plan was for a rectangular building the size of the present building, but without the two wings or pavilions at either end, or the great Ionic porticoes on the north and south façades. When the building was two-thirds constructed, and the walls had risen to about the middle of the second-level windows, the politicians decided that the structure was too plain and they asked the architect, Isaac Smith, to add classical porches and two corner pavilions. The corner structures were easy to incorporate. The great porticoes, however, required that the bases literally lean against the lower level, and that the architraves (the great blocks that support the roof from column to column) be constructed as flat arches consisting of a row of wedge-shaped blocks. This was because no pieces of stone large enough to fill the gap between the second and third columns could be found in the Nova Scotia quarries.

Knowing these problems and the last-minute changes makes the astonishingly coherent design of Province House all the more special, and the achievement of its builder, Isaac Smith, all the greater.

6 — GOVERNMENT HOUSE, FANNINGBANK

This Georgian-style wooden structure was finished to a design by Isaac Smith. It was built next to the city and has a spectacular view of the harbour on land that was set aside by Governor Fanning, the Island's second governor — hence the name Fanningbank.

The south or grand entrance was sheltered by a huge Ionic portico held up by four slender wooden columns. Wrapping around three sides of the house were verandas supported by Tuscan Doric columns, also made of wood.

FANNINGBANK

The east door, through which most visitors to the house entered, was framed by a single-storey Tuscan Doric portico. Because of its narrowness, it was supported by pairs of columns. This porch, missing since the 1870s, has recently been restored as part of a long-term project to bring the exterior and interior of the house as close as possible to their original appearance.

Originally the house was covered with wooden planks, which simulated masonry construction. In honour of the Prince of Wales's visit in 1860, these planks were removed and replaced with shingles. All architectural articulation disappeared. In 1864 the Fathers of

THE GARDEN AT
FANNINGBANK

Confederation, in town for the Charlottetown Conference, were photographed in front of the building. The same shingles against which they stood are there today.

The interior of the house consists of suites of rooms that circle the great empty two-storey space of the central hall or saloon. Above, this is circled by a balcony on three sides and a grand divided staircase lit by a huge Palladian window on the other side. For many years, dedicated volunteers have been tracking down original furniture and seeking to give the house an internal ambience redolent not only of its date but also of the succession of governors who have lived there. Fanningbank is open for house tours during the summer months.

7 — THE CARMICHAEL HOUSE, 238 POWNAL STREET

The Carmichael House was built in the 1820s by John Edward Carmichael, the son-in-law of the Island's fourth lieutenant-governor. This private residence is unique in Charlottetown and on the Island for its light-hearted treatment of the classical style. The design is typical of the style we call Picturesque, which flourished in the last years of the 18th century.

The exterior is fascinating and retains most of its original arrangement. A room above the central entrance

CARMICHAEL
HOUSE

HISTORIC HOUSES ON WATER STREET

extends so far as to form the boundary of a deep veranda. This extension is faced in the style of a classical temple, with the corner boards acting as pilasters holding up a triangular pediment or gable in which is placed a fashionable round window. The temple front is supported by pairs of columns which continue in pairs, providing support for the rest of the veranda. It is crested by a low balustrade in the Italian style. Charlottetown never saw such elegance and fancy again.

9 — CENTRAL CHIMNEY HOUSE, 222 SYDNEY STREET

When you look at this little storey-and-a-half house, now a private home, you are struck by the immense size of its centrally placed chimney. In Canada we call this a central chimney house, but it is the same as the American Cape Cod house. This example was probably built in the early 1800s.

The house at 222 Sydney has lost most of its interior finish, but the exterior front and sides preserve an elegant trim that was popular on the Island in the 1840s. The front door is stoutly panelled with a transom above it.

GAINSFORD HOUSE

10 — THE GAINSFORD HOUSE, 102–104 WATER STREET

"Next to Gainsford's brick house" or "across from Gainsford's brick house" was quite often told to people seeking directions in lower Charlottetown in the mid-1800s. John and Elizabeth Gainsford's brick house, located at 102–104 Water Street, was an important landmark because it was made out of brick in a city built largely of wood. This 1834 double tenement, now the oldest brick house in the city and used as a private residence, has recently been restored. In style, the house is austere Georgian row with the simplest architectural decoration.

The brick exterior of 102–104 Water Street was cleaned of old paint and repointed using appropriate soft lime mortar. What emerged was a wonderfully tactile surface of

Island brick, perhaps made in Mr. Gainsford's brickyard, with occasional vitrified bricks (those heated at much higher temperatures so that their surfaces became darker and glass-like), adding a new dimension of colour and texture to the whole.

POST-CONFEDERATION CHARLOTTETOWN

In July of 1866 a great fire swept through the city's old commercial district destroying several blocks of private and commercial buildings. In spite of the planning of the original founders, who insisted on broad north/south streets and slightly narrower east/west side streets to act as fire breaks, the fire spread and destruction was extensive.

Rebuilding began at once and it is significant that, by 1866, architectural styles had changed dramatically. The symmetrical, classical Georgian styles which had provided the basis of design for the city since its earliest days were now out of style. New exotic buildings, showing the

influence of Italy in particular, were now in vogue, and all over the burned-out area of the city there sprang up new shops and homes with round-headed windows, flat roofs supported by innumerable brackets, and, in the case of commercial buildings, more and more attempts to make the structures fireproof by the use of brick. The Island's significant brick industry would peak in the generation after the great fire.

Thus change began and the face of the city acquired a new, fashionable look that continues to this day.

2 — VICTORIA ROW, 128–134 RICHMOND STREET

After the great fire of 1866, the commercial district of Charlottetown moved closer to the centre of things and the block on the south side of Queens Square, between Queen and Great George Streets, became the focus of intensified activity. Tragedy struck again in 1884 when nearly all the buildings were destroyed. Within a few years, the various commercial establishments rose again, employing the talents of the architects of the day, individuals such as W. C. Harris and Phillips & Chappell. In the brief half-generation since the introduction of the Italianate style to

119

Charlottetown, new styles, this time modelled on the American brownstone tradition and on the new partly prefabricated structures of cast-iron store fronts, took over, and Victoria Row became home to the finest collection of late-Victorian commercial buildings in the city.

The new styles combined brick and stone in a manner that took advantage of the smoothness and regularity of brick and the rusticated or rough finish of stone. It gave us buildings that exuded an ostentatious pride of achievement in the great beehives of financial success. Victoria Row is now home to upper-floor offices, apartments, and an art gallery, on the upper floor, and street-level gift shops and restaurants, which offer sidewalk café service in the summertime.

VICTORIA ROW

LOWDEN HOUSE

3 — THE LOWDEN HOUSE, 2 HAVILAND STREET

George Lowden was a prominent Charlottetown merchant who died in 1864. Two years later, his house was destroyed in the great fire of 1866. When his widow Esther rebuilt, the house was in the latest Italianate style and it is still the best example of that style on the Island. Although the architect is not known, it may have been David Stirling, who was in town working on other projects and who was known to favour this new style.

The house is a square block with a large bracketed overhanging cornice. The sides are articulated by slightly projecting bays which are capped by pediments. The lower part of the front bay extends beyond the original line to form a porch. The crowning element is a magnificent belvedere, a small glassed-in room where one may sit and see a beautiful view. Today the building is the home of the Haviland Club, a private club.

4 — EDENHURST, 12 WEST STREET
The so-called Queen Anne house had nothing to do with Queen Anne but was a late Victorian name given to a hodge-podge of historical architectural elements that, taken

THE HISTORIC
CHARLOTTE
RESIDENCE ON
WEST STREET

together, could often produce results of great style and beauty. Edenhurst is one of the finest Queen Anne-style houses left in Charlottetown and displays its characteristic profile with its high conical tower and Georgian Revival pedimented gable with Palladian window. It has been restored as one of Charlottetown's most elegant bed-and-breakfasts.

This style, popular between 1885 and 1900, added tremendous variety to streetscapes dominated by the classical styles of the past. These houses were painted in the new bright, custom-mixed colours that became available late in the century and they sport fine plate glass windows contrasted with mood-enhancing stained glass accents in door surrounds and even along the top of the great clear panes themselves.

BEACONSFIELD

5 — BEACONSFIELD, 2 KENT STREET

In 1877, James Peake, one of the great shipbuilders at the end of the Island's golden age of shipbuilding, had this imposing structure built by nascent architect William Critchlow Harris, who probably adapted the Italianate mansard design from a book by Samuel Sloane published in 1859. Peake did not live long in the house because his finances took a turn for the worse and the building reverted to the mortgagee, Henry Cundall. Cundall eventually moved into the house and the family lived there until 1917. After that, it became a YWCA and then a residence for most of the province's nurses at the PEI Hospital. In 1973, it became the home of the Prince Edward Island Museum and Heritage Foundation; today it is the administrative headquarters of the provincial museum system, as well as a house restored to the Cundall period, open to the public for tours.

The house is a fine example of its style and time with paired windows sporting the newly available large panes of glass that permitted a two-over-two combination instead of the earlier six-over-six sashes. The roof is mansard and typical of the French Second Empire influence that began to combine with the Italianate styles of the time. Like the Lowden house, Beaconsfield, as it came to be called after Disraeli's elevation to the peerage, has a large belvedere overlooking the harbour.

The verandas that run along three sides of the house are the glory of the building because their very elaborate yet elegant tracery and elliptical arched tops provide a series of framed views of great beauty. In an earlier time, the trellis support would have been alive with vegetation, thereby enhancing what was already very beautiful.

8 — THE LONGWORTH HOUSE, 181 FITZROY STREET

LONGWORTH
HOUSE

This very large house, now called the Hillhurst Inn, was built in 1898 in the Georgian Revival style that the Americans call Colonial Revival. The Colonial Revival was a movement that began in America as far back as the Centenary of the American Revolution in 1876 when a wave of nostalgia seemed appropriate after a century of separation.

The interiors of Colonial Revival houses made great use of wooden panelling to create a warm but, at the same time, majestic front hall. This house is no exception. The hallway is finished in a glowing golden oak, and the mantelpiece in the front parlour is an architectural entity unto itself, with all the elements of a classical temple but the pediment.

DUCHESS OF KENT

NORTH CAPE

LOBIE DAUGHTON

North Cape
Seacow Pond
Norway
Anglo Tignish
Nail Pond
Judes Point
Tignish Shore
Skinners Pond
Tignish
Ascension
St-Felix
Fisherman's Haven Provincial Park
Kildare Capes
Waterford
Kildare
Pleasant View
Jacques Cartier Provincial Park
St. Edward
Miminegash
Ebbsfleet
Lauretta
Huntley
Alberton
Campbellton
Rosebank
Brooklyn
Northport
Bloomfield
Mill River East
Cascumpec
Cascumpec Bay
Fortune Cove
Murray Road
Foxley River
Freeland
Burton
Bloomfield Provincial Park
Mill River Provincial Park
Woodstock
Carleton
Inverness
Portage
East Bideford
Cape Wolfe
Knutsford
O'Leary
Coleman
Ellerslie
Bideford
Springfield West
Milo
Mount Pleasant
Tyne Valley
West Cape
Glenwood
Hebron
Brae Harbour
Enmore
Springhill
Grand
West Point
Cedar Dunes Provincial Park
Egmont Bay
Victoria West
Richmond
St-Chrysostome
Urbainville
Wellington
St-Raph
Abram-Village
Maximeville
Cap-Egmont
Mon
Car

Percival River
Foxley River
Conway Narrows

0   5   10
kilometres

12
14
2
153
152
151
150
145
143
148
142
14
136
174
163
133
132
179
124
177
127
11
2

**LIGHTHOUSE AT
CAP-EGMONT**

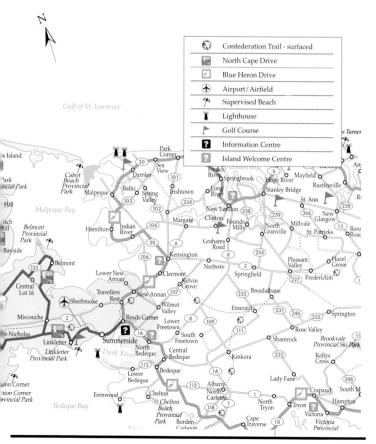

N

🌀	Confederation Trail - surfaced
🚗	North Cape Drive
🚗	Blue Heron Drive
✈	Airport/Airfield
🏄	Supervised Beach
⚓	Lighthouse
⚑	Golf Course
❓	Information Centre
❓	Island Welcome Centre

Gulf of St. Lawrence

Park Corner
Sea View
Darnley
London Bay
Park Provincial Park
Cabot Beach Provincial Park
French River
Springbrook
Hope River
Mayfield
Rusticoville
An
Malpeque
Baltic
Spring Valley
Irishtown
(101)
(20)
Long River
(6)
Stanley Bridge
St. Ann
R
Malpeque Bay
(103)
(102)
(234)
New London
(238)
(239)
(266)
New Glasgow
(258)
Margate
Clinton
Millvale
St. Patricks
(13)
Renr
Road
Hill
ich
Hamilton
Indian River
(104)
Founds Mills
North Granville
Belmont Provincial Park
(20)
(6)
Grahams Road
(8)
(254)
Pleasant Valley
Hazel Grove
Bayside
Kensington
Norboro
(2)
Springfield
Fredericton
(1)
Belmont
(123)
Lower New Annan
Clermont
Kelvin Grove
(232)
Breadalbane
(227)
Central Lot 16
Travellers Rest
New Annan
(107)
Wilmot Valley
(231)
(246)
Rose Valley
Springton
(225)
Miscouche
Sherbrooke
(2)
Reads Corner
Lower Freetown
(8)
(109)
Emerald
St-Nicholas
Linkletter
Summerside
South Freetown
(111)
Shamrock
Brookvale Provincial Ski Park
(13)
Linkletter Provincial Park
Dunk River
North Bedeque
Central Bedeque
Kinkora
(232)
Kellys Cross
(1A)
ion Corner
ion Corner
vincial Park
Fernwood
Lower Bedeque
Bedeque
(112)
Albany
North Carleton
Lady Fane
(246)
South M
Crapaud
Hampton
Chelton
(112)
(1)
North Tryon
Tryon
Victoria
Bedeque Bay
Chelton Beach Provincial Park
(118)
Cape Traverse
(10)
Victoria Provincial
Borden-Carleton

e Turner

![Aerial view of Summerside]

SUMMERSIDE FROM THE AIR

SUMMERSIDE CITY HALL

Picturesque communities, secluded beaches, historic architecture, beautiful churches and non-stop festivals and events: this is the North Cape Coastal Drive of Prince Edward Island, or what I'll call here "the Drive." This is where you can enjoy unspoiled natural wonders, succulent fresh seafood and an area rich in Acadian and Aboriginal culture.

Just twenty minutes from Confederation Bridge, Summerside, the Island's second-largest city, has a fine harbour and a rich history as a shipbuilding centre in the Age of Sail. Between 1840 and 1890, over 3,100 wooden vessels were constructed at 176 locations. The good timber is long gone, but ships from all over the world still dock in Summerside to load Island spuds.

It's worth getting out of the car for a walk among Summerside's stately heritage homes, built a century ago by wealthy shipbuilders and fox ranchers. A walking tour, published by the City of Summerside, is an excellent guide to the houses and their stories.

Summerside has come a long way in show-casing its historic waterfront, while also maintaining a working port. Visitors can stroll the new boardwalk, stop at the beach, browse the Shipyard Market, eat local seafood at the Little Mermaid or sip a refreshing brew at the Silver Fox club by the yacht basin. The boardwalk is dotted with pictures and plaques that detail area history.

Serious history buffs can find more inside the nearby Wyatt Centre, which houses the Eptek National Exhibition Centre. Eptek means "the hot place" in the language of the Mi'kmaq, who once used the area as the starting point for a portage across the Island's narrowest

WYATT CENTRE

point (just 6 kilometres across).

Just beside Eptek, Spinnaker's Landing has a boat shed displaying traditional 19th-century methods of boat-building. In the downtown area, large murals grace the library and the fire hall, and historical landmarks include the International Fox Museum and Hall of Fame, housed in the old Holman Homestead on Fitzroy Street. The College of Piping and Celtic Performing Arts, on Water Street East, hosts wonderful concerts throughout the summer and is home to world-champion pipers, drummers and dancers.

SPINNAKER'S LANDING

For the more active traveller, the Confederation Trail, formerly the railway route across PEI and now a groomed walking and biking trail, passes through the centre of Summerside and on through the heart of the region.

In Miscouche, about 8 kilometres west of Summerside on Route 2, the Acadian Museum offers a presentation depicting the story of Island Acadians and has access to 30,000 genealogical cards. The friendly, bilingual staff can answer questions on the history and attractions of the area. Turning right onto Route 12 at Miscouche leads to beautiful countryside dotted with heritage buildings. St. Patrick's Church in Grand River was designed by the architect William Critchlow Harris, brother of the famous

Fathers of Confederation artist Robert Harris.

As you head west along the Drive, a visit to Green Park Shipbuilding Museum and Yeo House offers an in-depth look at PEI's shipbuilding history. The museum's re-created shipyard traces the rise and fall of the

ST. PATRICK'S CHURCH

DOCTOR'S INN

industry. A tour through Yeo House reveals something of the lifestyle of "ship barons" of the 1800s. The impeccably restored residence has great views of Malpeque Bay from the cupola atop the roof. Green Park is a favourite camping spot with locals and visitors alike, with some cabins for rent.

Further along Route 12 is the pretty village of Tyne Valley, where you'll find the Doctor's Inn B&B. Owners Paul and Jean Offer also serve dinners (by appointment only) featuring poultry and produce from their large organic garden. Tyne Valley plays host to the annual Oyster Festival in August, as well as to the Larry Gorman Folk Festival (Larry worked in the Maine woods and his songs and verses have become folklore favourites). The Landing pub features microbrew beer while the Tyne Valley Studio showcases local art and knitwear.

A scant five-minute drive away in Bideford, the lovingly restored Victorian parsonage on Route 166 serves as a memento of L. M. Montgomery's first teaching post in 1894–95. Art on display in the tiny West Prince Gallery at the site of Montgomery's first one-room schoolhouse is worth a look. Back on Route 12, another William Harris–designed church, the small but lovely St. John's in Ellerslie, is open for visits.

LENNOX ISLAND

The Drive is home to the largest native population on PEI. Turning right off Route 12 onto Route 163 and driving over the causeway, you will come to the Lennox Island Reserve. Mi'kmaq crafts, food and culture are demonstrated at the cultural centre. An interpretive trail provides a great walking circuit and also a wheelchair-accessible route. Rumour has it that the café has the best food in Prince County!

After the reserve, a drive back to Route 12 will take you right towards Route 2, "the Western Road" at Portage (pronounced "Portidge"). Pretty well any side road that branches off Route 12 to the right will lead down to the shore. Windsurfers, boaters and kayakers can easily find places to launch and explore bays, inlets, beaches and barachois (the French name for the shallow saltwater lagoons that run between the offshore dunes and the mainland).

Beyond Portage, West Prince is certainly less developed than the centre of PEI. This can be a source of pleasure to the visitor looking for something different: quieter, slower-paced, less "touristy." The area's farms and fishing villages are still mostly peopled by descendants of the first European settlers.

The land is flat or gently rolling, but the real glory of West Prince is its seacoast: red sandstone cliffs, often carved into striking shapes and caves by waves and wind, with miles of red or white sand beaches. It's a beachcombers' and birdwatchers' heaven.

The best way to explore the coastline is to follow the Drive across the bridge over Foxley River and then across the Mill River towards Alberton. It was here that the silver

HORACE MCNEVIN AT MILO

RED SANDSTONE CLIFFS AT CAP EGMONT

TIGNISH HARBOUR

fox industry began. On an island in Alberton Harbour, Robert Oulton and Charles Dalton succeeded in raising the black foxes with white-tipped tails whose pelts created the equivalent of a gold rush on Prince Edward Island in the early 20th century. The boom collapsed, but the industry's affluence is reflected in the handsome three-storey residences — known as "fox houses" — many of which still stand in West Prince.

On the outskirts of Alberton, Northport Pier features a fine waterfront inn, marina and restaurant. You can indulge in delicious food and a glass of wine while enjoying a view over the bay. Birdwatchers will appreciate a tour on a pontoon boat or kayak along the shallow strip of water along the region's north shore, protected by ramparts of deserted sand dunes.

A few kilometres past Alberton, the Drive begins to hug the coastline. Jacques Cartier Provincial Park is named for the great French explorer who may have first come ashore here in 1534. The beach runs virtually unbroken, at low tide, all the way to North Cape.

Opportunities for side trips to the shore abound. A short walk through the churchyard of the little white Anglican church at Kildare Capes brings you to sandstone cliffs overlooking the gulf. The beach runs north as far as the eye can see and is often entirely empty. At low tide, you can wade to tiny "private" beaches sheltered on either side by the cliffs.

A few miles up the coast and a little inland, Tignish is a predominantly Roman Catholic community with strong co-operative traditions. The church dominates the landscape in the form of the soaring spire of St. Simon and St. Jude, a brick building unusual in this province of wooden churches. The magnificent pipe organ, built in Quebec, is almost as old as the 1860 church. Several years ago, the neighbouring convent was converted into the Tignish Heritage Inn.

At the Tignish Cultural Centre, visitors can learn about the early days of the Irish and Acadian settlers. The Green, an eco-tourism site, depicts the landing of the eight founding families in 1799. Certain surnames, such as Gaudet, Perry/Poirier, Gallant and Arsenault, still predominate to this day.

Approaching the tip of the Island, you come to Seacow Pond, a tiny harbour named for the walrus once slaughtered for their hides, tusks and oil. Walrus herds no longer visit, but seals are a common sight off western beaches. Keep your eyes peeled for the spout of a passing whale.

At North Cape, the lighthouse has been joined by the Atlantic Wind Test Site with its array of towering windmills and by an Interpretive Centre where visitors can learn all about this elegant, sustainable power source. A meal at the site's Wind and Reef restaurant offers spectacular views across the water. Running out from the cape is what may be the longest natural rock reef in the world.

You'll see many splendid draft horses in the fields of West Prince. Horses haul the scoops which rake up the Irish moss washed ashore after a storm. The moss is processed for carrageenan, a gelling agent used in a wide range of products, including ice cream. Carrageenan was a favourite dietary supplement for reggae legend Bob Marley, and you can try it for yourself at the Seaweed Pie café in Miminegash. Miminegash also boasts the childhood home of Canadian cultural icon, singer/songwriter Stompin' Tom Connors.

For swimmers, there are beaches all along the coastal route, or you can watch the fishing boats come in to tie up

NORTH CAPE
LIGHTHOUSE

HARVESTING IRISH
MOSS

CEDAR DUNES PROVINCIAL PARK

along the wharves at communities such as Howards Cove and Cape Wolfe. It is also the provincial light-house museum. At Cedar Dunes Provincial Park, there's prime white sand beach as well as camping facilities. The nearby West Point Lighthouse, built in 1874, was converted into a community-owned restaurant, inn and craft shop. Cedar Dunes makes a great stop for a refreshing snack, swim and stroll along the beach, or you can settle in for a long stay … West Prince is no place to rush.

From West Point, the Drive turns inland again through farms and woodland and back to Route 2, but you have options. With a left onto Route 2, then left on Route 142, you'll reach O'Leary, the home of the Prince Edward Island Potato Museum. You may be amused to find a whole museum devoted to a vegetable, but potatoes are to the Island what wheat is to the Prairies. Displays of machinery help to explain the central role that the potato has played in the province's agriculture. A 14-foot potato marks the entrance!

POTATO BLOSSOMS

Just a few miles farther west along Route 2 is the principal "tourist complex" in West Prince: the Mill River Provincial Park and resort. The 18-hole championship course is one of the best in Canada and the Rodd Resort is a family favourite, with everything from golf and nature walks to an indoor pool with waterslide. Less than a kilometre along the road is the Mill River Fun Park, with even bigger water slides and many other attractions.

Across the highway, MacAusland's Woollen Mill welcomes visitors to watch as wool is carded, spun and woven into the warm blankets for which MacAusland's is known. Knitters prize the wool, and both yarn and blankets are on sale.

Finally, visitors should not be reluctant to explore off the beaten track. Route 145, for example, will take you through some of the prettiest pastoral scenery in the province. Many roads lead to the coast. Even if you get lost, you're never far from somewhere, and even the smallest roads are shown on the maps that are available from any Tourism office or Visitor Information Centre. Feel free to ask a local for directions; people up west are helpful types and generous with their advice.

MACAUSLAND'S WOOLLEN MILL

LICENSE PLATE

A right turn from The Drive onto Route 2 brings you back towards Portage. After coming to Mount Pleasant – where a bustling Second World War airforce training base once stood – you regain The Drive as you take a right turn and follow Route 11 through Enmore and Victoria West, into the main francophone area of the Island.

NOTRE-DAME CATHOLIC CHURCH, MONT CARMEL

FISHERS' SHEDS

The next several miles follow the coastline along Egmont Bay into the heart of "La Région Évangéline" (named after Longfellow's famous poem about the Acadian deportation). Acadians are a lively bunch; local musicians and dancers know how to throw a party! Acadians love to eat as well, whether it's "râpé pie," tourtière or a lobster dinner. The Acadians are famous for their friendliness and hospitality, so you might find yourself planning to stay a while longer.

A tour around this French-speaking area will give you a taste of Acadian pride as well as Acadian food. The Acadian flag (a tricolour with a single star) adorns many houses, and local people are proud of their resilience to hard times. The region is known for beautiful churches, such as the Church of St. Phillip and St. Jacques in Egmont Bay and the Church of Our Lady of Mont Carmel. The people of the area are also renowned for their annual Agricultural Exhibition and Acadian Festival, held on Labour Day weekend in Abrams Village.

The Bottle Houses (Les maisons des bouteilles) in Cape Egmont feature over 30,000 bottles built into colourful buildings. A little further east in Mont-Carmel you'll find Le Village de l'Acadie, which includes the Acadian Pioneer Village, L'Auberge du Village (a comfortable inn), "La Cuisine à Mémé" dinner theatre (in both English and French) and the restaurant L'Étoile de Mer.

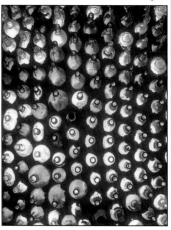

BOTTLE HOUSE, CAP EGMONT

UNION CORNER SCHOOLHOUSE MUSEUM

From Union Corner you can continue on The Drive, passing through St. Raphael and St. Nicholas, back into Miscouche. If you have time, Route 177 at Union Corner will take you into the little village of Wellington. By following Route 124 from Wellington to Route 2, you'll come across the Promenade Acadienne Boardwalk, which replicates the commercial architecture of the late 1880s with attractions such as the Évangéline Tourist Information Centre, and the Quilt Eco-museum. Another three kilometres west on Route 2, towards Richmond, finds Culture Crafts Co-op on the right-hand side. The co-op's artisans preserve and showcase age-old basket-making artistry. Their beautiful split ash baskets last for decades and are useful as well as decorative.

Whenever you want to head back towards the bridge to New Brunswick, the ferry to Nova Scotia or to central PEI, all roads will take you through Summerside. But you mustn't be in a hurry — if you're interested in shipbuilding, in natural history, or in Mi'kmaq, French, British, Irish, Scottish, Welsh and Loyalist history, or if you just like lush countryside and curving coastline, it's worth the wander through the western part of Prince Edward Island known as the Drive.

HORSE AND WAGON AT NORTH CAPE

135

ANNE'S LAND

H. SHIRLEY HORNE

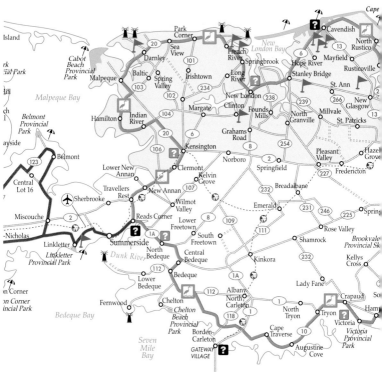

Gulf of St. Lawrence

Confederation Bridge

Of all the scenic beauty of Prince Edward Island some of the most striking is found along the north shore and in Prince Edward Island National Park. There you'll see views of the sparkling Gulf of St. Lawrence from the road that runs through the park and parallel to the gulf. Often there's a "sea on" and waves foam and splash up over the creamy pastel beaches. The sand dunes between the gulf and the road are the same pastel colour, but their cover of spiky green marram grasses makes a brilliant contrast. Along the roadside the grasses are interspersed with fragrant bay leaves and clumps of rugged spruce. The effect is as exhilarating as a breath of salt air. Marshlands and spruce groves line the opposite side of the road, and great blue herons, which feed in the ponds and harbours, can often be seen standing motionless, with one long, slim

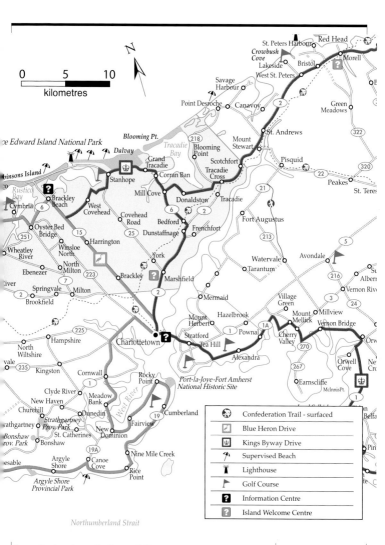

leg raised and crooked gracefully.

While admiring the grandeur of the shore, one cannot neglect the simple wonders inland. The park is also home to several woodland hiking trails. The Bubbling Springs Trail is a relaxing two-kilometre hike with a real bubbling spring and a bench from which to admire it. Along the trail you'll notice an old cemetery with small stubby headstones made of brown sandstone, although the names of sailors lost in the Yankee Gale of 1851 have long since worn away.

As you enter Prince Edward Island National Park at Dalvay, if the Island's most luxurious summer cottage seems vaguely familiar to you, you've probably seen it before. On the made-for-TV movie *Anne of Green Gables* or *The Road to Avonlea* TV series it appears as the White Sands Hotel.

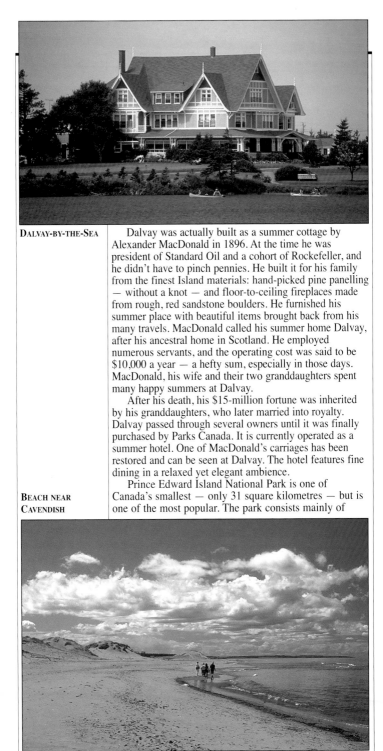

DALVAY-BY-THE-SEA

Dalvay was actually built as a summer cottage by Alexander MacDonald in 1896. At the time he was president of Standard Oil and a cohort of Rockefeller, and he didn't have to pinch pennies. He built it for his family from the finest Island materials: hand-picked pine panelling — without a knot — and floor-to-ceiling fireplaces made from rough, red sandstone boulders. He furnished his summer place with beautiful items brought back from his many travels. MacDonald called his summer home Dalvay, after his ancestral home in Scotland. He employed numerous servants, and the operating cost was said to be $10,000 a year — a hefty sum, especially in those days. MacDonald, his wife and their two granddaughters spent many happy summers at Dalvay.

After his death, his $15-million fortune was inherited by his granddaughters, who later married into royalty. Dalvay passed through several owners until it was finally purchased by Parks Canada. It is currently operated as a summer hotel. One of MacDonald's carriages has been restored and can be seen at Dalvay. The hotel features fine dining in a relaxed yet elegant ambience.

Prince Edward Island National Park is one of Canada's smallest — only 31 square kilometres — but is one of the most popular. The park consists mainly of

BEACH NEAR CAVENDISH

marshland and spruce woodlands, which include hiking trails and campgrounds. But its fine sandy beaches — some of the best in the world — are its main attraction. Wading in the clear salt waters of the Gulf of St. Lawrence, you can see your toes on the sandy bottom; you will be hard-pressed to find a stone on which to stub your toe.

BOARDWALK AT NORTH RUSTICO

This coastline was also the setting for the infamous but profitable rum-running trade. During prohibition days, when the Island was dry, ships sailed in from the French islands of St. Pierre and Miquelon, located off the south coast of Newfoundland. Laden with rum, they dropped anchor offshore and blinked their lights to signal fishermen standing by, their small boats at the ready. As soon as the coast was clear of Mounties they rowed out — usually after dark — to claim their booty. Fishermen carried on a brisk rum-running trade and many homes had clever hiding places such as false cupboards and floorboards.

It was along this coastline too, that wooden sailing ships were built and launched. Shipbuilding brought such prosperity to the Island during the mid-1800s that it was

referred to as "The Golden Age of Sail." In this particular area, 43 ships were built and launched from 1786 to 1890.

TRACADIE HARBOUR

As you travel the coastline of the Gulf of St. Lawrence, you will come to Brackley Beach where there are excellent beach houses with change and shower facilities. Located on Brackley Bay is Shaw's Hotel, a relaxing country lodge. This traditional inn, with its first-class dining room along with several cottages, is a favourite place for families. The inn was opened by the Shaws in 1860 and is still run by the family.

SHAW'S HOTEL

COVEHEAD LIGHT STATION

RUSTICO HARBOUR

Leaving Shaw's Hotel and Prince Edward Island National Park, stop by the Dunes Studio Gallery and Café. It's worth a stop even to see the interesting architecture, right from the outdoor gardens to the tiny water garden on the roof, to the view of the bay from the observatory gallery and tower called "The Muse." The Dunes, the Island's most elegant craft shop, displays beautiful crafts by Canada's finest artists and artisans. The owner, potter Peter Jansons, can often be seen at work in his studio. Also on display is one of the finest exhibitions of Prince Edward Island art. The Dunes has a reputation for its delicious and unique cuisine.

Back on the main road you will see the signs designating Blue Heron Drive. Along the way there are signs to Rustico, Anglo Rustico, South Rustico, Rusticoville and North Rustico. Rustico used to be mainly a fishing area with a few craft shops and some tourist accommodations, but new attractions have recently been added. The scenery is green and pastoral, with glimpses of Rustico Bay. Most fishermen here work in the lucrative lobster fishery during its season — the month of June — and then paint and "gussy up" their boats to take tourists out deep-sea fishing for the summer and fall. If you ask around the area you can usually arrange an excursion in a genuine fishing boat. Upon your return, you'll have a healthy appetite and a fresh catch for your supper.

The Rustico region was the first settled Acadian community in PEI after the expulsion, and is still thought of as Acadian. Though

FARMERS' BANK

ST. AUGUSTINE'S IN SOUTH RUSTICO

French inflections are still heard, very few of its residents speak French as a first language. For a flavour of Acadian history, one can turn right near Gallant's grocery store (Route 243) at South Rustico and visit Belcourt Centre. The centre is named after Father Georges-Antoine Belcourt who served in South Rustico in the mid-1800s. Father Belcourt was committed to helping the Acadians make a better life for themselves. One of his first projects was to establish the Farmers' Bank so that residents could borrow money at a preferred interest rate in order to buy seed.

The bank was operated as a co-operative, or credit union — one of the first in the country. The slate-roofed Island stone Farmers' Bank is now a museum. On display are numerous artifacts including Father Belcourt's robes, and one of the most recently acquired treasures, a handsome bronze bust of Napoleon III, which was brought from France with great ceremony in 2004. A forward-thinking man for his time, Father Belcourt is remembered as the first Islander to own a car. He is revered for his efforts on behalf of the Acadian people.

In Belcourt Centre stands St. Augustine's Church, the Island's oldest Roman Catholic church, with its lovely paired Gothic windows. For bed-and-breakfast accommodation in this area, the Barachois Inn across the road from the church is a fine old home, with a sloping mansard roof and antique furnishings. It is one of the Island's few rural five-star bed-and-breakfast establishments. The owner says she can provide "just about every imaginable comfort." The inn is open year-round.

Next door is the Belcourt Centre, once a convent used for teaching French, but now used for retreats. One of the most exciting and most recent additions to the centre is Doucet House. Built of logs in 1772, it was constructed in the Acadian style by Jean Doucet in the nearby community of Cymbria. Slated to be torn down, the building was rescued by the Friends of the Farmer's Bank, who had it moved to Belcourt Centre. Restored, furnished and staffed, it is an authentic example

DOUCET HOUSE

of early Acadian life. Connecting Doucet House and the Farmers' Bank is a landscaped boardwalk with benches, offering a fine place for a picnic.

Continuing on Blue Heron Drive (Route 6) to North Rustico, you will

FISHERIES MUSEUM pass the road down to the wharf to the Fisheries Museum and the nearby mussel café. After some fresh mussels and a pleasant walk along the seaside boardwalk, you might even work up an appetite for a lobster dinner at the Fisherman's Wharf Restaurant nearby.

A return to Route 6 to Cavendish, and a right turn at the intersection with traffic lights, will bring you to the Cavendish Information Centre. A short distance down the side road you will find the creamy sands of Cavendish Beach. A majority of the Island's first-time visitors feel

they can't miss Cavendish. For those travelling with young children it seems to be a must.

Another favourite attraction is Rainbow Valley. For a daily entrance fee, a family can enjoy the acres of grass and woodlands, ponds for pedal boats and canoes, waterslides and various fairy-tale attractions. Families often take along a picnic.

Another well-run attraction is

THE WHARF AT NORTH RUSTICO

CAVENDISH BOARDWALK

Sandspit, which includes racing cars, bumper boats, mini rides, mini-golf and a canteen. In Cavendish you can find every kind of fast food imaginable. Most kids — big and little — think they have to "do" the Cavendish scene at least once. There are those who berate the commercial

aspects of Cavendish, referring to it as a honky-tonk area, but no one can deny that the spacious green areas and beaches save it from that fate. On a summer's day you sometimes find a few thousand people there, sure proof that it holds an attraction for many.

GREEN GABLES

Many visitors will not want to leave Prince Edward Island without having their photo taken with Green Gables in the background. If you know the story, it is captivating to walk through the home which is believed to be the setting for the novel, *Anne of Green Gables*. It's easy to imagine yourself in the milieu where the spunky, much-loved, red-haired Anne used to roam and to walk into the kitchen and imagine Marilla at work. You'll even find Matthew's bedroom, with his big work boots under his patchwork-quilt covered bed. (Matthew had to sleep downstairs because of his bad heart.) Anne's little room upstairs is precious. There you see her tiny boots, the plain dresses she hated and, on the floor, the slate she cracked over Gilbert Blythe's head. But what many

visitors to Green Gables don't know about is the walking area behind the home. After a tour of the house, they can walk down Lovers' Lane and through the Haunted Wood. It's very beautiful there, with woodland paths leading over bridges and little streams.

SANDSPIT

VISITORS AT PEI PRESERVES, NEW GLASGOW

NEW LONDON SHOPS: GREEN GABLES STORE

It is not uncommon to see smiling young Japanese girls in traditional white wedding gowns, posing for photos at Green Gables. A number of couples come from Japan to the Island to be married. In Japan, the admiration for their heroine Anne, along with her creator, Lucy Maud Montgomery, is so great that it has inspired several fan clubs. The Japanese have even established a replica of Green Bush at Canada World in Japan.

Prince Edward Island has thousands of Japanese visitors every year, mainly because of "Anne of the Red Hair." The place where the young Japanese girls like to be married is the home of Montgomery's cousins at Park Corner, referred to as "Silver Bush" in her novels — now the Anne of Green Gables Museum. Montgomery herself was married at Silver Bush, and the Japanese girls want a wedding which is exactly the same.

There, young Maud used to spend happy times with her cousins, the Campbells. One of their descendants, George Campbell, has turned Silver Bush into a museum and he

NEW LONDON DEEP-SEA FISHING

delights in showing visitors around. On the grounds, they have built the charming Shining Waters Tea Room nestled in a grove of trees.

Montgomery's ivory-coloured wedding gown is kept at her birthplace at New London. This charming little home is probably where the ghost of Montgomery is felt most strongly. Her wedding dress, her old scrapbooks and samples of her writing are on display. When you go into the kitchen of the tiny home it's easy to imagine the young parents, Hugh Montgomery and Clara Macneill, living as a happy family with Maud, their vivacious, chattering toddler. But it's when you go upstairs and see Maud's room, with her baby furniture and pinafores, that the tragedy of this little family hits you. When baby Maud was just two years old her young mother was struck down with tuberculosis. The author later wrote in her journal: "My earliest memory is of being held in my father's arms and reaching down to touch my mother's cool cheek with my baby hand."

MALPEQUE HARBOUR

Another of the area's Anne-related attractions is
Avonlea Village. Here the church Maud attended,
and the schoolhouse where she taught, have been
brought together in a village constructed to look
like the period in which the *Anne* books were set.
There is an admission charge to the entire village,
but a horse-and-wagon ride around the square and
entrance to each of the buildings are free.

For a change of pace — especially if you have
children travelling with you, or if you have children
on your gift list — you might like to find Route 13
and tour the rolling hills to New Glasgow for a visit to the
Toy Factory. In this charming little factory toys are made
from Island wood and guaranteed to last a lifetime,
according to the proprietor. Children are welcome in the
factory and they can have their names stamped on their new
toys. While in the vicinity you could treat yourself to one of
the famous New Glasgow lobster suppers nearby.

For a pleasant way to finish the day, take an early
evening tour on Blue Heron Drive through French River to
Malpeque. This is one of the Island's most beautiful areas.
Glimpses of water are seen around each curve in the road.
Indeed, no Prince Edward Island community is more than
20 kilometres from the sea.

Further south on Blue Heron Drive is Indian River,
home to a world-class classical music festival. The French
Gothic-style St. Mary's Church is the largest wooden church
remaining on the Island. Built in 1902, it is an acoustical
wonder — the perfect setting for musical performance. The
festival attracts internationally known vocalists and
instrumentalists throughout the summer. The seats are hard
but the music is heavenly. A concert at St. Mary's Church is
a fitting finale to a visit to this particularly lovely section of
Prince Edward Island.

**ROADSIDE, NEAR
MALPEQUE**

ST. MARY'S CHURCH

NEW GLASGOW

CHARLOTTE'S SHORE

ANNE McCALLUM

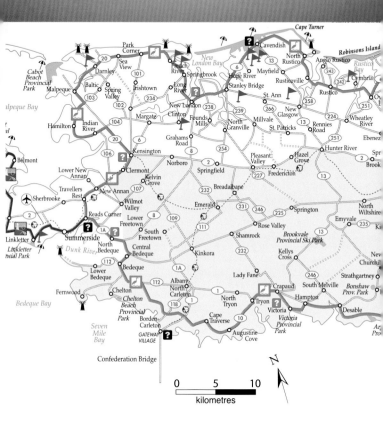

Charlotte's Shore is a patchwork of small farming
communities interspersed with natural woodlands and
bordered by a series of picturesque fishing villages along
the Northumberland Strait. What strikes you most when
you catch the first shimmering glimpse of Prince Edward
Island from the high centre point on Confederation Bridge
is the rich, red hue of the sandstone shoreline, especially if
the sun is setting. Much of the Island's natural beauty
comes from its strong colour contrasts — the burnished red
of the earth, the innumerable green shades of fields and
forests, and the brilliant blues of sky and ocean. These
colours dominate your first images of Charlotte's Shore
and stay with you long after the smaller details of your trip
have faded.

146

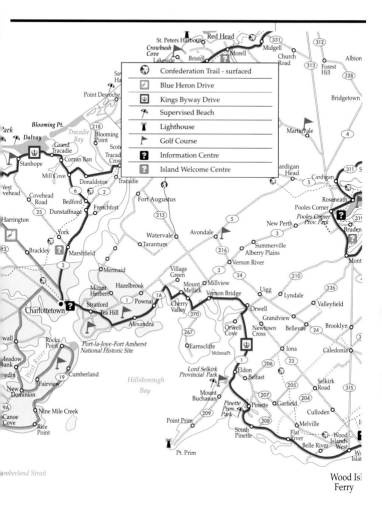

After you drive off the bridge near the village of Borden-Carleton, it is well worth spending an hour or so at Gateway Village, opened as part of the Confederation Bridge development to welcome visitors to the Island. You will notice it immediately to your right as you arrive. It is a first-rate interpretive centre where you will learn about the history, geography and economy of Prince Edward Island through a series of multimedia, interactive exhibits. You will be introduced to the work of some of the province's most creative craftspeople and find out how much effort and expertise it took to construct the world's longest continuous marine span bridge over ice-covered waters.

Just west of Confederation Bridge is Chelton Beach Provincial Park, the region's only dune beach. The water is

SANDSTONE CLIFFS

FARM ON ROUTE 1

POTATO FIELDS IN
BLOOM,
MEADOWBANK

warm and the park has supervised swimming and picnic tables.

Another point of interest in the area is Seacow Head lighthouse. It is an eight-sided wooden structure over 18 metres above water level, built in 1863 and moved back from the eroding cliff edge to its present location in 1979. Black guillemots lay their eggs on the cliff's ledges. Watch out for eiders, scoters and oldsquaws in the water.

Nearby Bedeque is a sleepy country village, but over a century ago it was a bustling shipbuilding centre. One of the most influential shipbuilders and merchants from the area was James Pope, the first Island premier after Confederation. You'll find the J. C. Pope historic site near Bedeque.

From Central Bedeque and Middleton, Route 225 will take you through the Island's potato-growing heartland. The area was initially settled by Loyalists, but, as the nearby place names of Shamrock and Emerald indicate, it became home in the first half of the 19th century to Irish immigrants. Every July residents celebrate their Irish heritage with a three-day festival in Emerald Junction.

The focal point of Kinkora is the "new" St. Malachy's Catholic Church, opened in 1901. Its Gothic Revival design and beautifully carved interior make it one of the region's most impressive churches.

Farming communities around Kinkora have flourished, thanks to the potato. The Island's most prized export, the white seed potato, was developed in this area. The immaculately cultivated fields of green foliage topped with white blossoms present a healthy, fertile image, but from an environmental perspective, some of today's potato production methods have proved less than benign. Soil

erosion and river siltation are serious problems in many areas where potato monoculture is common. Fortunately, the more progressive farmers now practise across-the-slope plowing and plant strip crops to conserve the Island's fragile topsoil from the ravaging effects of wind and water.

When you reach the Route 231 intersection at Rose Valley, travel north to Breadalbane. Ask at the library/community centre about the hiking trail that village residents have developed. Include a visit as well to Malcolm Stanley's pottery studio on Route 246, known locally as the Dixon Road. This little red road is home to numerous artists and musicians who settled on the Island in the 1970s as part of the "back-to-the-land movement." Rural life and nature provide the inspiration for the hand-painted Island scenes, trees and flowers on the Stanley family's hand-thrown pottery.

From Breadalbane, you can head north to join Route 2, one of two main roads running east-west from Summerside to Charlottetown. It passes through the picturesque village of Hunter River, where you might catch sight of a flock of Canada geese on the river below the Presbyterian Church. A less travelled route would be to backtrack from Breadalbane to Rose Valley and follow Route 225 through the rolling hills to North River. This is dairy farming country.

Throughout the summer, the hayfields and roadsides are ablaze with wildflower colour — dog daisies and dandelions, purple vetch and white clover, black-eyed Susans and Queen Anne's Lace. If you have young children along, you'll want to stop at the Toy Factory in

FARM NEAR VICTORIA

WILDFLOWERS IN BLOOM

PEI FACTORY OUTLETS, NORTH RIVER CAUSEWAY

New Glasgow, which offers an assortment of unique wooden toys handcrafted while you watch.

At North River, if you turn left onto the TransCanada and drive across the causeway — watching out for great blue herons, Bonaparte's gulls, and factory outlets as you do so — you will find yourself at the western entrance to Charlottetown.

If you turn right at North River and travel west to Cornwall, you will be at a perfect starting point to explore the bays and beaches of the south shore. South shore beaches are unsupervised and much coarser than those on the north shore. But the water is considerably warmer and, at low tide, they're great for digging clams or searching for sea treasures in nooks and crannies of rock pools. Turn left onto Route 19 and follow the Blue Heron Drive through Meadowbank. Cross the West River and follow Route 19 towards Rocky Point. At Fairview you'll see signs for Dunollie Travel Park. In mid-July, bluegrass bands from all over the Maritimes and the eastern US gather here for the annual Bluegrass Festival. At Rocky Point you'll have a panoramic view of Charlottetown Harbour.

Continue west about two kilometres on Route 19 to Fort Amherst/Port LaJoye, a national historic site. In the early 1700s the French established a settlement here. When the British took possession of the Island in 1758 they built Fort Amherst. At its peak the fort served an important military function. There is an interpretive centre where you can learn about early Island settlement. The grounds and shoreline are pleasant places to walk, picnic or fly kites.

CORNWALL UNITED CHURCH

If you follow Route 19 around Rice Point you will reach Canoe Cove. When the Island was in French possession, the Mi'kmaq took the British ashore in their canoes and it is said that those soldiers gave the name to the district. Some cove people of the past claim to have sighted a flaming sailboat or steamer off this shore. It is known in local folklore as "The Phantom Ship," and sightings have been reported from both sides of the strait. Swimming is good in this large sheltered cove. Argyle Shore Provincial Park, a few kilometres west, is another great swimming and picnicking spot.

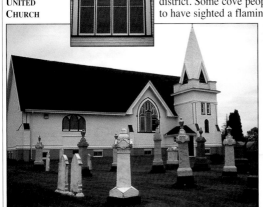

At Desable, Route 19 joins the TransCanada again. The Free Church of Scotland here reflects distinctive Scottish tradition in its architecture. Its steeple is topped with a thistle. The church holds 500 people, but is known to have held twice that number when the Reverend Donald McDonald preached in the mid-1800s. He established a local sect called the "McDonaldites." His powerful sermons in Gaelic and English attracted close to 5,000 followers.

VICTORIA-BY-THE-SEA

By following the coastline you will have missed Strathgartney Provincial Park in the Bonshaw Hills. It is well worth backtracking a few kilometres along Route 1 to Strathgartney to experience the excellent hiking trails that have been developed. The nearby Strathgartney Inn was built by landowner and land agent Robert Bruce Stewart in the mid-1800s. At St. Catherines Cove off Route 9 you can rent a canoe and paddle the tidal West River.

If you are travelling in July or August, you can pick your own strawberries or raspberries at local fruit farms. The area around South Melville is also a paradise for hikers and cyclists.

From Desable it is a short drive to Victoria-by-the-Sea. Many homes in this charming village are notable examples of 19th-century architecture. Victoria did not develop at random, but rather was built by design on one family's farm, to serve as a seaport for nearby

ORIENT HOTEL, VICTORIA

agricultural communities. In its heyday, it was the fourth-busiest port on the Island, but when transportation methods switched from water to land, it declined. In recent years it has enjoyed a resurgence because of its popularity among visitors.

Although a small village, Victoria offers quite a range of attractions. There is a warm-water beach and picnic area at Victoria Provincial Park — great for beachcombing. Look for bank swallows nesting on the cliff edge. Dunrovin Lodge, Victoria Village Inn and the Orient Hotel offer excellent accommodations in heritage surroundings. There is a chocolate factory, several tea rooms and some first-rate arts and crafts outlets. Professional repertory

ISLAND CHOCOLATES, VICTORIA

MRS. PROFITTS TEA ROOM

CONFEDERATION BRIDGE

theatre and musical concerts are presented nightly at the Victoria Playhouse. The hall's sloping floor design ensures that there isn't a bad seat in the house.

One of the Island's largest salt marshes is in this area — the Tryon Marsh. The Tryon River is of historical interest because it was the site of the Island's first woollen mill, built by Charles E. Stanfield in 1856.

From Tryon it is just a short drive back to the Confederation Bridge where, incidentally, you will be asked to pay a bridge toll if you are leaving. The fee actually pays for the two-way trip, but is collected on the Island side.

If you are staying, you can travel east to Route 13 from Crapaud to the north shore. This meandering route will take you past the Brookvale Demonstration Woodlot, where you can follow an interpretive walking tour. Brookvale is also the site of the Island's only downhill ski park, open from December to March. Route 13 continues through Hunter River. At this point you will be entering the popular tourist area known as Anne's Land.

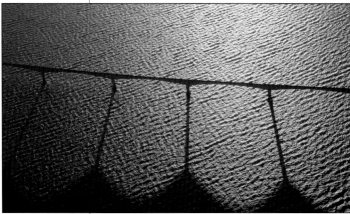

BAYS AND DUNES

KUMARI CAMPBELL

BOATING ON THE CARDIGAN RIVER

Unlike the busy central region of the province, life in the Bays and Dunes region is unhurried. Simple treasures of nature are abundant, and peace and solitude are tangible commodities. Unbelievable as it may seem, this is largely virgin territory, virtually undiscovered by the masses. So, if you promise to keep it a secret, I will share with you the natural riches of this region I call home.

A warning before we begin: you won't find any commercial attractions or grandiose structures along the way. The only items of large proportions here are the great outdoors and the hearts of our residents. But be assured, that is all you will need for a splendid vacation.

Residents of northeastern Prince Edward Island are determined that their region remain as close to nature as possible, and the Bays and Dunes region has developed a reputation as a "green tourism" destination. Two green tourism products help visitors get a closer look at the natural beauty of the region. The Confederation Trail, which uses the former railbed of the Prince Edward Island Railway as a hiking and biking trail across the province, had its beginnings in this region. This trail provides vistas of the interior that cannot be had from your car window. The Bays and Dunes Drive, which circles the entire region, offers the visitor a complete northeastern PEI experience, by

153

linking its natural, cultural and historic sites. Beginning at Pooles Corner, the first stop on the Bays and Dunes Drive will be Cardigan. One of many picturesque little villages that dot the shoreline of Prince Edward Island, this is a cohesive community where group spirit runs high. A new marina and interpretive centre, a five-kilometre section of the Confederation Trail through the village, a community centre, and a craft shop and tea room in the former Cardigan railway station are accomplishments of which residents are rightfully proud. You'll also find a lobster supper and a magnificent Tudor mansion on the Cardigan River that is now the five-star Cardigan River Inn.

Route 311 takes you around the Launching Peninsula. While Island woodlands are experiencing a period of intensive harvesting, this area has retained more of its woodlands than have other parts of the province. As you enter Launching, you can catch a glimpse of heavily wooded Boughton Island to your right. This is one of many islands off the coast of Prince Edward Island that provide nesting places

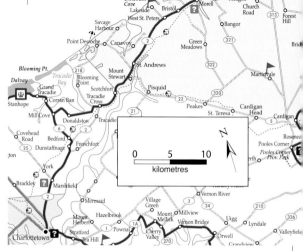

154

for colonies of terns, cormorants, and blue herons.

Driving down into Bridgetown, you will notice that the forests have given way to farm fields. In the adjoining community of Dundas, the annual Dundas Plowing Match has been celebrated for over 100 years.

The Fortune Peninsula has several secluded beaches that can be reached from side roads leading off Route 311. Local residents would be happy to provide directions. The area also has many interesting craft shops and accommodations. Of particular interest is The Inn at Spry Point, which also houses a distinctive restaurant. Nature trails and the local beach add to the allure of this charming hideaway.

A stroll through the Sailor's Hope Bog in Howe Bay will take you through an area rich in flora, such as the insect-eating sundew, pitcher plants, and calapogan orchids.

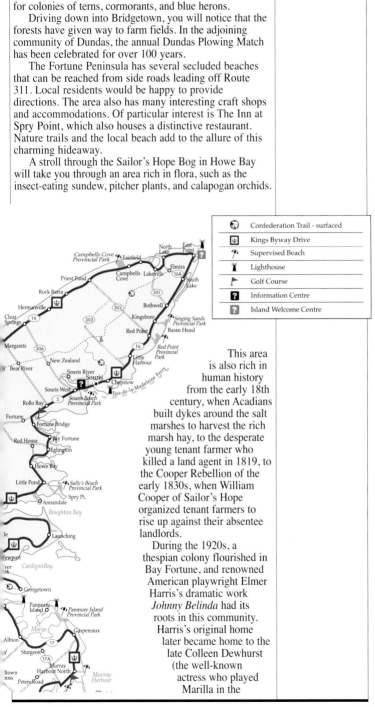

	Confederation Trail - surfaced
	Kings Byway Drive
	Supervised Beach
	Lighthouse
	Golf Course
	Information Centre
	Island Welcome Centre

This area is also rich in human history from the early 18th century, when Acadians built dykes around the salt marshes to harvest the rich marsh hay, to the desperate young tenant farmer who killed a land agent in 1819, to the Cooper Rebellion of the early 1830s, when William Cooper of Sailor's Hope organized tenant farmers to rise up against their absentee landlords.

During the 1920s, a thespian colony flourished in Bay Fortune, and renowned American playwright Elmer Harris's dramatic work *Johnny Belinda* had its roots in this community. Harris's original home later became home to the late Colleen Dewhurst (the well-known actress who played Marilla in the

THE INN AT BAY FORTUNE

MATTHEW HOUSE INN

motion picture *Anne of Green Gables*). Today, the home has been restored and houses an elegant inn and restaurant. The Inn at Bay Fortune certainly offers one of the Island's premier culinary experiences.

Stop for a few moments at the Rollo Bay scenic lookout and enjoy a long view of the bay with its salt marshes and the potato fields in the foreground. A short distance down the road is the home of the Rollo Bay Fiddle Festival, an important event for ardent fiddlers across the Maritimes.

Souris is the economic hub of the Bays and Dunes region, with retail stores, restaurants, and public services. Souris is also the terminus of the passenger ferry to the Îles-de-la-Madeleine or Magdalen Islands. The town's rather unusual name originated with several plagues of mice that beset the early 18th-century settlers of the area. Sailing into its harbour filled with floating dead mice, a group of French fishers dubbed it Havre à la Souris, or Mouse Harbour, which was eventually shortened to Souris. Here a Victorian heritage home, the four-star Matthew House Inn, offers charming accommodations.

For a change of pace, a drive down the Scenic Heritage Road on Route 303 can take you back a century. Scenic Heritage Roads are specially designated provincial clay roads, bordered by lush vegetation that often forms a leafy canopy overhead. If you follow this with a walk along the trails of the adjacent Townshend Woodlot, you will slip into a peaceful world of unspoiled natural beauty.

Some of the most spectacular beaches in the Maritimes are to be found east of Souris. Magnificent white pearly beaches stretch endlessly, bordered by delicate marram grass dunes. It is truly memorable to watch the sun rise as you walk along the sand and listen to the music of the

ABOVE: "SINGING SANDS," BASIN HEAD

waves, or spend a romantic evening admiring the sunset, to the cacophony of shore birds. Nature just does not get more exotic than this. Basin Head and Red Point, both situated within provincial parks, are the most popular beaches, while Little Harbour, Bothwell and South Lake are more secluded.

The South Side, as this area is called by residents, is simply awash with wildflowers between early spring and late autumn. Dandelions, marsh marigolds, ox-eye daisies, devil's paintbrushes, Queen Anne's Lace, clover, purple loosestrife, fireweed and tansy ragwort are some of the most common. But none is more beautiful and plentiful than the common lupin.

The fisheries museum at Basin Head will guide you through all the arcane aspects of the fishery as it is practiced on PEI. The Boardwalk boasts some charming craft and gift shops. While at Basin Head, be sure to walk on the beach and listen to the "singing sands" — a phenomenon caused by high silica content in the sand, and ages of polishing by heavy surf.

The little white church in South Lake, on the hill to your left, has long been called "The Fisherman's Church" because of the beacon it provides for home-bound fishermen. The nearby Elmira Railway Museum chronicles the history of railroading on the Island. One of the largest model railway collections in Canada, along with a miniature railway that offers rides around a beautiful woodland track, are sure to excite model railway buffs and youngsters alike. Elmira is also the easternmost entry point of the Confederation Trail. The rolling landscape of this area, with its prevalent ocean vistas and patchwork fields, makes this a singularly attractive drive. On a clear day, if you look to the horizon on your right, you can easily see Cape Breton.

East Point is land's end. You can climb to the top of the lighthouse and witness the meeting of the tides as the Gulf of St. Lawrence tides

EAST POINT LIGHTHOUSE

collide with those of the Northumberland Strait. If heights don't appeal to you the craft shop might. If you're lucky one of the guides may tell you a salty yarn or two.

Once you have rounded the point you are on the North Side. Campbell's Cove, a few kilometres down the road, is believed to be the jut of land that Cartier first spied when he spoke those memorable words, "the fairest land 'tis possible to see."

The landscape on the North Side is vastly different from that of the South Side. Here you see more woodland and a rugged coast. The white marram-grass-covered dunes are interspersed with red sandstone cliffs. The trees speak of cruel north winds — a very different kind of beauty.

In the Rock Barra–Hermanville area you will notice several hundred acres of blueberry barrens. Sometimes in August the fields are literally tinged with blue. Later, in the fall, the plants turn bright red, and present a feast for the eye. In recent years, blueberries have consistently increased in value as an agricultural crop on PEI. The four-star Johnson Shore Inn, which offers magnificent ocean vistas from every one of its rooms, is located in this community.

The North Side beaches are smaller than their South Side counterparts. But, for this very reason, they are less known and therefore offer greater privacy. They also have white sand beaches, although many have captivating red sandstone cliffs rising behind them. North Lake, Campbell's Cove, Johnston's, Bear River, Naufrage, Cow River and Cable Head are the most accessible of these beaches.

A typical rural lobster supper is served in the St. Margaret's Church hall. And a few kilometres to the west, there is not a more picture-perfect fishing harbour than Naufrage, with its unique hump bridge.

Just down the road at Monticello is a re-created, authentic one-room schoolhouse, which offers up a Scottish ceilidh every summer Sunday night.

A right turn at the large white church on the hill in the village of St. Peters will take you to the Greenwich dunes, an adjunct to the Prince Edward Island National Park. This spectacular parabolic dune system is the jewel of the region. Although they have existed for thousands of years, the dunes are nevertheless extremely fragile, being susceptible to the prevailing ocean winds that cause them to change shape and migrate. The immense parabolic, crater-like dunes, anchored by coarse marram grass, along with adjacent ponds, wetlands, forests, and attendant rare plant species, form this unique ecosystem now under the protection of Parks Canada.

Greenwich is also the guardian of an

CHURCH NEAR ST. PETERS

ancient cultural history legacy, as the site of confirmed human habitation dating back 10,000 years. Since receiving National Park status in 1998 the site has been developed to include a state-of-the-art interpretation centre, with many static exhibits and a delightful multimedia presentation entitled "Wind, Sea and Sand, the story of Greenwich." Trails, including a floating boardwalk over a pond teeming with plant and animal life, lead through the various features of the site. A commitment to maintaining the integrity of the dunes has necessitated certain ultra-sensitive areas being closed to public access, while sustainable energy and waste systems have been installed to service the site. There are only a handful of dune systems like Greenwich on the planet and given its accessibility, this one is well worth a visit.

ABOVE: THE INN AT ST. PETERS

CYCLISTS AT ST. PETERS

En route to Greenwich you will encounter the Inn at St. Peters, offering lovely four-star accommodations and fine dining. You may wish to stop for a few minutes at the beautiful wayside park in the little village of St. Peters, and visit the Estuary Interpretive Centre and Shops. Or take in a demonstration of pewter casting at the St. Peters Bay Craft and Giftware centre and stop for a bite at the popular Rick's Fish & Chips, which serves fresh catch from local waters and hand-cut PEI fries. If you happen by in the evening, enjoy some community theatre in the 130-year-old Courthouse Theatre, which served as a courthouse until the 1960s. In August, this community celebrates its ever-popular Blueberry Festival.

GOLFING AT THE LINKS AT CROWBUSH COVE

TRAILSIDE CAFÉ, MOUNT STEWART

The next sizeable community is Morell. The short jaunt to Red Head Harbour is recommended if you are in the market for fresh fish, lobster or the Island's most luscious Island Blue mussels. Not far from Morell is the challenging Links at Crowbush Cove, the Island's premier 4 1/2-star golf course, and the adjacent Rodd Crowbush Resort, the Island's only five-star resort.

At St. Andrews is the historic St. Andrews Chapel. Built in 1803, it was moved to Charlottetown in 1864, where it was used for over a century. Virtually destroyed by fire in 1987, the gutted structure was moved back to its original site in the late 1980s to be reconstructed and put back in use.

In the village of Mount Stewart the Hillsborough River Eco-Centre interprets the history of PEI's only National Heritage River. This rich and diverse river system provides habitat for salmon, trout, striped bass and one-third of the Island's oyster harvest. Mink, red foxes, bald eagles and ospreys live in the system's salt marshes. Across the road, at the rustic Trailside Café and Adventures, you can rent bikes for riding the adjacent Confederation Trail and canoes for paddling the river. When you return your rentals at day's end, stay for dinner and enjoy some of the Maritimes' most popular entertainers.

The final leg of the drive (along Route 22) passes through largely undeveloped areas, although the scenery continues to be beautiful. At Baldwin Road, the drive turns left onto Route 5. Just before this highway meets Route 4, on your right you will find the Cardigan Water Science Centre, which offers interpretive programs of the largest fish-rearing facility for stocking Island rivers, a U-fish facility, children's programming and nature trails. Minutes from this attraction, turn right onto Route 4, which will return you to Pooles Corner, right where you began.

A FARM NEAR CROWBUSH

HILLS AND HARBOURS

HUGH MACDONALD

SUNSET AT WOOD ISLANDS

At the beginning of the 18th century my mother's family came by the shipload to southern Kings County. However, by the time I was born, my branch of the family tree was firmly planted in Charlottetown — a city which, for all Islanders east of the Confederation Bridge, is the undisputed centre of the civilized world. But I still spent most of my holidays in southern Kings with grandparents and cousins, learning the joys of tossing steaming piles of manure into spreaders, and walking among wildflowers and gnarled apple trees. About a quarter-century ago I moved back to southern Kings for good. I have few regrets.

If you listen hard you can get some pretty bad advice about travelling to the Island. Don't listen to mythology about long ferry line-ups at Caribou, Nova Scotia. An authentic Island visit ought to involve a trip by ferry. Someone forgot to tell those weavers of misconception about the *Confederation*, the huge ferry that began its run in 1994, and the acquisition of the *Holiday Island*, another large-capacity vessel that joined the route in 1997. A run across Northumberland Strait by ferry is a genuine luxury — the poor person's ocean cruise. Especially for anyone coming from Cape Breton or mainland Nova Scotia (anywhere from Truro north), the trip by ferry is much cheaper and far more sensible than the Confederation Bridge. Motorists can lounge on a comfortable vessel enjoying scenery and cool ocean breezes, instead of being in a hot car burning up rubber and fuel along miles of asphalt.

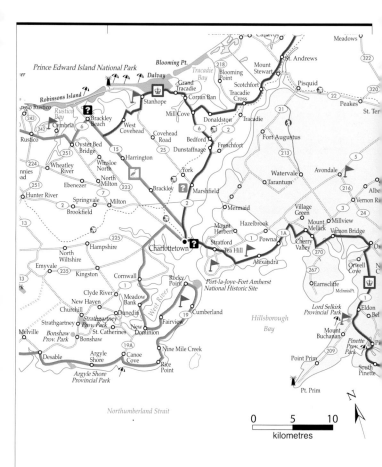

When the boat arrives at Wood Islands, most of the cars race along Route 1 to Charlottetown. All these tourists don't realize they've passed by the best part of the Island. Every year though, more and more people have been making a right turn off the TransCanada and discovering the rural delights of southern Kings and Queens Counties. For the most part we're not professional tourist handlers, but we're honest about our feelings and genuinely happy to see visitors who appreciate our part of the Island.

There are several ways to approach a trip through the hills and harbours of southern Kings. You could head down from Charlottetown and take Route 3 to Montague, the economic centre of the area. If you've arrived here from Nova Scotia by ferry at Wood Islands, the shortest way is a 20-minute drive along Route 315 — a road not without its attractions. The countryside in this area is hilly and a lush green.

Somehow though, I get the feeling you came to the Island because you're tired of being in a hurry. You need to slow down, to get out of the rat race and forget about things.

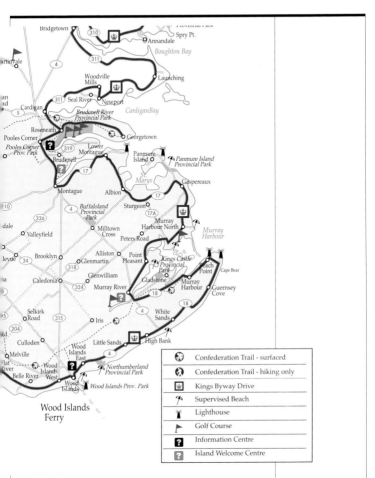

	Confederation Trail - surfaced
	Confederation Trail - hiking only
	Kings Byway Drive
	Supervised Beach
	Lighthouse
	Golf Course
	Information Centre
	Island Welcome Centre

If this is the case, when you leave the ferry terminal, turn off the TransCanada and look for Route 4. It's the long way, but you will visit some of the most beautiful acreage on earth. Pull into Northumberland Park. Take off those shoes and socks. Dip those sore toes into balmy salt water. Feel the sun-warmed sand beneath your feet. Perhaps you'll stay around here for a while. You can dig a few clams and bake them, or put on a snorkel and a mask and float out on the water, barely rippling the smooth surface.

When you leave the park a right turn will take you, six-and-one-half kilometres later, to the Rossignol Estate Winery. Here you can sample their award-winning fruit and table wines. It costs nothing to visit the meticulously tidy farm, winery, vineyard and art gallery. The owner, John Rossignol, is happy to chat about the beautiful sandy loam, or about how he is using former tobacco greenhouses for grape varieties previously considered too tender to grow on the Island. From this splendid farm you'll see breathtaking vistas of the Northumberland Strait.

These views of the strait, with Pictou Island and Nova

ROSSIGNOL ESTATE WINERY

Scotia in the distance, continue as you glide through the communities of Little Sands, High Bank and White Sands. Route 4 will become Route 18, and you'll veer to the right past Guernsey Cove where Huguenots, descendants of settlers from the Isle of Guernsey, have raised their families for generations. You'll pass through historic Cape Bear, where the first distress signal from the *Titanic* was heard, then back to the pavement and around Beach Point. By now you will probably have noticed the lovely orderliness of local fishing villages and you'll have watched dozens of Cape Island fishing boats rumble in and out of the harbour mouth. If you follow Route 18 to its end you'll visit two more working fishing villages, Murray Harbour and Murray River. You may decide to join a charter or a seal-watching expedition, or perhaps just explore the exquisite river systems or the Murray Islands. The entire area is a delight for the nature-lover, with its magnificent variety of birds and animals.

A visit to the Old General Store, famous for its mural, its quilts, linen and handicrafts, will take you back in time to a general store from the 1860s. If you haven't already discovered a small restaurant or purchased a feed of fresh Island seafood, you have a number of choices. If you aren't ready to eat yet, there are roads that lead in several directions. Route 24 is the shortest way to Charlottetown. It rolls and dips through the hills, all of it lovely farming country. At Kinross you can turn left onto Route 210 and be at the TransCanada in about 20 minutes.

But why not forget Charlottetown for a while? This neighbourhood is too good to leave. Watch for a sign on your right that announces the Orwell Corner Historic Village. Turn right again and pass the village entrance for now. We'll come back. A minute or two down the road, on your left, is the stone gate that marks the entrance to the Sir Andrew Macphail Homestead. The restored house and a cup of tea await. A series of walking trails take you under big pines and huge hemlock and yellow birch, especially the trail that goes down by the brook. Smell — here you can catch a glimpse of how the original forest cover of Kings County once looked. Some of the trees are over 150 years old. In the spring, the big linden in front of the house bursts into bloom and hums with thousands of bees.

OLD GENERAL STORE, MURRAY RIVER

The property has a tree nursery that specializes in native trees and shrubs.

After a while you'll want to return to the historic village at Orwell Corner. The village transports visitors back to a less complicated age. You can visit the store or the church, or wander at will. If you're lucky, there will be a ceilidh later in the hall. If not, there's always homemade ice cream to enjoy, or an ancient piece of farm machinery to climb on. Or some warm sun to sit in and dream.

The second way out of Murray River is Route 4. This is the shortest route to Montague. As you approach Milltown Cross, you may be surprised to see buffalo. Someone in the provincial government took advantage of a buffalo surplus in western Canada and the Island gained a herd of buffalo. These critters never roamed on Prince Edward Island, but kids love to roam Buffaloland Provincial Park and look at them.

SCHOOLHOUSE AT ORWELL CORNER

But you may prefer a third option. A turn onto Route 17 will take you along the coast, past numerous fishing

harbours. Local waterways are popular with yachting enthusiasts from all over the Island, partly because of their many beautiful, secluded inlets and coves. The Panmure Island Cultural Grounds are open for walking anytime, and for admiring their natural beauty. But in the third week of August you can join 4,000 people in a

MURRAY HARBOUR

celebration of Mi'kmaq culture, which even includes tasting some moose, deer or frybread. Panmure Island has wonderful beaches and a campground. Ask about Joe French's wharf, American privateers or my Macdonald ancestors.

Route 17 continues through scenic countryside and finally follows the Montague River up to Montague. The signs outside Montague welcome visitors to "Montague the Beautiful." There's lots of fast food but the kids will

GARDEN OF THE GULF MUSEUM, MONTAGUE

particularly love the Gillis' Drive-In Restaurant. It's a local institution, a real drive-in restaurant. The Dynasty Restaurant offers a Chinese menu, and the food is quite good at two motels, the Lobster Shanty and the Whim Inn, or at the Rusty Pelican by the marina. For fine dining, Windows on the Water sits on the north side of the bridge, just up from the boardwalk.

Montague boasts the Garden of the Gulf Museum, as well as good shopping, an excellent health food store, an indoor pool and fitness centre and a small marina. The Montague River flows from its source several miles above town, down toward Georgetown into Cardigan Bay. From Montague Bridge you can go seal-watching, or take a cruise and munch on locally grown blue mussels.

You may choose to stay in the area a few days. There's lots to do. A new park, Roma at Three Rivers, is an historic site commemorating a 1700s French settlement, Victorian shipbuilding and the birthplace of Father of Confederation A. A. Macdonald. There are archaeological displays, nature trails, picnic facilities, beach and river access, and occasional re-enactments.

PANMURE ISLAND

It's not a long drive to the Provincial Park, where the Brudenell Golf Course is world-class. It has excellent accommodations and a decent restaurant. Or, you may opt for one of the many bed-and-breakfasts in the area. They are run by friendly people who know the area intimately. You might try Brenda and Edgar Dewar's comfortable 1868 farmhouse just off Route 4 (take Dewar's Road on the right just before Pooles Corner). Named Roseneath, it is one of the most interesting and relaxing bits of real estate around. Edgar's family operated a mill there for generations and the house is chock full of art and artifacts from his and Brenda's years in the Near and Far East. Outside, it's paradise for birders or trout fishers who follow the walking trail along the Brudenell River to where it joins the Confederation Trail. Or, if you're a camping enthusiast, you can't do much better than the Brudenell River Campground. It's right beside the golf course, and features a marina, canoeing, horseback riding, campfires and not too many bugs.

If you continue on Route 3 past the resort, you'll arrive in Georgetown, the capital of Kings County. Lately it's been prospering. The Irvings recently began operating the shipbuilding plant, rejuvenating something that's been a part of this town since its inception. Shipbuilding is what my mother's people did for a living. Once, so I've been told, you could walk across the Georgetown harbour on the decks of wooden ships. Now it's a quiet little place, filled with friendly people, and it's an easy place to walk around. The King's Playhouse was built to replace the historic

MONTAGUE HARBOUR

HISTORIC SITE AT THREE RIVERS

ROSENEATH

King's Theatre, destroyed by fire in 1983, but once a regular stop on Eastern North America's theatre circuit. Behind the theatre is the A. A. Macdonald Memorial Gardens, honouring an ancestor of mine, the Father of Confederation who was a long-time resident of the town.

If you like lobster, Georgetown has two lobster pounds. At the foot of Queen Street, on the left, is Kinnear's. Or you can turn right onto Water Street and go to Georgetown Packers, the big red brick building on the large government wharf at the end. If you ask, they'll show you some big lobsters, or, even better, some weirdly coloured lobsters. If you ask me, lobster from southern Kings is the best in the Maritimes. If you buy a few pounds, it's easy to cook them yourself. You'll need a pot, a fire and some sea water or clean tap water laced with a fistful of pickling salt. Place the lobster in boiling water head first. When the water begins to boil again, cook for 12 minutes, then serve. The shells are packed tightly with tender, sweet meat. Enjoy the pleasure of digging it out with your fingers and getting messy.

CANOEING AT BRUDENELL RIVER

I have yet to mention my favourite summertime treat. Every year I like to leave home and head out into the countryside with no particular destination in mind. Sometimes I pack a lunch. Sometimes Sandra and the kids come with me; sometimes I travel alone. I pick a day when the sun paints the world lazy and a fat breeze shakes all the trees. Southern Kings has wonderful tree-lined red clay roads that are mostly used by farmers heading out to their fields. There are a million places to park a car and wander, or picnic in swaying fields of brown-eyed Susans and white-collared daisies. Pretend you're in heaven. You may never get closer.

CONTENTS

Getting There   **170**

By Bridge   170
By Sea   170
By Bus   170
By Air   170

Travel Essentials   **170**

Money   170
Passports   171
Customs   171
Taxes   171
Guides   172

Getting Acquainted   **172**

Time Zone   172
Climate   172
Metric System   172

Staying Healthy   **173**

Getting Around   **173**

By Bus   173
By Car   173

Lodging   **174**

North Cape   174
Anne's Land   175
Charlotte's Shore   176
Bays and Dunes   177
Hills and Harbours   178

Dining   **178**

North Cape   178
Anne's Land   179
Charlotte's Shore   180
Bays and Dunes   180
Hills and Harbours   181

Attractions   **181**

North Cape   181
Anne's Land   183
Charlotte's Shore   184
Bays and Dunes   185
Hills and Harbours   186

Genealogical Research   **187**

Festivals and Events   **187**

Island-wide   187
North Cape   187
Anne's Land   188

Charlotte's Shore   189
Bays and Dunes   189
Hills and Harbours   190

Night Life   **190**

Theatre   190
Pubs and Taverns   191

Craft Shops   **192**

North Cape   192
Anne's Land   193
Charlotte's Shore   193
Bays and Dunes   194
Hills and Harbours   195

Product Tours   **195**

Art Galleries   **195**

Outdoor Recreation   **196**

North Cape   196
Anne's Land   197
Charlotte's Shore   197
Bays and Dunes   197
Hills and Harbours   197

Golf   **198**

North Cape   198
Anne's Land   198
Charlotte's Shore   199
Bays and Dunes   199
Hills and Harbours   199

Boating and Sailing   **199**

Canoeing and Kayaking   **200**

Cycling   **200**

Fishing   **201**

Deep-Sea   201
Sport Fishing   201

Index   **202**

✴ denotes a location identified
by the publisher for its
exceptional quality

GETTING THERE

BY BRIDGE

There used to be only one way of bringing your car to Prince Edward Island, and that was by ferry. The Confederation Bridge, which opened on June 1, 1997, changed all that. Now it's an easy 10-minute drive across a 13-kilometre bridge that, unless you're in a truck or a van, seems for all intents and purposes a highway with high concrete sides. If you're a foot passenger, or on a bicycle, Strait Crossing offers a complimentary shuttle service from either side (accessed from the junction of the TransCanada Highway and Rte. 955 in New Brunswick, or at Gateway Village in Borden-Carleton, Prince Edward Island). Maximum wait time is two hours.

A return trip on the Confederation Bridge (payable when you leave the Island) costs $39.50 for a car, $15.75 for a motorcycle, $45.25 for a truck or recreational vehicle, $56.50 for a truck/trailer, and $226 for a bus, payable by cash, credit card, or debit card. Foot passengers and cyclists cross free of charge. The toll booth is on the Prince Edward Island side of the strait.

The bridge is sometimes closed to tall vehicles during high winds. For bridge conditions, call 1-888-437-6565, visit www.confederationbridge.com, or tune into the bridge's radio station at 93.9 FM.

BY SEA

Between May and December, Northumberland Ferries sail between Caribou, Nova Scotia, and Wood Islands, Prince Edward Island. Reservations are not required. Larger ferries have reduced wait times at the terminals in recent years. The trip takes an hour and 15 minutes, during which time you can stroll the decks, have a meal or light refreshments, or relax with a book in the lounge. The cost is $49.00 per car with any number of passengers, payable when you leave the Island. For a detailed schedule, call 1-888-249-SAIL (7245), or check their website, www.nfl-bay.com.

BY BUS

SMT (Eastern) Ltd. buses leave Charlottetown and other Island locations for the mainland twice daily, connecting in Moncton with coaches bound for major Canadian destinations. For information and schedules, call 1-800-567-5151. The SMT bus station in Charlottetown is located at 156 Belvedere Ave.; telephone (902) 628-6432. SMT buses also connect with VIA rail trains in Moncton; for information and reservations call 1-888-842-7245 (VIA RAIL).

BY AIR

Charlottetown is a 25-minute flight from Halifax, with connections to major cities in Canada and the U.S. Jazz, an Air Canada partner (1-800-565-3940), services Prince Edward Island with several flights daily throughout the year. Air Canada offers a direct flight from Toronto, and the low-cost Air Canada carrier Tango flies direct from Toronto on a seasonal basis. Direct service from Toronto is also provided by the low-cost carrier Jetsgo. Northwest Airlines now offers direct daily service from Detroit to Charlottetown with connections from U.S. cities as well as Asia. The service is available from July to mid-October. For flight information, check their website, www.nwa.com.

The airport is located about a 10-minute drive from downtown Charlottetown. Taxi service is available, with fares around $10 per passenger. Several car rental agencies have stands at the airport. For information on flights and services available at the Charlottetown Airport, check their website, www.flypei.com.

TRAVEL ESSENTIALS

MONEY

American currency can be exchanged at any Prince Edward Island bank or credit union at the going rate. Units of currency are similar to those of the United States, except for the Canadian two-dollar coin ("the Toonie"), and one-dollar coin ("the Loonie").

Travellers' cheques and major credit cards are accepted throughout Prince Edward Island, although you may require cash in some rural areas. Cheques issued by Visa, American Express, and Thomas Cook are widely recognized.

American visitors may also use bank or credit cards to make cash withdrawals from automated teller machines that are tied into international networks such as Cirrus, Interac, and Plus. These can be found in the larger communities on the Island.

PASSPORTS

American citizens are required to carry proof of citizenship, such as a U.S. passport or a birth certificate, plus photo identification. Naturalized U.S. citizens should carry a naturalization certificate, plus photo identification. Permanent U.S. residents who are not citizens are advised to bring their Alien Registration Card (Green Card) or a valid 1551 stamp in their passport. Note that other documents such as a driver's licence or voter registration card will not be accepted as proof of U.S. citizenship. Visas are not required for U.S. tourists entering Canada from the U.S. for stays up to 180 days.

Citizens of most other countries must bring a valid passport. Some may be required to obtain a visitor's visa. For details, please consult the Canadian embassy or consulate serving your home country.

CUSTOMS
Arriving

Visitors to Canada may bring certain duty-free items into the country as part of their personal baggage. These must be declared to Customs upon arrival in Nova Scotia or New Brunswick, and may include up to 200 cigarettes, 50 cigars, and 200 grams of tobacco. Visitors are also permitted 1.14 litres of liquor, 1.5 litres of wine, or 8.5 litres (24 341 ml cans or bottles) of beer.

Gift items — excluding tobacco and alcohol products — for Canadian residents that do not exceed $40 are also duty-free. Packages should be marked "gift" and the value indicated.

Boats, trailers, sporting equipment, cameras, and similar big-ticket items may enter Canada free of duty. However, Canada Customs may require a refundable deposit to ensure that these goods are not sold for profit. It might be better to register such items with customs officials in your own country, so that when you re-enter you have evidence that they were not bought in Canada.

Some items are strictly controlled in Canada. Firearms are prohibited, with the exception of rifles and shotguns for hunting purposes. Plant material will be examined at the border. Veterinary certificates are required for all pets.

For further information on Canadian Customs regulations call 1-800-668-4748 (inside Canada), 1-902-432-5608 (outside Canada) or visit the web site at www.ccra-adrc.gc.ca/visitors.

Departing

Visitors from the U.S. who have been out of the country for a minimum of 48 hours may take back goods to the value of U.S. $400 without paying duty (provided no part of the exemption has been used within the previous 30 days). Family members may pool their exemptions.

There are restrictions on alcohol and tobacco products, among others. Visitors may bring back one litre of alcohol free of duty and up to 200 cigarettes and 100 non-Cuban cigars.

To find out more about U.S. Customs regulations and what other restrictions and exemptions apply, contact your local Customs office or the U.S. Customs Service, Box 7407, Washington, DC, 20044; (202) 927-2095. Ask for a copy of "Know Before You Go."

Travellers from countries other than the U.S.should check on customs regulations before leaving home.

TAXES
Provincial Sales Tax (PST)

Prince Edward Island has a 10% sales tax on purchased goods and some services. Short-term accommodations and restaurant meals are subject to this tax. Articles of clothing and shoes are exempt, as are most basic grocery items. The PST is applied on top of the GST.

Goods and Services Tax (GST)
There is an additional 7% federal tax on almost all goods and services sold in Canada (basic grocery goods are excepted). Non-residents can get a GST rebate on goods purchased for use outside the country provided the goods are removed from Canada within 60 days of purchase. GST rebates are also available on short-term accommodation (less than 30 days). A rebate cannot be claimed for GST paid on restaurant meals, alcohol, car rentals, gas, and other services. Each receipt for goods must bear a minimum of $50 in eligible purchases, prior to taxes. In order to make your claim, you must have a minimum of $200 in eligible purchases. Rebate forms are available at the PEI Visitor Information Centres, or from the Visitor Rebate Program, Tax Centre, Summerside, PEI, C1N 6C6. Take your completed form, together with original receipts, to participating duty-free shops, or mail it to the Visitor Rebate Program. Claims may be submitted up to one year from the date of purchase, and up to four times a year. For more information, call 1-800-668-4748.

GUIDES
The Prince Edward Island Visitors Guide contains excellent accommodation, restaurant and attractions listings. To obtain a copy, write to Visitor Services, P.O. Box 940, Charlottetown, PEI, Canada, C1A 7M5, or, in North America, call toll-free 1-888-734-7529; outside North America, call (902) 368-4444 or fax (902) 368-4438. The Guide is also accessible on the Internet at www.peiplay.com and available at Visitor Information Centres throughout Prince Edward Island. To book accommodations, an online reservation system offers real-time vacancy information. The website is www.peiplay.com/bookonline. For further information, e-mail Tourism PEI at peiplay@gov.pe.ca.

GETTING ACQUAINTED

TIME ZONE
Prince Edward Island falls within the Atlantic Time Zone, which is one hour later than the Eastern TimeZone. Daylight Saving Time, when the clocks are advanced one hour, is in effect from early April until late October.

CLIMATE
Summers on Prince Edward Island are hot, but rarely humid. The average daytime temperature is 22°C (72°F). You'll be comfortable in a T-shirt during the day, with a light sweater or jacket for evening. Bring your bathing suit: the water here is as warm as any north of the Carolinas, thanks to our sheltered location in the Gulf of St. Lawrence. The fall is an especially beautiful time on Prince Edward Island, with warm clear days and gorgeous fall colours. We have lots of snow in the wintertime, which makes for great downhill and cross-country skiing, snowmobiling, and snowshoeing. Daytime high temperatures in winter are usually in the range of -8° to 2°C (18-36°F).

Average daily maximum temperatures for Charlottetown are:

Jan.	-3.4°C	25.9°F
Feb.	-3.6°C	25.5°F
Mar.	0.6°C	33.1°F
Apr.	6.3°C	43.3°F
May	13.8°C	56.8°F
June	19.6°C	66.9°F
July	23.1°C	73.6°F
Aug.	22.5°C	72.5°F
Sept.	17.8°C	64.0°F
Oct.	12.1°C	53.8°F
Nov.	5.9°C	42.6°F
Dec.	-0.3°C	31.5°F

METRIC SYSTEM
Prince Edward Island, like the rest of Canada, uses the metric system of weights and measures. Some useful conversions are:

1 kilometre = 0.62 miles
100 kph = 62 mph
4 litres = 1 U.S. gallon
1 metre = 3.28 feet
1 centimetre = 0.39 inches
1 kilogram = 2.2 pounds
20° Celsius = 68° Fahrenheit
To convert degrees Celsius to

Fahrenheit, multiply by 2 and add 30 (accurate within 2 degrees).

STAYING HEALTHY

If you are not a Canadian citizen, you should obtain or extend health insurance coverage before leaving home. Only prescriptions written by Prince Edward Island doctors can be filled here, so bring an adequate supply of medication. Hospitals are located in Alberton, O'Leary, Tyne Valley, Summerside, Charlottetown, Montague, and Souris. Clinics can be found in Tignish, O'Leary, Tyne Valley, Summerside, Bedeque, Kensington, Cornwall, Charlottetown, Montague and Souris.

For all emergency services, dial 911.

GETTING AROUND
BY BUS

Scheduled public transportation on PEI is limited: visitors headed off the beaten path must make their own arrangements. SMT offers daily service connecting Charlottetown and Borden-Carleton via Kensington and Summerside. From Charlottetown to Summerside costs about $11. The bus leaves Charlottetown daily at 7:45 am and 1:50 pm and Borden-Carleton at 11:15 am and 3:10 pm. On Friday, Saturday and Sunday, a second bus leaves Charlottetown at 5:15 pm, arriving at Borden-Carleton at 6:30 pm. In the peak season, another run later in the day is usually added. Schedules are subject to change, so call 1-800-567-5151 for current information, or check their website, www.smtbus.com.

A transit bus operates in Charlottetown. For information, call (902) 566-5664.

Shuttle Service
East Connection offers year-round passenger shuttle service from Charlottetown to Morell, St. Peters, Souris, Montague and Wood Islands. Island-wide tours are also available through this service. For information, call (902) 892-6760.

A beach shuttle service (902-566-3243) runs between Charlottetown and Cavendish Beach in the summer.

Several companies offer guided sightseeing tours by bus. Abegweit Tours and Travel (902-894-9966) offers six daily one-hour tours of Charlottetown, as well as tours of the north and south shores in a double-decker bus. Trius Tours (902-566-5664), Prince Edward Tours (1-877-286-6532), and Capture the Spirit of Prince Edward Island (1-866-836-4200) are among the companies that will arrange tours for groups and individuals.

BY CAR

The Prince Edward Island Visitors' Map is available at Visitor Information Centres throughout the province. Highways are generally well maintained. Gasoline prices range between 81 and 86 cents per litre (about $3.35 per U.S. gallon). Speed limits are as follows: 90 kilometres per hour along the main highways, 80 kph along secondary roads, and 50 kph in cities and towns. On Prince Edward Island, seat belt use is compulsory for driver and passengers.

A valid United States driver's license is also valid in Prince Edward Island. Evidence of the car's registration is required (a car rental contract will serve). U.S. motorists may obtain a Non-Resident Inter-Province Motor Vehicle Liability Insurance Card through their own insurance companies as evidence of financial responsibility within Canada.

Car Rentals
All major car rental agencies are represented in Prince Edward Island.
Avis
In the U.S. 1-800-331-2112
In Canada 1-800-879-2847
Budget
In the U.S. 1-800-527-0700
In Canada 1-800-268-8900
Hertz
Worldwide 1-800-263-0600
National (affiliated with National Interrent in the U.S.)
Worldwide 1-800-227-7368

Consult the Yellow Pages of the Prince Edward Island telephone directory under Automobile Renting for local numbers and agencies.

LODGING

For a complete list of accommodations in the province, consult the Prince Edward Island Visitors Guide. For visitors who are interested in B&B-style accommodation, a pamphlet called "PEI Bed and Breakfasts and Country Inns" is a good source of information. Write to P.O. Box 2551, Charlottetown, PEI, C1A 8C2.

There are three hostels in Prince Edward Island, at the following locations:

- The Midgell Centre, Morell Post Office, C0A 1S0; 961-2963. Hostel with a non-denominational Christian environment located in Midgell on Rte. 2, three km west of St. Peters. Open July–Sept. Daily $20.
- Hostel East @ A Place to Stay Inn, Box 607, 9 Longworth St., Souris, C0A 2B0; 1-800-655-STAY, or 687-4626. 14-bed dormitory. Open March 1–Jan. 31. Daily $22.
- Simple Comforts B&B and Bicycle Hostel, Box 5, Victoria, C0A 2G0; 658-2951. Open year round. Daily $20.

The following list of accommodations includes those already mentioned in this book and other selected locations. Immediately following the name of each establishment is an abbreviation indicating whether it is an inn (I), hotel/motel (H/M), resort (R), cottage (C), or hospitality home (HH). For detailed information on these categories, see the Visitors Guide.

Approximate prices are indicated, based on the average cost at time of publication, for two persons staying in a double room (excluding taxes): $ = under $100; $$ = $100–150; $$$ = more than $150.

The area code for all phone numbers is 902.

North Cape

- The Doctor's Inn (HH), Tyne Valley, C0B 2C0; 831-3057; www.peisland.com/doctorsinn. Rte. 167, 30 km west of Summerside. Beautiful gardens, organic vegetables. Breakfast included; dinner by reservation. Open year round. $
- Hotel Village sur l'Océan (I), Mont-Carmel, C0B 2E0; 854-2227; 1-800-567-3228; www.hotelvillage.ca. Rte. 11, 24 km west of Summerside. Country inn with exceptional architecture blends early 20th century with modern decor. Sheltered, wooded area. Restaurant specializing in Acadian cuisine. Dinner-theatre with English and French productions. Lounge, live entertainment weekly, art exhibit, craft shop, beach, tennis courts, bicycle rentals and tours. Bilingual. Open mid-June to Sept. $/$$
- Lakeview Loyalist Resort (H/M), 195 Harbour Drive, Summerside, C1N 5R1; 436-3333; 1-877-355-3500; www.lakeviewhotels.com. Traditional inn offering all the amenities of a luxury urban hotel overlooking the waterfront. Licensed dining room and lounge, conference facilities. Two rooms for physically challenged, craft shop, indoor pool, sauna, tennis courts, bike rental, outside patio. Open year round. $$/$$$
- Linkletter Inn and Convention Centre (H/M), 311 Market St., Summerside, C1N 1K8; 436-2157; 1-800-565-7829; www.virtuo.com/Linkletter. Convention facilities, family restaurant, licensed lounge. Indoor pool, outdoor patio. Small pets allowed. Inn has elevator, amenities for physically challenged. Open year round. $/$$
- Northport Pier Inn (I), P.O. Box 685, Alberton, C0B 1B0; 853-4520; 1-866-887-4520; www.northportpier.ca. Luxury oceanfront inn located directly on the beach. Two rooms available with wheelchair-accessible showers. On-premise restaurant, shops, marina, day adventure centre and Sea Rescue Interpretive Centre. Open May–Oct. $$/$$$
- Quality Inn — Garden of the Gulf (H/M), 618 Water St. E., Summerside, C1N 2V5; 436-2295; 1-800-265-5551; www.qualityinnpei.com. Rte. 11 off Rte. 1A. Waterfront property, close to downtown Summerside. Indoor and outdoor pools, free 9-hole golf, shuffleboard, bicycling, gift shop, coffee shop, Brothers Two Restaurant and Dinner Theatre.

Open year round. $$/$$$
- Rodd Mill River Resort (R), Woodstock, O'Leary, C0B 1V0; 859-3555; 1-800-565-7633; www.rodd-hotels.ca. Rte. 2, 57 km west of Summerside. Three-floor hotel resort. Lounge, conference facilities, licensed dining room. Gift shop, indoor swimming pool, sauna, whirlpool, water slide, two squash courts, Nautilus exercise room, 18-hole championship golf course, pro shop, tennis courts, canoeing, windsurfing, bicycling. Open Jan.–Oct. $$/$$$
- Silver Fox Inn (HH), 61 Granville St., Summerside, C1N 2Z3; 436-1664; 1-800-565-4033; www.silverfoxinn.net. Historic house built in 1892. Antiques, claw-foot tubs, antique shop. Tree-top balcony, water gardens, afternoon tea. Buffet breakfast included. Open year round. $$
- Tignish Heritage Inn (HH), Tignish, C0B 2B0; 882-2491; 1-877-882-2491; www.tignish.com/inn. Elegantly restored convent. Guests welcome to use kitchen, dining area, laundry room. Continental breakfast included. Children under 6 free. Open mid-May to mid-Oct. $/$$
- West Point Lighthouse Inn, Restaurant & Museum (I), 859-3605; 1-800-764-6854; www.westpointlighthouse.com. Rte. 14. Canada's first inn in a functioning lighthouse. Enjoy the sea at your doorstep, supervised swimming, nature trails, clam digging, fishing, biking. Museum, licensed dining room, patio, two rooms with whirlpool tub. Open late May to early Oct. $/$$

ANNE'S LAND

- Barachois Inn (HH), Hunter River RR3, C0A 1N0; 963-2194. Rustico; www.barachoisinn.com. Church Road, Rte. 243. Six km from PEI National Park; 17 km from Charlottetown. Heritage Victorian house, built 1870, works of art, whirlpools, Victorian tubs, four suites with kitchenettes and fireplaces. Meeting rooms, sauna, exercise room. View of Rustico Bay. No pets or smoking please. Bilingual. Full breakfast included.

Open year round. $$$
- Dalvay-by-the-Sea Inn (I; C), Little York, C0A 1P0; 672-2048; www.dalvaybythesea.com. Rte. 6 in PEI National Park. Victorian inn (1895). Magnificent endless beach. National Historic Site. Fine dining, breakfast and dinner included. Tennis court, bike rentals, croquet, lawn bowling, golf practice range, lake, canoes, 2-hole fairway, children's recreational area, nature trails. $$$
- My Mother's Country Inn (HH; C), Box 172, Hunter River, C0A 1N0; 964-2508; 1-800-278-2071; www.mymotherscountryinn.com. Restored heritage home (c. 1860) on Rte 13 in the picturesque village of New Glasgow. Rooms with whirlpool tubs, breakfast. Housekeeping cottages and deluxe executive cottage. Open June 1– Sept. 30. $/$$/$$$
* Shaw's Hotel and Cottages (I; C), Brackley Beach, C1E 1Z3; 672-2022; www.shawshotel.ca. Rte. 15. Oldest family-operated inn and resort in Canada. Located on a 75-acre peninsula overlooking Brackley Bay. Antique-furnished guest rooms, cottages, luxury chalets. Walking distance to Brackley Beach in the Prince Edward Island National Park. Many recreational activities. Meals included. Open May–Oct. Chalets open year round. $$$
- Shining Waters Country Inn and Cottages (HH; C), Cavendish, C0A 1N0; 963-2251; 1-877-963-2251; www.shiningwatersresort.com. Historic inn overlooking ocean. Luxury suites and cottages with air conditioning, fireplaces and whirlpool tubs. Playgrounds, two heated pools and exercise room. On-site restaurant and conference centre. No pets, please. Open May–Oct. $/$$/$$$
- Stanhope by the Sea Resort & Inn (R), Covehead, C0A 1P0; 672-2047; 1-877-672-2047; www.stanhopebythesea.com. Rte. 25 (Bay Shore Road) overlooking Covehead Bay and Prince Edward Island National Park. Country inn since 1817. Smoke-free rooms in original historic inn, new inn, motel units, cottages. Designated smoking

rooms. Fine dining. Bilingual. Tennis, croquet, volleyball, horseshoes, playground, heated pool. Laundromat. Open June 1–Oct. 15. $/$$/$$$

• Stanley Bridge Country Resort (H/M; I; C), Kensington, C0B 1M0 886-2882; 1-800-361-2882; www.stanleybridgeresort.com. Rte. 6, Stanley Bridge. Country inn, housekeeping cottages. Convention facilities, heated pool, exercise room, playground, dinner theatre, Stanley Bridge Studios on-site. No pets, please. Open May–Oct. $/$$/$$$

CHARLOTTE'S SHORE

• Briarcliffe Inn (HH), Salutation Cove Rd., Fernwood, C0B 1C0; 887-2333; 1-866-887-3238; www.briarcliffeinn.com. Restored 1914 farmhouse. Antique-filled rooms, gourmet breakfast. Open year round. $/$$

• The Delta Prince Edward (H/M), 18 Queen St., Charlottetown, C1A 8B9; 566-2222; 1-866-894-1203; www.deltaprinceedward.pe.ca. Located at the foot of Queen St., Harbourside, Olde Charlottetown. Shopping, offices, attractions, and theatre nearby. Saunas, jacuzzis, golf simulator, indoor pool, spa, restaurants, lounge, indoor mall. Food and beverages billable to your room at Fox Meadow Golf and Country Club. Ballroom plus meeting rooms. Open year round. $$$

• Duchess of Kent Inn (HH), 218 Kent St., Charlottetown, C1A 1P2; 566-5826; 1-800-665-5826; www.duchessofkentinn.ca. Heritage home (1875) with antiques, downtown. No pets or smoking. Separate fully equipped kitchen, living room. "Turret" suites available. Breakfast extra. Open year round. $/$$

• The Dundee Arms (I; H/M), 200 Pownal St., Charlottetown, C1A 3W8; 892-2496; 1-877-638-6333; www.dundeearms.com. Picturesque inn located in heart of Charlottetown. Furnished in period decor and antiques. Dining room and lounge. Open year round. $$/$$$

• Edenhurst Inn (HH), 12 West St.,

Charlottetown, C1A 3S4; 368-8323; www.peisland.com/edenhurst/inn.htm. Built in 1897, Edenhurst is a designated heritage property located in historic downtown Charlottetown. Rooms decorated with period antiques, some with fireplace and jacuzzi. Air conditioning and off-street parking. Open May 1–Oct. 30. $$/$$$

• Elmwood Heritage Inn (HH), 121 North River Rd., Charlottetown, C1A 3K7; 368-3310; 1-877-933-3310; www.elmwoodinn.pe.ca. W.C. Harris–designed house (1889) antiques, quilts, artwork, fireplaces, whirlpool, and Victorian tubs. Bicycles. Wireless high-speed internet. Private, personal, friendly service. Includes breakfast. $$/$$$

• Fitzroy Hall (HH), 45 Fitzroy St., Charlottetown, C1A 1R4; 368-2077; www.peisland.com/fitzroyhall. Stately Victorian mansion built in 1872. Recently restored, antique furnishings. Relax by the fireplace or in the garden. No smoking or pets. Open year round. Full breakfast included. $$/$$$

• The Great George (I), 58 Great George St., Charlottetown, C1A 4K3; 892-0606; 1-800-361-1118; www.innsongreatgeorge.com. Completely restored buildings. Suites, flats, stylishly appointed with antiques, fireplaces; Jacuzzi and claw-foot tubs available. Breakfast included. Open year round. $$$

• Hillhurst Inn (HH), 181 Fitzroy St., Charlottetown, C1A 1S3; 894-8004; 1-877-994-8004; www.hillhurstinn.com. Heritage home (1897) two blocks from city centre. Elegant setting, period furnishings, Island art. Two whirlpools. Wireless high-speed internet. Breakfast included. No smoking. Open year round. $$/$$$

• Orient Hotel (HH), Box 55, Main St., Victoria-by-the-Sea, C0A 2G0; 658-2503; 1-800-565-ORIENT (6743); www.theorienthotel.com. Heritage inn (circa 1900). Located in a picturesque seaside village with views of countryside and shore. Smoke-free. Open May 15–Oct. 15. $/$$

• Rodd Charlottetown (H/M), Box

159, Charlottetown, C1A 7K4; 894-7371; 1-800-565-7633; www.rodd-hotels.ca. Kids eat free in July and August, seniors' discounts. Indoor pool, waterslide, whirlpool, sauna, licensed dining room, pub and eatery. Golf and theatre vacation packages available. Open year round. $$/$$$

- The Shipwright Inn (HH), 51 Fitzroy St., Charlottetown, C1A 1R4; 368-1905; 1-888-306-9966; www.shipwrightinn.com. Elegant 1860s heritage home, lovingly restored in nautical theme, fireplaces, antiques, books, art. Secluded garden, balconies, whirlpool. Business centre with computer, fax, wireless LAN. Memorable breakfast and afternoon tea. No smoking. Open year round. $$/$$$

- Victoria Village Inn & Restaurant (B&B), Victoria-by-the-Sea, C0A 2G0; 658-2483; www3.pei.sympatico.ca/victoriavill ageinn. Victorian sea captain's home next to Victoria Playhouse. Classically-trained chef/owner serves innovative cuisine. No smoking. Full breakfast included. Open year round. $

BAYS AND DUNES

- Cardigan River Inn (HH), Cardigan, C0A 1G0; 583-2331; 1-800-425-9577;www.cardiganriver inn.com. Classic Tudor mansion on 26 acres overlooking Cardigan River. Period antiques, fireplaces, whirlpool baths. Elegant fireside breakfast. Open mid-June to Oct. $$/$$$

* The Inn at Bay Fortune (I; C), Souris RR4, C0A 2B0; 687-3745; (860) 563-6090; www.innatbayfortune.com. On Rte. 310, overlooking Fortune Harbour. Restaurant featuring contemporary creative cuisine using seasonal produce. Dinner only. 18 rooms, 14 with fireplace. Relaxed, casual atmosphere. Two guest homes located off premises. Full breakfast included. Open late May to mid-Oct. $$$

- Inn at Spry Point (I), Souris, C0A 2B0; 583-2400; (860) 563-6090; www.innatsprypoint.com. Off Rte. 310. Striking inn at the tip of a 110-acre peninsula. Walking trails, secluded beach, meeting facilities, dining. Near three world-class golf courses. Full breakfast included. Open mid-June to Oct. $$$

- The Inn at St. Peters (I), Greenwich Road, St. Peters Bay, C0A 2C0; 961-2135; 1-800-818-0925; www.innatstpeters.com. Luxury inn on waterfront, minutes from golf, PEI National Park at Greenwich. Antique furnishings, fireplaces, waterfront dining, award-winning chef. Full breakfast and gourmet dinner included. Pets welcome. Open late May to Oct. $$$

- The Johnson Shore Inn (HH), Hermanville, Souris RR2, C0A 2B0; 687-1340; 1-877-510-9669. Country inn located on a high, rocky red cliff with spectacular ocean views. Full breakfast included. Open May 1–Oct 31. $$/$$$ $120–300

- The Matthew House Inn (HH), Box 151, Souris, C0A 2B0; 687-3461; www.matthewhouseinn.com. Award-winning heritage inn, near Magdalen Islands ferry. Renowned for hospitality, ambience. Close to beaches, golf, fishing. No smoking. Multilingual. Elegant fireside breakfast included. Real Italian organic dinner packages. Open late June to early Sept. $$/$$$

- Rodd Crowbush Golf & Beach Resort (R), Lakeside, C0A 1S0; 961-5600; 1-800-565-7633; www.rodd-hotels.ca. Golf and ocean vistas, access to white sand beach. Indoor and outdoor pools, whirlpool, tennis. Restaurant, lounge and conference facilities. Internationally-acclaimed championship golf course, The Links at Crowbush Cove on site. Pets welcome. Children under 16 free with parents or guardians. Open mid-May to mid-Oct. $$$

- Rollo Bay Inn (I), Rollo Bay, Souris RR1, C0A 2B0; 687-3550; 1-877-687-3550. Elegant Georgian-style inn in peaceful country setting. Conference facilities. Walking distance to beach. No pets please. French spoken. No charge for children under 12 occupying same room as parents. Open year round. $

HILLS AND HARBOURS

- Bayberry Cliff Inn (HH), Little Sands, Murray River P.O., C0A 1W0; 962-3395; 1-800-668-3395; www.bayberrycliffinn.com. Secluded post-and-beam, cliffside lodge with panoramic view of seals, dolphins and sunsets from your own private deck. Full breakfast included. No smoking. Pets permitted. Open June 1–Sept. 30. $$

- Lobster Shanty — Atlantic Resorts, Restaurant & Lounge (H/M), 102 Main St. South, Montague, C0A 1R0; 838-2463; 1-800-418-9430 (off-Island only); www.auracom.com/~lobshant. Scenic river view, rustic atmosphere. Licensed lounge and dining room. Golf, swimming, seal-watching cruises nearby. Playground, laundromat. Access to nearby fitness centre and pool. Breakfast included. Open year round. $/$$

- Maplehurst Properties (HH; C), Panmure Island, Box 1447, Montague, C0A 1R0; 838-3959; (954) 752-2548; www.maplehurstproperties.com. Secluded 25-acre beachfront estate. Decorated with artwork and period antiques. Full gourmet breakfasts. Beachfront cottage located on site. Open late May to late Oct. $$/$$$

- Rodd Brudenell River (R; C), Roseneath, Box 67, Cardigan, C0A 1G0; 652-2332; 1-800-565-7633; www.rodd-hotels.ca. Kids program. Hotel, riverside chalets, conference facilities, licensed dining room, Two 18-hole championship golf courses, golf academy, pro shop, tennis, canoeing, windsurfing, trail riding, lawn bowling, indoor and outdoor pool, sauna and fitness centre. Family, golf, romance packages available. Restrained pets allowed. Children under 16 free. Open mid-May to mid-Oct. $$/$$$

- Roseneath Bed & Breakfast (HH), Cardigan, C0A 1G0; 838-4590; 1-800-823-9833; www.rosebb.ca. Adjacent to Brudenell Golf Course, half-hour from Charlottetown. Peaceful country retreat, historic 1868 home with antiques, artwork, gardens, walking trails. Smoke-free, no pets. Full breakfast. Open May 1–Oct. 31. $/$$

DINING

When it comes to food, there's more to Prince Edward Island than just potatoes. Taking advantage of the freshest produce grown in this "Garden of the Gulf," as well as the bounty of the sea, restaurant owners cook up a wide variety of meals to suit the most discriminating diner. We're home to the Culinary Institute of Canada: what more could one expect?

Island cuisine benefits, too, from a variety of cultural influences, including Scottish, Dutch, Lebanese, Acadian, Indian, and German. Check out our many restaurants and cafés. And drop by the Charlottetown Farmers' Market on Saturdays from 9 to 2, and taste for yourself!

NORTH CAPE

- Brothers Two, Water St. East, Summerside, 436-9654; www.brotherstwo.ca. Seafood, steak, fresh lobster suppers, succulent mussels, chicken and skillets. Fresh desserts, handcrafted microbrew beer and kids' menu. Fully licensed. Open year round.

- Le Cajun Jacques Restaurant, at Hotel Village sur l'Ocean, Mont-Carmel, on Rte. 11; 854-2227; 1-800-567-3228; www.hotelvillage.ca. Cajun/Acadian food, seafood, lobster suppers. Bilingual service. Open mid-June to Sept.

- Centre Expo—Festival Centre, Rte. 14, Abram-Village; 854-3300. Lobster suppers Acadian-style. Open July and Aug., Sun., 4–8 pm.

- The Doctor's Inn, Tyne Valley, on Rte. 167, 831-3057. International cuisine using fresh organic produce from their own garden. Recommended in *Where to Eat in Canada*. Evening dining by reservation only. Open year round.

- Hernewood Dining Room, Rodd Mill River Resort, Woodstock, Rte. 136; 859-3555. Licensed dining room. Full a la carte menu, specializing in fresh Island cuisine. Open seasonally.

- The Pier Restaurant, Rte. 152,

Northport Pier Inn, Northport; 853-4510; www.northportpier.ca. Located in an original boathouse on the waterfront. Fresh seafood and locally inspired cuisine. Outdoor patio. Licensed. Open June 1 to late Sept.

- Prince William Dining Room, Lakeview Loyalist Resort, 195 Harbour Dr., Summerside; 436-3333; www.lakeviewhotels.com. Seafood, steaks, Island delicacies. Licensed. Open year round.
- West Point Lighthouse Inn, Restaurant & Museum, West Point, off Rte. 14; 859-3605; 1-800-764-6854; www.westpointlighthouse.com. Serving chowders, seafood and full menu. Vegetarian, children's and senior's dishes available. Open end of May to Oct.
- Wind and Reef Restaurant, North Cape, 882-3535. Where the two tides meet. Serving fresh Island clams, mussels, lobsters; steaks and prime beef. Reservations recommended. Open mid-May to mid-Oct.

ANNE'S LAND

- Blue Mussel Café, North Rustico; 963-2152. Fresh mussels and seafood located oceanside at North Rustico Harbour. Seasonal.
- Chez-Yvonne, Cavendish, on Rte. 6; 963-2070; www.chezyvonne.com. Family dining room and take-out specializing in fresh seafood and steaks. Bakery, gift shop. Licensed. Open late May to early Oct.
- * Dalvay-by-the-Sea, Grand Tracadie, on Rte. 6; 672-2048; www.dalvaybythesea.com. Executive chef creates innovative cuisine with local ingredients. Extensive wine list, panoramic views. Afternoon High Tea served July and Aug. Reservations recommended. Open June 15–Sept. 30.
- * The Dunes Café and Studio Gallery, Brackley Beach, Rte. 15; 672-1883; www.dunesgallery.com. Inspired cuisine featuring local produce, seafood, sumptuous desserts, beautifully presented on the Dunes' handmade pottery. Vistas of flowering water gardens and ocean dunes. Open June 15–Sept. 30.
- Fisherman's Wharf, North Rustico,

on Rte. 6; 963-2669; 1-877-289-1010. Fresh seafood, lobster, steaks, ham, scallops and 60-ft. salad bar. Open mid-May to mid-Oct.

- Fyfe's Landing, Stanley Bridge Country Resort; 886-2882; www.stanleybridgeresort.com. Breathtaking views of New London Bay and Cavendish Dunes. Quality seafood, weekend buffets, lobster dinners and dinner-theatre. Children's menu. Open June–Sept.
- Millstream Family Restaurant, Brackley Beach, Rte. 15; 672-2644. Home-cooked, large-portion meals. Seafood pizza. Open seasonally.
- New Glasgow Lobster Suppers, New Glasgow; 964-2870; www.peilobstersuppers.com. Lobster, fresh from the pound, chowder, mussels, salads and dessert. Children's menu. Open late May to early Oct.
- Prince Edward Island Preserve Co. Restaurant, New Glasgow; 964-4300. Famous fresh salads, sandwiches, fish cakes and homemade fruit pies. Casual dining with a great water view. Open late May to early Oct.
- Rachael's Restaurant, Cavendish Corner; 963-3227. Three separate dining areas including ocean-view deck. Italian specialties and traditional favourites. Open June–Oct.
- St. Ann's Church Lobster Suppers, Hope River, off Rte; 224, 621-0635; www.lobstersuppers.com. Non-profit organization offering home cooking and professional service. Luncheon specials. Licensed. Open mid-June to late Sept.
- * Shaw's Hotel and Cottages, Brackley Beach; 672-2022; www.shawshotel.ca. Fresh local ingredients in season, including several seafood dishes. Sunday buffet evenings during July and Aug. Open late May to Oct. 1.
- Shining Waters Tea Room, Anne of Green Gables Museum at Silver Bush, Park Corner; 1-800-665-2663 (Mon.–Fri.); 886-2884 (Sat. & Sun.); www.annesociety.org/anne. Raspberry cordial, flavoured teas, and homemade treats. Open May to late Oct.

CHARLOTTE'S SHORE

- Cedar's Eatery, 81 University Ave., Charlottetown; 892-7377. Canadian and Lebanese food served in a nostalgic setting. Recommended in *Where to Eat in Canada*. Open year round.
- Claddagh Room, 131 Sydney St., Charlottetown; 892-9661; www.oldedublinpub.com. Seafood specialty house with Irish atmosphere. Irish pub with entertainment upstairs. Open year round.
- Gahan House, 126 Sydney St., Charlottetown; 626-2337; www.peimenu.com. Pub and brewery. Brewery tours, Charlottetown's Brown Bag Fish and Chips. Open year round.
- Griffon Dining Room, Dundee Arms Inn, 200 Pownal St., Charlottetown; 892-2496; 1-877-638-6333; www.dundeearms.com. Local favourite for its great food and historic atmosphere. Reservations recommended. Open year round.
- Landmark Café, across from Victoria Playhouse, Victoria; 658-2286; www.peisland.com/landmark/index.html. Licensed, air conditioned, full menu. Open June–Sept.
- Mavor's Bistro and Bar, Confederation Centre of the Arts, 145 Richmond St., Charlottetown; 628-6107; www.confederationcentre.com. Light modern cuisine in a chic atmosphere. Open-air garden and pre-theatre dining. Open year round.
- The Merchantman Pub, corner of Queen and Water Sts., Charlottetown; 892-9150; www.merchantmanpub.com. Full menu served 11:30 am–10 pm. Located in historic property. Thai and Cajun fare, fresh seafood, imported and local draught beer on tap. Open year round 11:30 am–midnight.
- * Off Broadway Café, 125 Sydney St., Charlottetown; 566-4620; www.peimenu.com. Intimate surroundings in cozy rooms and attentive service. Specializing in crépes, steaks, and luscious desserts. Open year round.
- The Pilot House, 70 Grafton St., Charlottetown; 894-4800; www.thepilothouse.ca. Fresh seafood, prime rib and steaks, and fine wines in a beautiful heritage building. Pub with local and imported draughts. Open year round.
- The Selkirk Room, Delta Prince Edward Hotel, 18 Queen St., Charlottetown; 894-1208. Fine dining room with innovative menu, elegant atmosphere, and continental service. Open year round.
- Sirenella Ristorante, 83 Water St., Charlottetown; 628-2271; www.sirenella.ca. Northern Italian cuisine, grilled seafood, veal, and homemade pasta. Outdoor patio. Open year round.
- Victoria Village Inn, off Rte. 1, Victoria; 658-2483; www3.pei.sympatico.ca/victoriavillageinn. Classically trained chef/owner serves innovative cuisine. Open year round.

BAYS AND DUNES

- Cardigan Lobster Suppers, Cardigan; 583-2020; www.peisland.com/sailpei. Licensed waterfront dining at reasonable prices. Five-course lobster supper and full family menu. Open early June to Oct.
- * The Inn at Bay Fortune, Bay Fortune, on Rte. 310; 687-3745; www.innatbayfortune.com. Recommended by *Where to Eat in Canada*. Contemporary creative cuisine in a country inn setting. Dinner only. Open late May to mid-Oct.
- Inn at St. Peters, next to Greenwich, Prince Edward Island National Park, St. Peters; 961-2135; www.innatstpeters.com. Award-winning executive chef, produce from on-site garden. Reservations recommended for dinner. Open mid-May to Oct.
- Inn at Spry Point, off Rte. 310, Little Pond; 583-2400; www.innatsprypoint.com. The finest ingredients are harvested locally. Airy dining room and patio. Open May–Sept. for dinner only.
- Red Stone Restaurant, North Lake; 357-2222. Located on a sandy beach at a fishing harbour famous for giant Bluefin tuna. Specializing in fresh Island seafood. Open mid-June to

mid-Oct.
- Rick's Fish 'N' Chips and Seafood House, Rte. 2, St. Peters; 961-3438. Seafood specialties, pizza, freshly battered fish and fresh-cut fries. Vegetarian items. Open early May to Oct.
- St. Margarets Lobster Suppers, Rte. 16, St. Margarets; 687-3105. Licensed dining room serving lobster and ham dinners. Children's menu. Open mid-June to mid-Sept.
- Trailside Inn Café and Adventures, 109 Main St., Mount Stewart; 676-3130; 1-888-704-6595; www.trailside.ca. Delightful café on the Confederation Trail, featuring local entertainment most weekends, seafood chowders, pizza, home-baked bread, desserts. Open July–Aug., daily. Reduced hours in the off season.

HILLS AND HARBOURS
- Dynasty Restaurant, 6 Rink St., Montague; 838-4118. Chinese and Canadian food, take-out. Licensed. Open year round.
- Gillis' Drive-In, Rte. 4, Montague; 838-2031. Drive-in restaurant featuring fast food and take out. Seasonal.
- Lobster Shanty Motel & Restaurant, Rte. 17, Montague, 838-2463; 1-800-418-9430; www.auracom.com/~lobshant. Full menu dining, three-course lobster dinner. Open year round.
- Point Prim Chowder House, Point Prim; 659-2023. Chowders, seafood, and famous Irish moss dessert. Oceanfront location at Point Prim Lighthouse. Open June–Sept.
- The Rusty Pelican Café, 1 Station St., Montague; 838-2233. Seafood, chowder, desserts, ice cream. Overlooking Montague Marina. Open May 15–Oct. 15.
- Sir Andrew Macphail Homestead, Orwell, off Rte. 1; 651-2789; www.isn.net/~dhunter/macphailfoundation.html. Tea room and restaurant featuring heritage meals from the 1900s. Lunch, dinner and afternoon tea. Open mid-June to late Sept.
- Stillwaters Fine Foods & Spirits, Rodd Brudenell River Resort, Roseneath; 652-2332; www.rodd-

hotels.ca. Bistro-style restaurant overlooking the Brudenell River. Specializing in fresh Island ingredients from the land and sea. Dinner only, reservations recommended. Open June–Sept.
- The Whim Inn, junction of Rtes. 3 and 4, Pooles Corner; 838-3838; www.whiminn.com. Home-cooked meals. Lounge with pub food. Open year round.
- Windows on the Water Café, 106 Sackville St., Montague; 838-2080. Locally grown produce, casual country dining. Eat on the deck and enjoy a lovely view of Montague Harbour. Reservations recommended. Open May 1–Sept. 30.

ATTRACTIONS

Admission fees are subject to change.

NORTH CAPE
- Acadian Museum/Musée Acadien, Miscouche, on Rte. 2, west of Summerside; 432-2880; www.peimuseum.com. History of the Island Acadians from 1720 to present, visitor information, genealogy. Open year round. Admission charged May–Oct.
- Alberton Museum & Genealogy Centre, 457 Church St., Alberton; 853-4048. Artifact collection depicting activities carried out by PEI's early settlers. Historical photographs and genealogical information. Open June–Sept., daily 10 am–5 pm; Sun., 1–5 pm. Admission by donation.
- Bideford Parsonage Museum, on Rte. 66, Bideford; 831-3133. Community museum with displays depicting the shipbuilding era, the role of the parsons in the community and the residency of L.M. Montgomery as a school teacher. Open June–Sept., daily, 9:30 am–5:30 pm. Admission: $3 adults, $2 students, $10 family.
- The Bottle Houses/Maisons de Bouteilles, Cap-Egmont, on Rte. 11; 854-2987; www.bottlehouses .com. Fantasy-like buildings made out of over 30,000 coloured bottles. Open May 30–Sept. 30. Admission: adults $4.50, seniors and children $4, children 6–16 yrs. $2,

preschoolers free.

- College of Piping and Celtic Performing Arts of Canada, 619 Water St. E., Summerside; 436-5377; 1-877-BAGPIPE; www.collegeofpiping.com. Performances, demonstrations of bagpiping, Highland dancing, stepdancing, fiddling. Concert series and Celtic Gift Shop. Celtic Festival July and Aug; interpretive and interactive exhibit open year round.
- Ellerslie Shellfish Museum, Ellerslie; 831-2933. Aquariums featuring live native fish and shellfish, artifacts relating to species identification, the history of oyster cultivation, and the growth and culture of shellfish. Open June 30–Sept. 1. Admission charged.
- Eptek Art & Culture Centre, Waterfront Properties, 130 Harbour Dr., Summerside; 888-8373; www.peimuseum.com. Art gallery featuring Island artists and touring Canadian exhibitions. Open year round. Admission by donation.
- Green Park Shipbuilding Museum and Historic Yeo House, Port Hill, Rte. 12, west of Summerside; 831-7947; www.peimuseum.com. Restored house of shipbuilder James Yeo Jr., re-created shipyard. Gift shop. Open June–Sept. Admission charged.
- Historic Site at the Green, off Rte. 12 north of Tignish at Founder's Lane; 882-3398. Visit the landing site of the eight founding families of the area. An eco-tourism site with trails, a protected archeological area, observation deck and amphitheatre. Open June–Oct., daily.
- International Fox Museum and Hall of Fame Inc., 286 Fitzroy St., Summerside; 436-2400; www.isn.net/~foxpei. This museum tells the story of the fox industry on PEI. Open June–Sept. Admission by donation.
- Lennox Island Aboriginal Eco-tourism Centre; 831-5423; 1-866-837-5423; www.lennoxisland.com. "Malpeque Discoveries" program, guided tours of museum, community and Lennox Island Nature Trail. Traditional Mi'kmaq food, craft demos and ecotourism information.

Open late June to early Sept., Mon–Sat. 10 am–6 pm, Sun. noon–6 pm. Off-season by appointment.
- MacAusland's Woollen Mill, Bloomfield, on Rte. 2; 859-3508. Watch while wool is carded, spun and woven. Shop on premises. Open July–Aug., 9:30 am–6:30 pm, Sun. noon–6 pm; June–Sept., Mon.–Sat. 10 am–5 pm. Admission free.
- Mill River Fun Park, Woodstock, on Rte. 2; 859-3915. Family activities for all ages: children's pool with waterslides, swimming pool, mini-golf, bumper boats, play area, sea of balls, giant twister slide and the Aqua Rage. Open mid-June to Labour Day, daily, 11 am–7 pm, weather permitting.
- North Cape Nature and Technology in Perfect Harmony, North Cape; 882-2991/3535. Atlantic Wind Test site, Irish Moss harvesting by horse, low-tide walks along rock reef. Black Marsh Nature Trail, North Cape Interpretive Centre, and restaurant. Open mid-May–mid-Oct.
- Prince Edward Island Potato Museum, 1 Dewar Lane, Centennial Park, O'Leary; 859-2039; www.peipotatomuseum.com. Interpretive display of the potato's history to present day. Collection of farm equipment. Gift shop and resource room. Open May 15–Oct. 15, Mon.–Sat. 9 am–5 pm, Sun. 1–5 pm. Admission: $5 per person, $12 per family.
- Seaweed Pie Café & Irish Moss Interpretive Centre, Miminegash, on Rte. 14; 882-4313. Learn all there is to know about Irish Moss through displays and videos. Gift shop and Seaweed Pie Café. Open early June to late Sept., daily 10 am–7 pm. Admission: $2 adults, $1 seniors and children 12 & under, preschoolers free.
- Spinnakers' Landing, on the waterfront, Summerside; 436-6692; www.summersidewaterfront.com/ spinnakers. Boardwalk along the edge of the water, shopping, outdoor entertainment, Boat Shed display, Interpretive Centre, Visitor Information Centre in a lighthouse. Open daily early June–late Sept., daily. Free admission, free parking.
- Shipyard Market, 370 Water St.,

Summerside; 436-8439. Open-air building with shopping, events and entertainment, and historic boat building. Saturday Farmers' Market. Licensed café and boardwalk. Open May–Oct.

- Tignish Cultural Centre, Maple St., Tignish; 882-1999. Interpretive Centre/Museum with displays depicting the natural history of the area and the arrival of the Acadian and Irish settlers who founded the area. Visitor information and library. Open year round. May–Sept., 8 am–4 pm; Oct.–April, 8:30 am–5 pm.

- Union Corner School House Museum, Union Corner, on Rte. 11; 854-2992. Old Schoolhouse brought back to life with original pictures of teachers and students. Open mid–June to Labour Day, daily, 9 am–5 pm. Admission: adults $3, seniors $2.50, students $2.

- West Point Lighthouse Inn, Restaurant & Museum, West Point, on Rte. 14; 859-3605; 1-800-764-6854; www.westpoint lighthouse.com. Climb to the top of the Island's tallest functioning lighthouse. Museum. Open late May to early Oct.

- Wyatt Heritage Properties, downtown Summerside; 432-1327; www.wyattheritage.com. Features MacNaught History Centre and Archives, historical and genealogical resources at 75 Spring St.; the Wyatt Historic House, 1867 home and gardens of distinguished Islander Dr. Wanda Wyatt at 85 Spring St.; and LeFurgey Cultural Centre, 19th-century shipbuilder's mansion now an arts and culture centre, at 205 Prince St. Open year round.

ANNE'S LAND

- Avonlea — Village of Anne of Green Gables, Cavendish, Rte. 6, across from Rainbow Valley; 963-3050; www.avonlea.ca. The Belmont Schoolhouse where Lucy Maud Montgomery taught in 1896 and the restored 1872 Long River Church where she attended, surrounded by reproductions of buildings and gardens of the time. Barnyard animals, horse and wagon rides, games with Anne and Diana,

and entertainment. Open June–Sept., daily. Admission charged.

* Anne of Green Gables Museum at Silver Bush, Park Corner, on Rte. 20; 886-2884; 436-7329; www.annesociety.org/anne. L.M. Montgomery often visited the home of her uncle John Campbell and aunt Annie Campbell. She was married here in 1911. Open late May to late Oct., daily. Admission: adults $2.55, children $1.

- Brackley Beach Drive-In Theatre and Mini Golf, Rte. 15, Brackley Beach; 672-3333; www.drivein.ca. One of the most unusual drive-in theatres in Canada. Two first-run movies nightly. Full-service canteen. Seasonal.

- The Fantazmagoric Museum of the Strange and Unusual, Cavendish, Rte. 6, beside Sandspit; 963-3242; www.cavendishsavings.com. Strange and unusual facts presented in thought-provoking displays and dioramas. Open mid-June to mid-Sept., 10 am–10 pm. Admission: $5.95; children 6–12 and seniors $4.95; preschoolers $2; children under 2 free.

- The Farmers' Bank of Rustico Museum, Rte. 243, Rustico; 963-3168. A National Historic Site operated from 1864 to 1894 as the first people's bank. The Doucet House adjacent to the bank is a restored 1772 Acadian period log house. Open June–Sept., daily.

* Green Gables — Prince Edward Island National Park of Canada, Cavendish, on Rte. 6; 963-7874; www.pc.gc.ca. Built in the mid-1800s, this house inspired the novel *Anne of Green Gables*. Nature trails; farm demonstrations and interpretive programs by bilingual staff in July and Aug. Open May–Oct., daily. Admission charged.

- The Keir Memorial Museum, Rte. 20, Malpeque; 836-3054. Exhibits illustrating household, religious, farming and oyster-fishing activities. Open June 1–Labour Day, daily. Admission: $2 adults, $1 children under 12, $5 family.

- Kensington Train Station, Rte. 20, Kensington; 836-3031; 1-877-836-3031; www.kata.pe.ca. Historic train station housing the library and PEI Railway Heritage Museum.

Tourist information and local crafts available in Kensington Railyards and Welcome Centre adjacent to the Train Station. Open May–Oct. 31, 9 am–9 pm.

* Lucy Maud Montgomery's Birthplace, New London, at Rtes. 6 and 20; 886-2099; 436-7329. Interior is decorated with authentic Victorian period pieces. The writer's wedding dress and personal scrapbook are among the items on display. Open early May to mid-Oct., daily 9 am–5 pm; July–Aug., 9 am–6 pm. Admission: adults $2.50, children 6–12 $0.50.

• Lucy Maud Montgomery Heritage Museum, Rte. 20 at Park Corner; 886-2807/2752. Guided tours of Lucy Maud Montgomery's Montgomery family home. Original furnishings, autographed first editions and more. Open June–Sept., daily. $2.50 adults, children under 12 free.

* Prince Edward Island National Park of Canada, Cavendish to Dalvay, off Rte. 6; 672-6350; www.pc.gc.ca. The park preserves 40 km of the Island's north shore. Facilities for camping, swimming and other activities. Admission charged. Family passes and season passes available.

• Rainbow Valley, Cavendish, Rte. 6, 963-2221; www.rainbow valley.pe.ca. Atlantic Canada's largest privately owned amusement park. Boat rides, monorail, waterslides, games, live animals, etc. Canteen and picnic area. Open mid-June to early Sept., weather permitting. Admission: adults $15, seniors $14, children $12, preschoolers free.

• Ripley's Believe It Or Not! Museum, Cavendish, Rte. 6; 963-2242. Exciting collection of wonders and curiosities in over 200 exhibits in 12 galleries with 10 video screens. Open early June to late Sept., daily. June and Sept., 9:30 am–5:30 pm; July and Aug., 9 am–10 pm. Ticket sales close one hour prior to closing time.

• Rustico Harbour Fishery Museum and Gift Shop, Harbourview Dr., North Rustico; 963-3799. Learn about the history of the fishing industry in the area. Open mid-May to Sept. 30.

• Sandspit, Cavendish, on Rte. 6; 963-2626; www.sandspit.com. Enjoy 14 attractions including Can-Am racers, ferris wheel, carousel, bumper boats, miniature golf, etc. Canteen and picnic facilities. Open mid-June to Labour Day. No admission charge to the grounds. All-day bracelet packages, or pay-as-you-go.

• Site of Lucy Maud Montgomery's Cavendish Home, Cavendish, on Rte. 6; 963-2231; www.peisland.com/lmm. Homestead fields, quiet woods, and gardens surround stone cellar of old farm house where Montgomery was raised by her Macneill grandparents. Bookstore and gift shop. Open mid-May to mid-Oct., 10 am–5 pm; July–Aug., 9 am–6 pm. Admission: adults $3, children $1, families $8.

• Woodleigh Replicas and Gardens, Rte. 234 in Burlington; 836-3401; www.woodleighreplicas.com. Large-scale replicas of castles and legendary buildings, English gardens, fountains, picnic area, playground and gift shop. Open early June to late Sept.: July and Aug., 9 am–7 pm; off season, 9 am– 5 pm. Admission: $8.50 adults, $8 seniors, $4.50 children 6–17 yrs., under 6 free.

CHARLOTTE'S SHORE

• Ardgowan National Historic Site of Canada, 2 Palmers Lane, Charlottetown; 566-7626; www.pc.gc.ca. Country home of William Henry Pope, a newspaper editor, politician and one of the Fathers of Confederation. The house was once the centre of high-society life and has been restored to its Victorian grandeur. Grounds open to the public.

* Beaconsfield Historic House, 2 Kent St., Charlottetown; 368-6603; www.peimuseum.com. Designed by W.C. Harris and built in 1877, one of the Island's finest residences. Historically furnished rooms, summer teas, music and theatre. Open year round. Admission charged May–Oct.

• Capital Area Recreation Inc. (CARI), University of Prince

Edward Island, University Ave., Charlottetown; 569-4584; www.caripei.ca. Leisure pool, hot tub and toddler's pool. Scheduled family swims. Waterslide, family change room. Open year round. Call, or check the website, for rates and schedules.

* Confederation Centre of the Arts, 145 Richmond St., Charlottetown, 628-1864; 1-800-565-0278; www.confederationcentre.com. Three theatres, Atlantic Canada's largest art gallery, library, gift shop, restaurant. Home of the Charlottetown Festival. Open year round, 9 am–5 pm. Extended hours May–Oct.

• Confederation Players Walking Tours, historic downtown Charlottetown; 368-1864; 1-800-955-1864; www.foundershall.ca. Three guided tours through the streets of Olde Charlottetown. Re-live history with "The Ghostly Realm," the "Historic Great George Street" and "The Settlers" guided walking tours. Tickets and departures from Founders' Hall. Mid-June to late Sept.

* Founders' Hall — Canada's Birthplace Pavilion, historic Charlottetown Waterfront; 368-1864; 1-800-955-1864; www.foundershall.ca. Live the nation's history from 1864 to present day through state-of-the-art displays, multimedia, holivisuals and new technology. Open mid-May to mid-Oct.

• Gateway Village, Borden-Carleton at the foot of the Confederation Bridge. Museums, exhibits, dining and shopping. Free parking. Open year round. Free admission.

* Government House, Victoria Park, Charlottetown; 368-5480; www.gov.pe.ca. Built in 1832, Fanningbank is the official residence of the Lieutenant Governor of PEI. House open to the public during July and Aug. Tours Mon.–Fri., 10 am–4 pm. Donations accepted.

• Harbour Hippo (Land and Sea Tours), Lower Prince St. Wharf, Charlottetown; 628-8687. Land and sea tours of historic Charlottetown and Charlottetown Harbour aboard an amphibious vehicle. Tours

June–Sept., daily, 10:15 am–8 pm (running every hour and 15 minutes). $23 adults, $16 children (5–12 yrs.), 4 and under free.

• Harness Racing Entertainment Centre, Kensington Road, Charlottetown. New state-of-the-art facility with live seasonal racing, a simulcast lounge, full-service tiered dining, enclosed grandstand, and an entertainment centre offering an assortment of gaming products. Open year round.

• Port-La-Joye/Fort Amherst National Historic Site of Canada, Rocky Point, off Rte. 19; 566-7626; www.pc.gc.ca. The French established Port-La-Joye in 1720. The British captured the area in 1758 and built Fort Amherst. Today, only the earthworks remain. Visitors' centre features audio-visual presentation. Grounds open May–Nov.; Visitor centre open mid-June to late Aug., daily 9 am–5 pm with bilingual guide service. Site admission.

* Province House National Historic Site of Canada, corner of Richmond and Great George Sts., Charlottetown; 566-7626; www.pc.gc.ca. Considered the "Birthplace of Canada," the first meeting to discuss federal union was held here in 1864. Several rooms restored to period. Home of the provincial legislature. Open year round. Bilingual guides. Donations accepted. Group fees apply.

BAYS AND DUNES

• Basin Head Fisheries Museum, Basin Head, off Rte. 16; 357-7233; www.peimuseum.com. Boats, gear and photographs depict the lifestyle of an inshore fisher. Saltwater aquariums, boardwalk to beach, children's play area. Open June–Sept., daily. Admission charged.

• Cardigan River Heritage Centre & Marina; 583-2445. Full-service marina, showers and laundry facilities. Local history centre, retail outlets, souvenir and ice-cream shop. Open May–Oct.

• East Point Lighthouse & Welcome Centre, East Point, off Rte. 16; 357-2718. Guided tours available mid-June to Aug. 31. Adults $3, students and seniors \$2, children \$1, preschoolers free.

- Elmira Railway Museum & Miniature Railway, Elmira, Rte. 16A; 357-7234; www.elmirastation.com. History of railroading on PEI. Home to the PEI Miniature Railway and one of the largest railway collections in Canada. Open mid-June to Sept. 30, daily. Admission charged.

* Greenwich Interpretation Centre, Prince Edward Island National Park of Canada, off Rte. 313, St. Peters; 961-2514; www.pc.gc.ca. A rare system of parabolic sand dunes and sites of Aboriginal, French and Acadian occupation. Three walking trails, beach facilities, interpretive centre with multimedia displays of the site's natural and cultural features. Open mid-May to early Oct.; call for off-season information. National Park entrance fees apply.

- Hillsborough River Eco-Centre, 104 Main St., Mount Stewart; 676-2811. Interpretive displays portraying the natural and cultural history of PEI's first Canadian Heritage River. Guided tours, entertainment. Open July–Sept., daily, 10 am–6 pm. Reduced hours year round.

- St. Andrew's Chapel, St. Andrew's, on Rte. 2; 676-2442. The church began its life in 1803, and was moved down the ice on the Hillsborough River in 1864 to become a girls' school. It was returned to the original site in 1990 and restored. Open June–Aug., 10 am–7 pm. Donations in lieu of admission.

- St. Peters Landing, St. Peters Bay, www.stpeterslanding.com. Bayside Landing Park with boardwalk and retail shops featuring fine art, Island crafts and cuisine. Island Blue Cultured Mussel Interpretive building. Seasonal.

HILLS AND HARBOURS

- Ben's Lake, Rte. 24, Bellevue; 838-2706; www.benslake.com. Trout fishing on 18-acre lake. Catch-and-release fly fishing and fee fishing. Fishing tackle available for rent. Open April–Sept. 30. \$4/pound for catch.

- Buffaloland Provincial Park, Milltown Cross, on Rte. 4; 652-8950. A boardwalk leads to a deck overlooking an enclosure where herds of buffalo and white-tailed deer graze. Open year round. Admission free.

- Cape Bear Lighthouse & Marconi Museum, off Rte. 18 at Cape Bear; 962-2917; www.eaglesviewgolf.com. Four-storey lighthouse built in 1881. Replica of the Cape Bear Marconi Station believed to be the first Canadian land station to receive distress signals from the *Titanic*. Open mid-June to mid-Sept., daily, 10 am–6 pm. Admission: \$2.75 adults, \$2.50 seniors, \$1.50 children 6–12 yrs., preschoolers free.

- Garden of the Gulf Museum, 564 Main St., Montague; 838-2467. Exhibit and interpretive programs on the natural history of the Three Rivers area. Open early June to late Sept., Mon.–Sat. 9 am–5 pm. Admission: adults \$3, children under 15 free.

- Orwell Corner Historic Village, Orwell, off Rte. 1; 651-8510; www.orwellcorner.isn.net. Experience the 1800s atmosphere of PEI's agricultural heritage. Farmhouse, church, school, community hall, smithy, shingle mill and barns. Events throughout the summer. PEI Agricultural Museum depicts the heritage of Island agriculture. Open May–Oct. Admission charged.

- Panmure Island Lighthouse, Rte. 347; 838-3568. PEI's oldest wooden lighthouse. Climb to the lantern and view the beach. Gift shop. Open July–Aug., daily. Reduced hours in June and Sept. Admission to climb tower.

- Pinette Raceway, Rte. 1 in Pinette; 659-2736. Community race night Wednesday evenings during the summer months.

- Point Prim Lighthouse, Point Prim, on Rte. 209; 659-2412. PEI's oldest lighthouse (1845). Climb 24 metres (80 ft.) above sea-level to view the Northumberland Strait in this round brick structure. Chowder House on site. Open July–Aug., guided tours. Admission by donation.

- Roma at Three Rivers, Rte. 319

north of Montague; 838-4590; www.romapei.com. Historic site commemorating 1700s French settlement, and Victorian shipbuilding. Archeological displays. Open July 1–Aug. 30, 10 am–6 pm.

- Rossignol Estate Winery, Little Sands, on Rte. 4; 962-4193; www.rossignolwinery.com. The Rossignol family's winery, vineyard and art gallery. Wine-tasting of premium fruit wines. Open May–Oct., Mon–Sat. 10 am–5 pm, Sun. 1–5 pm. Admission free.
- Sir Andrew Macphail Homestead National Historic Site, Orwell, off Rte. 1; 651-2789; www.isn.net/~dhunter/macphailfou ndation.html. Restored historic house, museum, nature trails, ecological forestry project on site. Restaurant serves lunch and dinner (with reservations). Open mid–June to late Sept., Tues.–Sat., 9 am–4 pm; Sun., 1–5 pm. Free admission.
- Wood Islands Lighthouse & Interpretive Museum; 962-3110; www.woodisland.ca. Photos, displays and documentation. Over 200 artifacts. Craft and gift shop. Open June to early Sept., 9:30 am–6 pm. Admission charged.

GENEALOGICAL RESEARCH

Check out the PEI website for further information on genealogy and on-line census: www.gov.pe.ca/infopei/Arts_ Culture_and_Heritage/Genealogy/ind ex.asp
- Alberton Museum and Genealogy Centre, 457 Church St., Alberton; 853-4048; www.auracom.com/~alberton
- Acadian Museum of PEI/Musée Acadien de l'I-P-E, Miscouche; 432-2880; www.peimuseum.com.
- The Farmers' Bank of Rustico Museum, Rte. 234, adjacent to St. Augustine's Church, Rustico; 963-3168; sleep@barachoisinn.com
- The History Room, 12 Heritage Lane, Kingsboro, off Rte. 16, east of Souris; 357-2116; www.islandregister.com/leard.html
- MacNaught History Centre & Archives, Wyatt Heritage

Properties, 75 Spring St., Summerside; 432-1327; www.wyattheritage.com
- PEI Collection, UPEI Robertson Library; 566-0536; www.upei.ca/ ~library/about/peicoll.html
- Public Archives and Records Office, The Hon. George Coles Building, Richmond St., Charlottetown; 368-4290.

FESTIVALS AND EVENTS

Hardly a weekend goes by in the spring, summer, and fall when there isn't a celebration happening somewhere in the province. Included here is a selective listing of events highly recommended if you're in striking distance. Many Island communities also go all out for Canada Day on July 1. For detailed information on Festivals & Events, check out the websites www.festivalspei.com and www.peiplay.com/festivals.

ISLAND-WIDE
September:
- Prince Edward Island Studio Tour Weekend. Island-wide; 368-6300; www.peibusinessdevelopment.com. Open houses at artists' and craft producers' workshops and studios.

NORTH CAPE
June
- Summerside Highland Gathering, College of Piping, Summerside; 436-5377; 1-877-BAGPIPE; www.collegeofpiping.com. Competitions for pipe bands, drummers, stepdancers, and heavy-weight athletes. First-rate Celtic entertainment.

July/August
- Celtic Festival, College of Piping, Summerside; 436-5377; 1-877-BAGPIPE; www.college ofpiping.com. A nine-week concert series featuring piping, drumming, dancing, fiddling, singing and storytelling. July–Aug., Sun–Thurs.

July
- Evangeline Area Bluegrass & Old-time Music Festival, Abrams

Village. A weekend of bluegrass and old-time fiddle music. Local and international artists; 854-3300

- PEI Potato Blossom Festival, O'Leary; 859-1865/1487; www.exhibitions-festivalspeiae .com. Farm show, gospel concert, parade, outdoor music festival, fireworks, dances.
- St. Ann's Sunday Celebrations, Lennox Island; 831-5423; 1-866-837-5423; www.lennoxisland.com. Mi'kmaq food and culture.
- Summerside Lobster Carnival, Summerside; 436-4925/3650; www.exhibitions-festivalspeiae.com. Lots of lobster, a parade, talent contest, midway, nightly entertainment.
- Tignish Irish Moss Festival, Tignish; 882-2476; www.exhibitions-festivalspeiae.com. Miss Irish Moss pageant, parade, dance, food, entertainment, lobster suppers.
- West Point Lighthouse Festival & Boat Race, West Point; 859-1274/2343; www.exhibitions-festivalspeiae.com. Dances, children's events, fishing boat races, antique car show, parade, competitions and food.

August

- Larry Gorman Folk Festival, Britannia Hall, Tyne Valley; 831-2191.
- Prince County Exhibition, Alberton; 853-3013/2455; www.peiwest.com. Various competitions, shows and displays, midway, parade.
- Tyne Valley Oyster Festival, Tyne Valley; 831-3294. Fiddling and step dancing championships, Canadian Oyster-shucking championship, adult dance, oyster and scallop dinners.

September

- L'Exposition Agricole et le Festival Acadien, Abram-Village; 854-2324/3300; www.expositionfestival.com. Acadian entertainment, parade, demonstrations and lobster suppers.

ANNE'S LAND
June-Sept.

- Avonlea Concert, Avonlea Village, Cavendish; 963-3050. Island singing, step dancing and fiddling in the restored 1872 Long River Church.

July-August

- Indian River Festival, St. Mary's Church, Indian River, Rte. 104, 5 km north of Kensington; 836-4933; 1-866-856-3733; www.indianriverfestival.com. Chamber music, jazz and choral concerts by international musicians enhanced by breathtaking acoustics of the church.

July

- British Car Days Across the Bridge, Cymbria Lions Centre, Rustico; 964-3294; 569-5337; www.bmapei.com. British car and motorcycle show with vehicles from Eastern Canada and USA.
- Festival Rendez-vous Rustico Festival, Rte. 243, Rustico; 963-3011; www.rendezvousrustico.com. An Acadian festival of traditional, contemporary and classical music, dance, food, and games. Lennie Gallant in concert.

August

- Fiddlers and Followers Weekend, Cavendish, Rainbow Valley Amusement Park; 963-2221; www.rainbowvalley.pe.ca. Four big fiddle shows featuring Maritime fiddle champions, step dancers, barbecues, lobster parties, and picnics.
- Lucy Maud Montgomery Festival, Cavendish and area; 963-7874; www.lmmontgomeryfestival.com Traditional music, readings from L.M. Montgomery's work, writers' workshops, traditional and children's entertainment.
- Woodleigh Highland Games, Burlington; 836-3401; www.woodleighreplicas.com. Bag piping, drumming, highland dancing and Celtic activities.

September

- Annual Cymbria Music Festival, Rustico at Cymbria Campground; 963-2458; www.cymbria.ca. A

weekend featuring independent Maritime artists with original works. Special guest appearances.
- Island Rally, Brackley Beach, Vacationland RV Park, Brackley Beach; 569-3913

CHARLOTTE'S SHORE
May
- Festival Port-La-Joie de Charlottetown; 368-1895; www.festivalacadiendecharlottetown .ca. A three-day festival featuring the best of Acadian musicians, dancers and performers.
- PEI Wine Festival, The Delta Prince Edward, Charlottetown; www.peilcc.ca. Wine-tasting sessions, wine boutique, gala dinner and silent auction.

May-October
- Capture PEI Writers & Photographers Workshops & Tours, Charlottetown; 566-9748; www.gotocreativeconnections.com. Learn writing, publishing, photography with professionals.
- Ceili at the Irish Hall, Benevolent Irish Society, 582 North River Rd., Charlottetown; 892-2367; www.irishisland.ca. Irish, Scottish and traditional music, song and dance. PEI's best traditional performers. Every Fri., 8–10:30 pm.

June/July
- Atlantic Superstore Festival of Lights, Charlottetown waterfront; 1-800-955-1864; www.visitcharlottetown.com/lights. Buskers, midway, fireworks, concerts, pub tents.

July
- Crapaud Exhibition, Crapaud; 658-2787; www.exhibitions-festivalspei ae.com. Animals, competitions, food, children's activities, entertainment.
- Emerald Junction Irish Festival, Emerald Community Centre, Rte. 113; 886-2400. Great Irish music, food, beer garden, children's activities, rough camping.
- Gay & Lesbian Pride Festival, Charlottetown and various locations across PEI; 894-5776; 1-877-380-5776; www.pridepei.com. Parade,

entertainment and dance, sporting activities.

August
- Old Home Week/ PEI Provincial Exhibition, Charlottetown Civic Centre and Driving Park; 629-6623; www.exhibitions-festivalspei ae.com. Horses and livestock shows, harness racing, parade, midway, exhibits, and entertainment. The Gold Cup and Saucer Race is one of eastern Canada's most prestigious harness races.

September
- PEI International Shellfish Festival, Charlottetown waterfront; 1-866-955-2003; www.peishellfish.com. Maritime entertainment, PEI/Eastern Canadian Oyster-Shucking Championships, PEI International Chowder Championships.

September/October
- Cornfest Festival, APM Centre, Rte. 1, Cornwall; 628-6260. Annual community celebration.

October
- Prince Edward Island Marathon, Brackley Beach to Charlottetown; 628-1861; www.princeedwardislandmarathon. com. Distant running event for the whole family. Health and Fitness Expo.

BAYS AND DUNES
Year round
- Monticello Ceilidhs, Monticello Hall, Rte. 16; 628-1254. Island fiddling, singing and dancing. Sundays, 8 pm. Admission charged.

July
- PEI Bluegrass & Oldtime Music Festival, Rollo Bay; 566-3011; www.bluegrasspei.com/rollobay.htm. Bluegrass and oldtime bands from Canada and the U.S.
- Rollo Bay Fiddle Festival, Rollo Bay; 687-2584; www.rollobayfiddlefest.com. Open-air concert featuring talent from all over North America.
- Souris Regatta "Festival of the Sea," Marine Terminal Wharf, Souris; 687-2157;

www.sourispei.com. Boat races, boat poker run, Queen-of-the-Sea pageant, marine trade show, midway, children's entertainment and barbecues.

August
- Provincial Plowing Match and Agricultural Fair (Dundas); 583-2723; www.exhibitions-festivalspeiae.com. Country fair celebrating the land, its bounty and people. Agricultural displays, livestock, food and entertainment.
- St. Peters Wild Blueberry Festival, St. Peters Park; www.isn.net/~festival. Open-air concert, dances, entertainment, blueberry pancake brunch, and parade.

HILLS AND HARBOURS
June-October
- Ceilidh at the Corner, Orwell Corner Community Hall; 651-8510; www.orwellcorner.isn.net. Traditional song, stories and dance. Wed., 8 pm.

July
- Northumberland Provincial Fisheries Festival, Murray River, Northumberland Arena; 962-3327. Pageant, golf tournament, fisherman's challenge, variety show, dances, lobster suppers.
- PEI Street Rod Association Show 'N' Shine, Brudenell; 962-4140. Outdoor car show featuring street. rod, antique, special interest and classic cars.

August
- Annual Mi'kmaq Pow-Wow, Panmure Island; 831-5423. A celebration of Mi'kmaq culture with traditional foods and entertainment.
- Caledonia Club of PEI Annual Highland Games, Eldon, Lord Selkirk Provincial Park; 659-2337. Piping, dancing, and traditional athletic competitions. Lobster suppers.
- Wendell Boyle Celtic Festival, Orwell Corner Historic Village; 651-8510; www.orwellcorner.isn.net. Outdoor concerts featuring PEI's best traditional musicians and fiddlers.

September
- Fête Roma, Roma at Three Rivers, Rte. 319; 838-4590; www.romapei.com. Celebrating 1730s life in PEI. Tours, re-enactments, music, food and dance. Pick up a copy of *The Buzz* magazine or visit its website at www.buzzon.com to find out what's going on during your visit.

NIGHT LIFE
THEATRE

NORTH CAPE
- Feast Dinner Theatre, at Brothers Two, Water St. Station, Summerside; 888-2200; 1-888-748-1010; www.feastdinnertheatres.ca. Dinner theatre, music and comedy. Seasonal. Mon.–Sat., 6:30 pm. Reservations recommended.
- Harbourfront Jubilee Theatre, 124 Harbour Drive, Summerside; 888-2500; 1-800-708-6505; www.jubileetheatre.com. Shows and musicals celebrate the culture and tradition of the Maritimes. Open year round.
- La Cuisine à Mémé Dinner-Theatre, L'Hotel Village sur l'Ocean, Mont-Carmel; 854-2227; 1-800-567-3228; www.hotelvillage.ca. French and English dinner theatre. Shows July–Aug., Tues.–Sat., 6:30 pm. Reservations required.
- V'nez Chou Nous Acadian Dinner Theatre Productions, Rte. 2, Tignish; 882-0475. Funny storyline based on local characters combines original and traditional Acadian song and dance. Mid-July to mid-Aug. by reservation only.

ANNE'S LAND
- The Barn, Rte. 6, Stanley Bridge. Musical acts, comedy and storytelling. Seasonal.
- Eddie May Murder Mystery Dinner Theatre, Stanley Bridge Country Resort, Rte. 6, Stanley Bridge; 569-1999; 1-888-747-4050; www.eddiemay.ca. Murder mystery dinner-theatre with audience participation. Mid-July to late Aug., Thurs. at 7 pm.

CHARLOTTE'S SHORE

- The Arts Guild, 111 Queen St., Charlottetown; 894-7272. Featuring a variety of local entertainment including sketch comedy, musical acts and plays. Open year round.
- The Charlottetown Festival, Confederation Centre of the Arts, 145 Richmond St., Charlottetown; 566-1267; 1-800-565-0278; www.confederationcentre.com. Home of Canada's longest-running musical, *Anne of Green Gables— The Musical* ™. The centre features two main-stage musicals (including Anne) each year. As well, MacKenzie Theatre offers musical theatre in a cabaret-style setting and there are free outdoor performances by the Confederation Centre Young Company from July to late August. Festival runs late May to mid-Oct.
- Eddie May Murder Mystery, Piazza Joe's, 189 Kent St., Charlottetown; 569-1999; 1-888-747-4050; www.eddiemay.ca. Murder mystery dinner-theatre with audience participation. Mid-July to late Aug., Tues. and Sat. at 7 pm.
- Feast Dinner Theatre, Rodd Charlottetown — A Rodd Signature Hotel, Charlottetown; 629-2321. Actors serve a choice of entrée, salad, steamed mussels and dessert at the same time keeping up the plot line and lively music. Mid-June to early Sept., Tues.–Sun., 6:30 pm. Reservations recommended.
- Victoria Playhouse Festival, Victoria, off Rte. 1; 658-2025; 1-800-925-2025; www.victoria playhouse.com. A charming location for professional repertory theatre and musical concerts. Fine dining and café a few steps away. Late June to late Sept.

BAYS AND DUNES

- St. Peters Bay Courthouse Theatre, Rte. 2, St. Peters Bay; 961-3636; www.courthousetheatre.com. Music, storytelling and dramatic productions with some of the best local talent. Open June–Sept.

HILLS & HARBOURS

- Kings Playhouse, Georgetown; 652-2591; www.kingsplay house.com. Featuring local performers including musical acts, plays, comedy and storytelling. Seasonal.

PUBS AND TAVERNS

CHARLOTTETOWN

- Baba's Lounge, 81 University Ave.; 892-7377. Friendly bar featuring up-and-coming Island performers.
- D'Arcy McGee's, 185 Kent St.; 894-3627. Live entertainment on Friday and Saturday nights. Open year round.
- Dundee Arms, 200 Pownal St.; 892-2496; 1-877-638-6333; www.dundeearms.com. Live entertainment in the Hearth and Cricket Lounge, Fridays, 7:30 pm. Open year round.
- Myron's Restaurant and Pub, 151 Kent St.; 892-4375; www.myrons.com. Downstairs is the pub and grub scene. Upstairs is PEI's premier dance club for the young crowd. Occasional live performances by local or touring acts.
- Olde Dublin Pub, 131 Sydney St.; 892-6992; www.oldedublinpub.com. A regular line-up of lively traditional music for an equally lively crowd. Live music nightly mid-June to mid-Oct.
- Peake's Quay Restaurant and Bar, Charlottetown Waterfront; 368-1330; www.peakesquay.com. PEI's largest outdoor deck with bar. Live entertainment. May–Sept., Thurs.–Sun.
- St. James Gate, 129 Kent St.; 892-4283. Restaurant and pub. Live entertainment on selected nights with local musicians. Open year round.
- Victoria Row, Richmond St. Enjoy a regular line-up of blues, jazz and local acts on an outdoor stage while dining on one of the patios along the pedestrian mall. Seasonal.
- The Wave, 550 University Ave.; 566-0530. The campus bar for the University of Prince Edward Island. Student crowd and frequent live acts.

NORTH CAPE

- The Silver Fox, Summerside Waterfront Property; 436-2153. Live music, mostly country. Nice

view of yacht club boats.
• The Landing Oyster House and Pub, Tyne Valley; 831-3138. Live local music, Thurs.–Sat., and many impromptu sessions.

ANNE'S LAND

• Thirsty's Roadhouse, Rte. 6, Cavendish; 963-2441. Where the young and the restless congregate in the summertime. Eclectic mix of workers in the hospitality industry and those they're hospitable to. Top-40 music. Open mid-June to Sept.

CRAFT SHOPS

NORTH CAPE

• Abram-Village Handcraft Co-op, Abram-Village, at Rtes. 124 and 165; 854-2096. Acadian crafts, weaving, quilts, rugs, pottery, mini-museum. Open June 1–Sept. 30, Mon.–Sat. 9:30 am–6 pm.
• Back Road Folk Art, Rte. 151, Lauretta; 853-3644; www.backroadfolkart.com. Folk art, antiques, birdhouses, carvings, rustic furniture, and studio. Open year round, Mon.–Sat., 9 am–5 pm; evenings and Sundays by chance or appointment.
• Bedeque Crafts Centre, Central Bedeque, off Rte. 1A. Operated by artisans. A large variety of all locally made crafts. Gallery of quilts. Open year round. Mid-May to mid-Oct., Mon.–Sat., 9 am–6 pm; Sun., 10 am–6 pm.
• Boutique A-Point, Rte. 165, Mont-Carmel; 854-2895. Handmade clothing, crafts, and souvenirs. Open year round. Mon.–Sat., 9 am–5 pm; open Sundays during July and Aug.
• Celtic Gift Shop, The College of Piping, 619 Water St., Summerside; 436-5377; 1-877-BAGPIPE; www.collegeofpiping.com. A wide selection of music, books, highland supplies, instruments, tartans and clan items. Open year round.
• The Cinnamon Tree, 20 Water St., Summerside; 436-5041; www.islandtelecom.com/~ctree. Specializing in country products and home accents and folk carvings. Open year round. July and Aug., Mon.–Wed. and Sat. 10

am–6 pm, Thurs. and Fri., 10 am–8 pm; Sun., 12 noon–5 pm.
• Culture Crafts Co-op, Rte. 2 east of Richmond; 854-3063; 831-2484; www.sun-sea.pe.ca. Basket weaving and Island crafts. Workshops. Open June 1–Sept. 30: June 1–Sept. 2, Mon.–Sat., 9 am–5 pm; Sept. 3–30, Mon.–Fri., 9 am–4 pm.
• Indian Art and Craft of North America, Lennox Island, on Rte. 163, off Rte. 12; 831-2653. Contemporary and traditional First Nations' crafts from across North America. Specializing in Mi'kmaq ash-splint baskets and Micmac Productions pottery and figurines. Open mid-May to mid-Oct., Mon.–Sat., 9 am–6 pm; Sun., 10 am–6 pm.
• The Old Mill Craft Company, Bloomfield, on Rte. 2; 859-3508. Adjacent to MacAusland's Woollen Mill. Featuring traditional Island gifts and crafts including woollen items, weaving, sheepskins and hand-hooked rugs. Hand-carved decoys. Open July and Aug. 9:30 am–6:30 pm, Sun. 12 noon–6 pm; June and Sept., Mon.-Sat. 10 am–5 pm.
• Shoreline Lobster Pattern Sweaters — Tyne Valley Studio, Rte. 12, Tyne Valley; 831-2950. Knitwear featuring the "lobster pattern" sweater. Open June–Sept., Mon.–Sat., 10 am–5 pm.
• Spinnakers' Landing, Waterfront Properties, Summerside; 436-6692; www.summersidewaterfront.com/ spinnakers. A boardwalk location on Summerside Harbour, featuring giftware, crafts, retail outlets and antiques. Food outlets, ice cream, free entertainment, and free parking. Open early June to late Sept., daily.
• Tignish Treasures Gift Shop/ Holiday Island Productions, School St., Tignish; 882-2896; www.tignishtreasures.com. Off Maple St., near St. Simon & St. Jude Church. Clay miniature replicas of historic buildings, handcrafted soaps, Christmas ornaments and PEI souvenirs. Free studio tours. Open June–Sept.
• West Point Lighthouse Craft Shop, West Point, on Rte. 14, through Cedar Dunes Provincial Park; 859-

3742. Locally made crafts. Open June 1 to late Sept.: July and Aug., daily 9 am–8 pm; June and Sept., 10 am–6 pm.

ANNE'S LAND

* The Dunes, Brackley Beach, on Rte. 15; 672-2586; www.dunesgallery.com. Excellent selection of contemporary pottery designs by owner Peter Jansons, along with works by other Island artists and imports. Jewellery, glassware and other art items also on sale in gallery-restaurant. Open mid-May to mid-Oct., daily 9 am–5 pm; evenings in summer.
* Dyed in the Wool, St. Ann, on Rte. 224; 621-0699. Wool from studio's flock goes to hand-knit designer sweaters. Tanned sheepskins, woven wall hangings, afghans, pillows and rugs. Open June–Oct.
* Gaudreau Fine Woodworking, Rte. 6, Rustico; 963-2273; www.woodmagic.ca. Fine crafts gallery features designer hardwood accessories, pottery, demos. Open year round: July–Aug. 9 am–9 pm; shoulder season, 10 am–5 pm. Call for winter hours.
* Memories Gift Shop, New London, at corner of Rtes. 6 and 8; 886-2020. Two floors of high-quality Canadian crafts. Anne dolls and Victorian accessories. Open mid-May to mid-Oct., daily, 10 am–5 pm; July–Aug., 9:30 am–5:30 pm.
* Prince Edward Island Preserve Co. Ltd., junction of Rtes. 224 and 258, New Glasgow; 964-4300; 1-800-565-5267; www.preservecompany.com. Craft and gift shop featuring fine preserves prepared for market on premises. On-site restaurant, ice cream take out, and 12-acre New Glasgow Country Gardens. Open mid-April to early Oct.: July 1 to early Sept., 8 am–9 pm; reduced hours in the off season.
* Sandscript, Rte. 8, New London; 886-3303; www3.pei.sympatico.ca/ ~sandscript. Handcrafted sand treasures, Island- and Canadian-made gifts. Open mid-May to mid-Oct., 10 am–5 pm.
* Seasway Hammock Shop, Churchill Ave., North Rustico; 963-2846. Hammocks handmade by

retired fisherman on the premises. Open year round, 10 am to dusk.
* Stanley Bridge Studios, Stanley Bridge, on Rte. 6; 886-2800; 621-0314. A large selection of pottery, reproductions in tin lighting, fine jewellery, glass, collectibles, Anne dolls, etc. Open late May to early Oct., 10 am–5 pm; July–Aug., daily, 9:30 am–dusk.
* The Toy Factory, New Glasgow, on Rte. 13; 964-2299. Assortment of unique wooden toys handcrafted while you watch. Lots of toys for play-testing too. Open mid-May to mid-Oct.: June 15–Aug. 31, Mon.–Sat., 9 am–9 pm, Sun., 10 am–5 pm; off season, Mon.–Sat., 9 am–5 pm., Sun., 11 am–4 pm.
* Trout River Pottery, Rte. 239, Millvale; 621-0498; www.pei pottery.com. Off Rte. 254. Hand-thrown porcelain and stoneware pottery. Open mid-May to mid-Oct., Mon.–Sat., 9 am–6 pm.
* Village Pottery, Rte. 6, New London; 886-2473; www.pei.welcome.to. Pottery made on-site, Island crafts, jewellery, weavings and paintings. Open May–Oct., daily.

CHARLOTTE'S SHORE

* Cavendish Figurines Ltd., Gateway Village, Borden-Carleton; 437-2663; 1-800-558-1908; www.cavendishfigurines.com. Island souvenirs and giftware. Figurines made on premises, free bilingual tours. Open year round.
* Charlottetown Farmers' Market, 100 Belvedere Ave., Charlottetown; 626-3373. In addition to a vast array of locally grown produce, fresh meats, seafood, baked goods, pastries, international foods, fresh flowers and locally roasted coffees, a number of local crafts people also market their products. Open year round, Sat. 9 am–2 pm. July–Aug., Wed. and Sat. 9 am–2 pm.
* Froggies Used Clothing Store, 9 Jordan Cres., Charlottetown; 892-4606. Quality used clothing and costuming items and accessories. Open year round. Mon.–Thurs. and Sat., 8:30 am–6 pm; Fri., 8:30 am–9 pm. Extended hours in the summer.
* Happy Red's Train Station, Folk

Art Store & Dairy Bar, Rte. 1, Hazelbrook; 628-3846; www.capngrumpy.com. Maritime folk art, pottery, handknitting and "Cap'n Grumpy's Lobster Tings" (lobster trap furniture and accessories). Open mid-May to Sept.

- Home Accents, 74 Queen St., Charlottetown; 368-8909. Local and world crafts, marine brass, glass, prints and garden centre. Open year round. Mon.–Sat., 10 am–5 pm. Extended hours in the summer.

- The Island Crafts Shop, 156 Richmond St., Charlottetown; 892-5152; www.peicraftscouncil.com. A vast array of crafts made by members of the PEI Crafts Council. Pottery, batik, woodwork, stained glass, knitting, and other unique items. Open year round. Oct.–May, 10 am–6 pm, closed Sun.; June–Sept., 9 am–9 pm, Sun. 11 am–6 pm.

- Moonsnail Soapworks and Nature Store, 85 Water St., Charlottetown; 1-888-771-7627; www.moonsnailsoapworks.com. Special Island soaps and natural body treats, all handcrafted on site. Open year round.

- The Official Island Store ™, Gateway Village, Borden-Carleton; 437-6421. Fine crafts by more than 80 Island artisans. Open May–Oct.

- Peake's Wharf — Historic Waterfront Merchants, located at the foot of Great George and Prince Sts., Charlottetown; 629-1864; 1-800-955-1864; www.visit charlottetown.com/waterfront. Crafts, clothing, gifts, homemade ice cream, restaurants, bars and live entertainment. Open mid-May to mid-Oct.

- The Reading Well Bookstore, 87-A Water St.; 566-2703; www.rebel reader.com. Specializing in children's books and local Island writers. The store also sells Ten Thousand Villages Crafts from the Third World. Free coffee. Open year round, Mon.–Sat., 10 am–5 pm. Extended hours during the summer.

- The Showcase — Confederation Centre of the Arts, 145 Richmond St., Charlottetown; 628-6149/6129; www.confederationcentre.com. Handcrafts from across Canada, books and Anne of Green Gables

products. Contemporary art for rent or purchase. Open year round.

- Stanley Pottery and Weaving Studio and Shop, Breadalbane, Rte. 246; 621-0316. Rural life and nature inspire the hand-painted scenes. Open May 1–Oct. 31, daily 10 am–6 pm.; off-season by chance or appointment.

BAYS AND DUNES

- Cardigan Craft Centre and Tea Room, Cardigan, off Rte. 5; 583-2930. A co-operative centre for handcrafts produced mainly by its members, featuring rug hooking, quilting, weaving, soft-sculpture knitting, sheepskin products, free-hand pottery, ceramics, etc. Open June to early Oct., Mon.–Sat. 10 am–5:30 pm.

- East Point Lighthouse Craft Shop, East Point, off Rte. 16; 357-2106. Handmade souvenirs and handcrafts. Open June 1–Oct. 1.

- Glenroy Gallery, located in the Mount Stewart Eco-Centre; 676-2262; www.virtuo.com/glenroy. Island-made products — fine woodworking, art and crafts. Open July 1–Sept. 30, daily, 10 am–6 pm.

- Log Cabin Arts & Crafts, 30 Main St., Souris 687-3046. Locally made crafts including souvenirs, quilts, paintings, ceramics, knitting, dried florals, weaving and books. Open May–Oct.

- Naturally Yours, 31 Beach Ave., Souris; 687-2571; www.peisland. com/islandeast/naturally. Home-grown flowers and herbs (fresh and dried), oil paintings of local landscapes, refinished antiques, natural souvenir items. Open June–Sept., Mon.–Sat. 11 am–5 pm.

- St. Peters Bay Craft and Giftware, Northside Rd., St. Peters Bay; 961-3223; www.stpetersbay.net. High quality pewter jewellery, pewter gifts, nature collectibles, leather figurines, books, photos and prints by local artists, and traditional music. Demonstrations in pewter casting. Open May 1–Nov. 30. Tours May 1–Oct. 30, Mon.–Fri., 9 am–4 pm.

HILLS AND HARBOURS

- Koleszar Pottery, Rte. 204, Melville; 659-2570. Delicate porcelain pottery, decorated with an eye to beauty and the sweetness of nature. Open May 1–Nov. 15, 9 am–12 noon and 2–5 pm. Closed Tues.
- Miss Elly's Genteel Gifts & Stuff, Main St., Murray Harbour by the wharf; 962-3555. Linens, lace, quilts, Island-wool blankets, hooked mats, Island pottery, prints, paintings and collectibles. Open mid-June to late Sept., Mon.–Sat., 10 am–5 pm, Sun., 1–5 pm. Evenings by chance.
- The Old General Store, Main St., Murray River; 962-2459. Turn-of-the-century general store featuring quality linens, quilts, clothing, jewellery, handcrafts, books, artwork and music. Open mid-June to late Sept. and Canadian Thanksgiving weekend, daily. Other times by chance or appointment.
- Spit'N Image — Creator of Fine Alpaca Knitwear, 649 Dover Rd., Murray River; 962-2031; www3.pei.sympatico.ca/micron. Handcrafted sweaters and cardigans in a variety of styles, handcrafted from certified organic fibres. Meet alpacas "Carmen" and "Maple." Open year round, daily.
- Plough the Waves Centre, intersection of Rtes. 1 and 4, Wood Islands. Gift shops, visitor information and liquor store on premises. Landscaped grounds with gazebo for relaxation and picnics. Open May–Oct., daily.
- Wooly Wares, 1570 Valleyfield Rd., Valleyfield, on Rte. 326; 838-4821. Sheep farm and craft studio specializing in "Cozy Toes" slippers, designer blankets, unique sheep doorstops, footstools, ornaments, sheepskins. Tanning and felting displays. Open June 1–Sept. 30.

PRODUCT TOURS

- Anne of Green Gables Chocolates, Avonlea Village, Cavendish; 963-3403. Premium chocolates and fudge. View chocolates being made on site and feel free to sample. Seasonal.
- CheeseLady's Gouda, Rte. 223 off Rte. 2, Winsloe North; 368-1506. Come see how Gouda cheese is made. Sample herb, onion, peppercorn and garlic-flavoured cheeses. Farm with calves, sheep and llamas. Open year round, Mon.–Sat. 9 am–6 pm; off season, Tues.–Sat., 10 am–5 pm.
- Island Chocolates, Main St., Victoria; 658-2320; 1-800-565-2320. Chocolates handmade using Belgian chocolate and fresh PEI fruits. Hands-on workshops. Open June–Sept. 30, daily: July and Aug., 9:30 am–8 pm; June and Sept., 9:30 am–5 pm.
- Paderno Cookware Factory and Outlet Store, 10 McCarville St., West Royalty Industrial Park; 629-2360; 1-800-263-9768; www.paderno.com. Surgical stainless steel cookware, guaranteed for 25 years. Open Mon.–Sat., 9 am–5 pm.
- PEI T-Shirts, Mount Stewart, off Rte. 2; 676-2146; www.bestofpei.com. An open-concept factory featuring Island-made T-shirts. Watch textiles being cut, sewn, and screen printed. Open May–Nov., 9 am–5 pm, Sun. 11 am–5 pm.
- Prince Edward Island Preserve Company, corner of Rtes. 224 and 258, New Glasgow; 964-4300; 1-800-565-5267; www.preservecompany.com. See, hear, smell, and taste fine preserves being prepared for market in a 1913 butter factory in the scenic village of New Glasgow. Gift shop and café. Open mid-April to early Oct.: July and Aug., 8 am–9 pm; reduced hours in the off-season.

ART GALLERIES

- Art Gallery of Tony Diodati, off Rte. 20 in Springbrook; 886-3009. Featuring original art and limited-edition reproductions of Prince Edward Island scenes by owner/artist Tony Diodati. Open late May to late Sept., daily.
- * Confederation Centre Art Gallery, 145 Richmond St., Charlottetown; 628-6142. Atlantic Canada's largest gallery featuring the works of Canadian artists. Open year round.
- Details Past and Present, 166

Richmond St., Victoria Row, Charlottetown; 892-2233. Featuring the works of local artists. Open year round, Mon.–Sat.

* The Dunes Studio Gallery, Brackley Beach, on Rte. 15; 672-2586; www.dunesgallery.com. A good cross-section of Island contemporary art in a beautiful setting. Open early May to mid-Oct., daily 9 am–5 pm. Evenings in summer.

• Ellen's Creek Gallery, 525 North River Rd., Charlottetown; 368-3494. Various Island artists. Open year round, Mon.-Sat., 9 am–5:30 pm.

• Eptek Centre, 130 Harbour Dr., Summerside; 888-8373; www.peimuseum.com. National exhibition centre with regular showings of Island artists. Open year round. Tues.–Fri., 10 am–4 pm; Sun., 12 noon–4 pm. Admission by donation.

• Gallery in the Guild, 111 Queen St., Charlottetown; 894-7272. Exhibits by PEI Arts Guild members.

• Glasgow Road Gallery, Wheatley River, on Rte. 224; 964-2055; www.islandprints.com. The paintings of Hugh Crosby. Open June 1–Sept. 30: June and Sept., 10 am–5 pm; July and Aug., 10 am–8 pm.

• Lefurgey Cultural Centre, 205 Prince St., Summerside; 432-1327; www.wyattheritage.com. Small gallery of Island art. Open year round.

• Mermaid Art Gallery and Framing, 131 Grafton St., Charlottetown, in Confederation Court Mall; 626-3001; www.mermaidart.com. Featuring the works of Island and Atlantic Canadian artists. Open year round.

• Pinette Studios, 159 Pinette Rd., off Rte. 1 at Eldon; 659-2330. Paintings, stained glass and prints of Island landscapes and wildlife. Open May–Oct., Tues.–Fri., 10 am–5 pm.

• The Showcase Art Sales and Rentals, Confederation Centre of the Arts, 145 Richmond St., Charlottetown; 628-6129/6149; www.confederationcentre.com. Fine Canadian art available for sale or rent. Open year round.

• The Studio Gallery, Victoria, on Rte. 116; 658-2733; www.studiogallery.com. The work of Island artists including artist-in-residence Doreen Foster. Open June–Oct., Mon.–Sat. 10 am–5 pm, Sun. 12 noon–5 pm or by appointment.

OUTDOOR RECREATION

The variety of landscapes and activities offered by the Island's parks is astounding. Calm south shore beaches, rolling wooded hills, marshland full of wildlife, quiet meadows for picnicking — it's your choice. About half of PEI's 29 provincial parks have camping facilities. Many also have day programs providing guided nature walks, concerts, evening campfires, and children's activities.

NORTH CAPE

• Belmont Provincial Park, off Rte. 123, Belmont. Camping, unsupervised beach, picnicking, showers, flush toilets, change house.

• Campbellton, off Rte. 14. No facilities, unsupervised beach.

• Cedar Dunes Provincial Park, off Rte. 14. Camping, supervised beach, picnicking, showers, flush toilets, change house, nature trail, interpretive programs, camping, wheelchair accessible washrooms.

• Fisherman's Haven, Tignish Shore, off Rte. 12. Camping, unsupervised beach, picnicking, flush toilets.

• Green Park Provincial Park, off Rte. 12, Port Hill. Camping, unsupervised beach, picnicking, nature trails, showers, flush toilets, change house, floating dock.

• Jacques Cartier Provincial Park, Kildare Capes, off Rte. 12. Camping, supervised beach, picnicking, showers, change house, canteen, interpretation.

• Linkletter Provincial Park, on Rte. 11, Linkletter. Camping, unsupervised beach, picnicking, showers, change house, flush toilets.

• Mill River Provincial Park, on Rte. 136. Camping, unsupervised beach, picnicking, showers, flush toilets, change house, wheelchair-accessible washrooms, marina.

• Miminegash Pond, off Rte. 14,

south of the harbour. No facilities; interpretive program, camping, unsupervised beach.
- Nail Pond, off Rte. 12. No facilities, unsupervised beach.
- St.-Chrysostome, off Rte. 11. No facilities, unsupervised beach.
- Union Corner Provincial Park, off Rte. 11, Union Corner. No facilities, unsupervised beach.

ANNE'S LAND

In the Prince Edward Island National Park:
- Brackley Beach. Group camping, supervised beach, information centre, flush toilets, change house, showers, canteen, wheelchair access.
- Cavendish Beach. Camping, supervised beach, information centre, flush toilets, change house, showers, canteen, wheelchair access.
- Dalvay Beach. Supervised beach, picnicking.
- North Rustico Beach. Supervised beach, toilets, change house.
- Robinsons Island. Unsupervised beach, camping.
- Stanhope Lane Beach. Camping, supervised beach, flush toilets, change house, showers, canteen, wheelchair access.

Outside Prince Edward Island National Park:
- Blooming Point Beach. Off Rte. 218 at Blooming Point. No facilities, unsupervised.
- Cabot Beach Provincial Park. Camping, supervised beach, picnicking, showers, flush toilets, change house, interpretive program.
- Cousins Shore, off Rte. 20 at Darnley. No facilities, unsupervised beach.

CHARLOTTE'S SHORE

- Argyle Shore Provincial Park, on Rte. 19, Argyle Shore. Unsupervised beach, picnicking, showers, flush toilets, change house.
- Brookvale Provincial Ski Park, Kelly's Cross. Walking trails.
- Chelton Beach Provincial Park, off Rte. 10. Supervised beach, picnicking, showers, flush toilets, change house, canteen.
- Fort Amherst/Port-La-Joye National Historic Site, Rocky Point. Information centre.
- Strathgartney Provincial Park, Strathgartney. Camping, picnicking, walking trails, wheelchair-accessible washrooms.
- Tea Hill Provincial Park, off Rte. 1, Tea Hill. Unsupervised beach, picnicking, showers, flush toilets, change house, canteen, recreation programs.
- Victoria Beach Provincial Park, off Rte. 1, Victoria. Unsupervised beach, picnicking, showers, flush toilets, change house.

BAYS AND DUNES

- Basin Head Day Park, on Rte. 16, Kingsboro. Outdoor showers, washroom facilities, gazebo, picnic tables, gift shop, canteen, ice cream, supervised beach.
- Boughton Bay, off Rte. 310 near Little Pond. No facilities, unsupervised beach.
- Campbell's Cove Provincial Park, on Rte. 16, Campbells Cove. Camping, unsupervised beach, picnicking, showers, flush toilets, change house.
- Greenwich, Prince Edward Island National Park, Rte. 313, Greenwich. Supervised beach, showers, change house, interpretive centre, walking trails.
- Red Point Provincial Park, on Rte. 302, Red Point. Camping, supervised beach, picnicking, showers, flush toilets, change house.
- Sally's Beach Provincial Park, off Rte. 310, near Inn at Spry Point, Spry Point. Facilities relating to resort, unsupervised beach, change house, picnicking.
- Savage Harbour Beach, Rte. 218, Savage Harbour. No facilities, unsupervised beach.
- Souris Beach Provincial Park, on Rte. 2. Unsupervised beach, picnicking, showers, flush toilets, change house.

HILLS AND HARBOURS

- Brudenell River Provincial Park, on Rte. 3, Roseneath. Camping, supervised beach, picnicking, showers, change house, flush toilets, interpretive program, canteen, camping, nature trail.
- Irvings Cape Beach, off Rte. 17 near Murray Harbour North.

Unsupervised beach.
- Kings Castle Provincial Park, Gladstone, off Rte. 18. Camping, unsupervised beach, picnicking, toilets.
- Lord Selkirk Provincial Park, on Rte. 1, near Belfast. Camping, unsupervised beach, picnicking, showers, flush toilets, change house, camping, supervised swimming pool.
- MacLeod's Beach, off Rte. 4, between White Sands and Little Sands. No facilities, unsupervised beach.
- Northumberland Beach Provincial Park, on Rte. 4, near Wood Islands. Camping, unsupervised beach, picnicking, flush toilets, showers, change house, recreational programs.
- Panmure Island Provincial Park, off Rte. 17, Panmure Island. Camping, supervised beach; picnicking, showers, change huts, flush toilets, canteen.
- Pinette Provincial Park, on Rte. 1, Pinette. Unsupervised beach, picnicking, showers, flush toilets, change house.
- Seal Cove, off Rte. 17, near Murray Harbour North. Unsupervised beach, nearby campground has picnicking facilities and toilets.
- Wood Islands Provincial Park, on Rte. 4. Unsupervised beach, picnicking, flush toilets, change house, canteen.

GOLF

For more information on golf courses, visit www.golfpei.com, and for a tip-to-tip, week-long itinerary, visit www.peiplay.com/golf

NORTH CAPE
- Mill River Provincial Golf Course (18-hole, par 72), Mill River Provincial Park and Rodd Mill River Resort, off Rte. 2; 1-800-235-8909 (for reservations); www.golflinkspei.com. May–Oct.
- St. Felix Golf & Country Club (9-hole, par 36), Greenmount Road, Rte. 153, St-Felix; 882-2328; 1-877-311-2328; www.stfelixgolf.ca. May–Oct. Green fees: $30.
- Summerside Golf Club (18-hole, par 72), Linkletter, Rte. 11 west of

Summerside; 436-2505; 1-877-505-2505; www.summersidegolf.com. May–Oct. Green fees: $29–42.

ANNE'S LAND
- Andersons Creek Golf Club (18-hole, par 72), Rte. 240, Stanley Bridge; 886-2222; 1-866-886-4422; www.andersonscreek.com. June–Oct. Green fees: $40–70.
- Darnley Greens Golf & Cottages (9-hole, par 27), Lower Darnley Rd., Darnley, off Rte. 20; 836-4355; 1-866-836-4355; www.darnleygreens.com. May–Oct. Green fees: $12.
- The Eagles Glenn Golf Course (18-hole, par 72), Rte. 6, Cavendish; 963-3600; 1-866-963-3600; www.eaglesglenn.com. May–Oct.
- Forest Hills Golf Course (9-hole, par 36), Cavendish, on Rte. 6; 963-2887; www.foresthills.ca. May–Oct.
- French River Golf Course (18-hole, par 67), Rte. 263, French River; 886-2098. April–Dec. Green fees: $14–20.
- Glasgow Hills Resort & Golf Club (18-hole, par 72), Rte. 13, New Glasgow; 621-2200; 1-866-621-2200; www.glasgowhills.com. May–Oct. Green fees: $50–70.
- * Green Gables Golf Course (18-hole, par 72), Cavendish in the Prince Edward Island National Park, on Rte. 6; 963-2488; www.greengablesgolf.com. May–Oct. Green fees: $30–55.
- Red Sands Golf Course (9-hole, par 32), Kerrytown Road, Rte. 107 off Rte. 6, Clinton; 886-3344; 1-877-886-3344; www.golfredsands.com. May–Oct.
- Rustico Resort Golf and Country Club (18-hole, par 73), Rustico, on Rte. 6; 1-800-GOLF-PEI (465-3734); 963-2909; www.rusticoresort.com. May–Oct. Green fees: $33, reduced rates in the afternoon.
- Serenity Valley Golf Course (9-hole, par 36), Howatt Road, Rte. 263, French River; 886-2098. May–Oct. Green fees: $12, children $6.
- Stanhope Golf and Country Club (18-hole, par 72), Stanhope, Rte. 25; 672-2842. May–Oct. Green fees: $45.

CHARLOTTE'S SHORE

- Clyde River Golf Club (18-hole, par 72), Clyde River, on Rte. 247; 675-2585; www.clyderiver golf.com. May–Oct. Green fees: $33.
- Countryview Golf Course (9-hole, par 36), Rte. 19, Fairview; 675-2800; www.countryviewgolf.com. May–Oct. Green fees: $22.50 (includes GST and range balls).
- Fox Meadow Golf & Country Club (18-hole, par 72), 167 Kinlock Road, Stratford; 569-4653; 1-877-569-8337; www.foxmeadow.pe.ca. Packages available.
- Glen Afton Golf Course (18-hole, par 70), Nine Mile Creek, on Rte. 19; 675-3000; www.glenaftongolf.com. May–Oct. Green fees: $32.
- Vistabay Golf Course (9-hole, par 34), Rte. 1A, Alexandra; 569-2252; www.vistabay.ca. May–Oct. Green fees: $12–20.

BAYS AND DUNES

- Beaver Valley Golf Club (18-hole, par 70), Martinvale; 583-3481; 1-877-351-GOLF (4653); www.peisland.com/beavervalley. May–Oct. Green fees: $27.
- * The Links at Crowbush Cove (18-hole, par 72), Lakeside, on Rte. 350, off Rte. 2; 1-800-235-8909 (for reservations); www.golflinkspei.com. May–Oct.
- Rollo Bay Greens (9-hole, par 35) Rte. 2, Rollo Bay; 687-1586; www.rollobaygreens.com. May–Oct. Green fees: $29.

HILLS AND HARBOURS

- Avondale Golf Course (18-hole, par 72), Vernon River; 651-4653; www.golfavondale.com. May–Oct.
- Belfast Highland Greens (9-hole, par 37), Eldon, off TransCanada Hwy.; 659-2794. May–Oct.
- * Brudenell River Golf Course (18-hole, par 72), in Brudenell Provincial Park, Roseneath, off Rte. 3; 1-800-235-8909 (for reservations); www.golflinkspei.com. May–Oct.
- * Canadian Golf Academy, at Brudenell River Resort, Roseneath; 652-2044;1-888-698-4653; www.canadiangolfacademy.ca. Programs for beginners to budding professionals, half-day to 3-day schools, private lessons, short games, and junior camps.
- Dundarave Golf Course (18-hole, par 72), in Brudenell River Resort, Roseneath, off Rte. 3; 1-800-235-8909 (for reservations); www.golflinkspei.com. May–Oct.
- Eagle's View Golf Course & Interpretive Centre (9-hole, par 36), Murray River; 962-4433; 1-866-962-4433; www.eagles viewgolf.com.
- Seal Cove Golf Course (9-hole, par 3), Murray Harbour North, on Rte. 17; 962-2745; www.sealcove golfcourse.ca. June–Sept. Green fees: $10–14.

BOATING AND SAILING

- Cardigan Sailing Charters, Cardigan; 583-2020; www.peisland .com/sailpei. Seasonal, 10 am–3 pm. Lobster lunch.
- Cruise Manada, Montague; 838-3444; 1-800-986-3444; www.tourpei.ca/seals/. Mid-May to Sept. 30. Four departures daily during July and Aug (call to reserve). Interpretive river cruise.
- Marine Adventures Seal Watching, Murray River; 962-2494; 1-800-496-2494; www.sealwatching.com. May 15–Sept. 30. Four departures daily from June to early Sept.
- Peake's Wharf Boat Tours, foot of Great George St., Charlottetown; 566-4458. June 1 to mid-Sept. Tour the Charlottetown Harbour. Four departures daily.
- Saga Sailing Adventures, Charlottetown Harbour; 672-1222; www.virtuo.com/sagasail. June–Sept., three departures daily.
- Sandhills and River Tours, 253 Matthews Lane, off Rte. 12 near Alberton; 853-2518; 1-888-272-2246; www.briarwood.ca. May–Oct. Pontoon boat tours.

Mariners may launch their own boats at concrete-slab haul-out sites or at slipways. Boats may be docked at Quartermaster Marine and the Yacht Club in Charlottetown, and at the Silver Fox Yacht Club in Summerside. Floating dock facilities are available in the Hills and Harbours region at the Municipal Marina in Montague, in

Murray River, Georgetown, Cardigan, Brudenell, and Murray Harbour. Wood Islands also offers a protected small-vessel harbour. Foreign pleasure craft are obliged to report to the nearest Canada Customs Office upon arrival. Charlottetown Customs: 628-4287, 94 Euston St., 1-800-461-9999.

CANOEING AND KAYAKING

With so much water around, it seems a shame not to go boating while on the Island. Beginners can go out for a quick paddle, while adventurers can chart their way through scenic river systems.

Some waterfront accommodations rent canoes, kayaks, and other vessels. Here are some other sources:

- By The Sea Kayaking, Victoria; 658-2572; 1-877-879-2572; www.bytheseakayaking.ca. June–Oct.
- Kingfisher Outdoors Inc., Leo F. Rossiter Angler's Park, Morell; 961-2080; morellcap.peicaps.org/kingfisher.html. Kayak tours on Morell River. Bike rentals. July 1 to mid-Sept.
- Malpeque Bay Sea Kayak Tours, Rte. 105 at Malpeque Bay; 432-0111; www.peikayak.ca. Tours and rentals. Open late June to Aug. 31.
- Outdoor Pursuits — Canoe Tours, Tracadie Harbour Wharf; 672-2000; www.pcpages.com/canoeing/travels.html. Explore the shoreline of Blooming Point in an eight-passenger replica of a Mi'kmaq open-water canoe. $20/paddler. Open June–Sept.
- Outside Expeditions, Brudenell, and North Rustico Harbour; 963-3366; 1-800-207-3899; www.get outside.com. Canoe and kayak rentals and excursions. June 1–Sept. 30.
- PEI Kayak Adventures and Rentals, Lower Montague; 838-4206; 1-888-838-4206; peikayakadventures.tripod.com. Mid-June to mid-Sept.
- St. Catherine's Cove Canoe Rental Inc., St. Catherine's; 675-2035; www3.pei.sympatico.ca/~ajlucock/canoeskayaks/HomePage.html. West off Rte. 9, on St. Catherines Road. Canoes and river kayaks.

Phone ahead for best times and tides. May–Sept.
- Venture Out Cycle and Kayak, 8 Main St., Souris; 687-1234; www.peisland.com/ventureout. Open May–Oct.
- Wagner's Outdoor Adventure, Rte. 174, Murray Road; 831-3079; www3.pei.sympatico.ca/eric.wagner. Canoe and kayak rentals. July–Sept. or by reservation.

CYCLING

There are few better ways to see Prince Edward Island than by bicycle. Sport PEI has information on cycling day tours, and Nimbus Publishing of Halifax has published *The PEI Cycle Guide*. Many inns, resorts and campgrounds rent bicycles. The following companies also rent bikes, sell package deals, and make other arrangements:

- Annandale Bicycle Rental & Repair Service, 274 Annandale Wharf Rd., Annandale; 583-2045/969-3099; bbcanada.com/8133. May 1–Oct. 30.
- Freewheeling Adventures, Cathy and Philip Guest, RR #1, Hubbards, NS; 857-3600; 1-800-672-0775; www.freewheeling.ca. End-to-end van-supported multi-day trips with guides, or custom trip-planning, and bicycle rentals.
- MacQueen's Island Tours — Bicycling Specialists, 430 Queen St., Charlottetown; 368-2453; 1-800-969-2822; www.macqueens.com. Independent and guided tours, bike and equipment rentals and repairs. Open year round.
- Outside Expeditions, North Rustico Harbour; 963-3366; 1-800-207-3899; www.getoutside.com. Self-guided and custom tours and rentals. June–Sept. 30.
- Paul's Bike Shop, 104 Chaisson Rd., St. Edward; 882-3750. Rentals and repair service available. Open year round.
- Plover Bike Rentals, St. Peters Bay; 961-3223. All sizes available. Open May 1–Oct. 31.
- Ricky's Bike Rentals, Montague Waterfront; 969-8826; 962-3085; www3.pei.sympatico.ca/~sds/fam/. A variety of bike styles and sizes for rent including hybrids,

mountain bikes, tandems, children's and buddy bikes. June–Oct.
- Smooth Cycle, 308 Queen St., Charlottetown; 566-5530; 1-800-310-6550; www.smoothcycle.com. Rentals, repairs and sales. Guided tours, route maps and shuttle service. Open year round.
- Trailside Inn, Café and Adventures, 109 Main St., Mount Stewart; 676-3130; 1-888-704-6595; www.trailside.ca. Quality bike rentals, route maps, gourmet picnics, and shuttle service, situated on the Confederation Trail. Open July and Aug., daily. Reduced hours in the off season.
- Venture Out Cycle and Kayak, 8 Main St., Souris; 687-1234; www.peisland.com/ventureout. May–Oct.
- Village Cycling Adventures, Rte. 11 at Hotel Village sur l'ocean, Mont-Carmel, 854-2227; 1-800-567-3228; www.hotelvillage.ca. Rentals and packages, designated highway tours, and cycling boutique.

FISHING

DEEP-SEA
- Aiden Doiron's Deep-Sea Fishing; www.peifishing.com. North Rustico; 963-3522/2288; 1-866-510-3474.
- Barry Doucette's Deep-Sea Fishing; Capts. Jamie & Jason Doucette, North Rustico; 963-2465/2611.
- Bearded Skipper's Deep-Sea Fishing; 963-2334/2525. Capt. Norman Peters, North Rustico Wharf.
- Beauty and the Beast Deep-Sea Fishing; www.gofishingpei.com. Capt. Chad Gallant, North Rustico; 963-3130/2085.
- Bob's Deep-Sea Fishing; www3.pei.simpatico.ca/~bobsdeepsea. Capt. Bob Doucette, North Rustico; 963-2666/2086.
- Dale's Deep-Sea Adventures; Capt. Dale Wall, Malpeque; 836-3393/439-3693.
- Graham's Deep-Sea Fishing; Capt. Marvin Graham, Stanley Bridge; 886-2491/2077; 439-1742.
- Joey Gauthier's Deep-Sea Fishing; www.joeysfishing.com.

Capt. Jamie Gauthier, Rusticoville; 963-2295/2191.
- MacKinnon's Deep-Sea Fishing; Capt. Lloyd MacKinnon, Red Head; 961-2873; 628-5343.
- MacNeill's Tuna & Deep-Sea Fishing; www.peitunacharters.com. Capt. Jeffrey L. MacNeill, North Lake; 357-2858.
- New London Wharf Deep-Sea Fishing; Capt. Wade Graham, New London Wharf; 886-2647/2124.
- Richard's Deep-Sea Fishing, Capt. Richard Watts, Covehead Harbour; 672-2376/2260.
- Salty Seas Deep-Sea Fishing; www.virtuo.com/salty. Capt. Lonnie MacDonald, Covehead Harbour; 672-3246/2681.
- Sea Run Deep-Sea Fishing; www.searun.ca. Capt. Ewen Clark, Malpeque; 888-7524.
- Tony's Tuna & Deep-Sea Fishing; www.tonystunafishing.ca. Capt. Tony MacDonald, North Lake; 357-2207.
- Wade's Deep-Sea Fishing; www.wadesdeepseafishing.com. Capt. Wade Gallant, North Rustico; 963-3064.

SPORT FISHING
- Ben's Lake; www.benslake.com. Ken and June Moyaert, Bellevue on Rte. 24; 838-2706; Trout fishing. Pay by the pound for catch.
- Mooney's Pond; Morell River Management Co-op, Rte. 22; 583-3144; Atlantic salmon, trout, equipment rental, guide service, interpretive centre and picnic area.

A.A. Macdonald Memorial Gardens, 168
Abrams Village, 52, 134
Abram-Village Handicraft Co-op, 103, 192
Acadian Festival. *See* L'Exposition Agricole et le Festival Acadien
Acadian Museum/Musée Acadien, 108, 127, 181, 187
Acadian Pioneer Village, 134
Acadians, 19, 130–31, 134–35, 140–42, 155
Agricultural exhibitions, 92, 134
Agricultural Museum, 43
Aiden Doiron's Deep-Sea Fishing, 201
Air Canada, 170
Airport, 170
Alberton, 40, 70, 129–30
Alberton Museum & Genealogy Centre, 109, 181, 187
Alien Registration Card, 171
All Saints Church, 85
Andersons Creek Golf Club, 65, 198
Annandale Bicycle Rental & Repair Service, 200
Anne of Green Gables attractions, 32–37, 93, 106–7, 108, 128, 143–45, 181
See also Montgomery, Lucy Maud, and L.M. Montgomery
Anne of Green Gables Chocolates, 195
Anne's Land, 136–43, 175–76, 179, 183–84, 190, 192, 193, 197, 198
Ann of Green Gables Museum at Silver Bush, 106, 144, 183
Annual Cymbria Music Festival, 188-89
Annual Mi'qmaq Pow-Wow, 190
Ardgowan National Historic Site of Canada, 184
Argyle Shore Provincial Park, 56, 150, 197
Art galleries, 195–96
Art Gallery of Tony Diodati, 195
Arts Guild, 95–96, 191
Atlantic Superstore Festival of Lights, 189
Atlantic Wind Test Site, 76, 131
Atwell Stone House, 84
Auburn Demonstration Woodlot, 74
Avis, car rental, 173
Avondale Golf Course, 64, 199
Avonlea Concert, 188
Avonlea—Village of Anne of Green Gables, 44, 145, 183

Baba's Lounge, 191
Back Road Folk Art, 103, 192
Bain Bird Count, 61
Barachois Inn, 141, 175
Barn Theatre, 95, 190
Barry Doucette's Deep-Sea Fishing, 201
Basin Head Beach, 55, 157
Basin Head Day Park, 197
Basin Head Fisheries Museum, 55, 96, 111–12, 157, 185
Bayberry Cliff Inn, 178
Bays and Dunes, 153–68, 177, 180–81, 185–86, 189–90, 191, 194, 197, 199
Beaches, 53–61, 131–32, 156–57, 158, 166
See also Camping
Beaconsfield Historic House, 110, 122, 184
Bear River beach, 158
Beaton/Leard House, 85
Beauty and the Beast Deep-Sea Fishing, 201
Beaver Valley Golf Course, 64, 199
Bedeque, 70, 148
Bedeque Crafts Centre, 192
Belcourt, Georges-Antoine, 83, 141
Belcourt Centre, 141–42

Belfast Highland Greens, 64, 199
Belmont Provincial Park, 196
Belvedere Golf Club, 64
Ben's Lake, 43, 186, 201
Bideford Parsonage Museum, 108, 128, 181
Birding, 58–61, 130, 154–55, 167
Black Marsh Nature Trail, 76
Blooming Point Beach, 55, 197
Blue Mussel Café, 179
Boat tours, 199
Bob's Deep-Sea Fishing, 201
Bothwell beach, 157
Bottle Houses/Maison de Bouteilles, 134, 181-82
Boughton Bay, 197
Boutique A-Point, 192
Boutique à Point, 103
Bowler, George, 86
Brackley Beach, 39, 54, 139, 197
Brackley Beach Drive-In Theatre and Mini Golf, 46, 183
Breadalbane, 149
Briarcliffe Inn, 176
Bridgetown, 155
British Car Days Across the Bridge, 91, 188
Brookvale Demonstration Woodlot, 74, 152
Brookvale Provincial Ski Park, 152, 197
Brookvale Nordic Ski trails, 59
Brookvale Provincial Forest, 76
Brothers Two, 178, 190
Broughton Island, 154
Brown, George, 23
Brudenell River Campground, 167
Brudenell River Provincial Park, 40, 57, 166, 197
Brudenell River Resort. *See* Rodd Brudenell River Resort
Brudenell River Golf Course, 64, 65–66, 167, 199
Bubbling Springs/Farmlands Trail, 39, 61, 137
Buchanan, Alan, 95
Budget, car rental, 173
Buffaloland Provincial Park, 165, 186
Burden, P. John, 81
Bus service, 170
Buzz magazine, 190
By the Sea Kayaking, 200

Cable Head, 158
Cabot Beach Provincial Park, 44, 55, 197
Caledonia Club of PEI Annual Highland Games, 90, 190
Campbell, Annie, 29
Campbell, John, 29
Campbell's Cove, 158
Campbells Cove Provincial Park, 197
Campbellton, 70, 196
Camping, 128, 196–98
Canada Customs Office, Charlottetown, 199
Canada Day, 88
Canadian Golf Academy, 65, 199
Canoe Cove, 150
Canoeing and kayaking, 129, 151, 167, 200
Cape Bear, 60, 164
Cape Bear Lighthouse & Marconi Museum, 111, 186
Cape Tryon, 60
Cape Wolfe, 132
Capital Area Recreation Inc., 47, 184–85
Capture PEI Writers & Photographers Workshops & Tours, 189
Cardigan, 154

Cardigan Craft Centre and Tea Room, 98, 194
Cardigan Lobster Suppers, 51, 180
Cardigan River Heritage Centre & Marina, 185
Cardigan River Inn, 154, 177
Cardigan Sailing Charters, 199
Cardigan Water Science Centre, 160
Carmichael House, 117–18
Car rentals, 173
Cavendish, 38–39, 142
    activities for children, 44–45,142–43, 145
    cottages, 38
    L.M. Montgomery at, 28, 30, 32–33, 34, 44
Cavendish Beach, 28, 54, 197
Cavendish Figurines Ltd., 193
Cedar Dunes Provincial Park, 56, 76, 132, 196
Cedar's Eatery, 180
Ceili at the Irish Hall, 189
Ceilidh at the Corner, 190
Celtic Festival, 90, 187
Celtic Gift Shop, 192
Central Chimney House, 118
Centre Expo-Festival Centre, 52, 91, 178
Charlotte's Shore, 146–52, 176–77, 180, 184–85, 189, 191, 193–94, 197, 199
Charlottetown
    boardwalk, 73–74
    pubs and taverns, 191
    walking tour, 114–23
Charlottetown Conference, 22–23, 26, 87–88
Charlottetown Driving Park, 47
Charlottetown Farmers' Market, 101, 193
Charlottetown Festival, 88, 191
Charlottetown Festival's Young Company, 46
Cheese Lady's Gouda, 195
Chelton Beach Provincial Park, 56, 147–48
Chez-Yvonne, 179
Church of Christ, 86
Church of Our Lady of Mont Carmel, 134
Church of St. Phillip and St. Jacques, 134
Church of St. Simon and St. Jude, 80, 130
Church of the Immaculate Conception, 80–81
Cinnamon Tree, 192
Claddagh Room, 180
Clyde River Golf Club, 64, 199
College of Piping and Celtic Performing Arts of Canada, 43, 90, 102, 127, 182, 187
Collings, Donna, 111
Confederation Bridge, 170
Confederation Centre Art Gallery, 195
Confederation Centre Library, 110
Confederation Centre of the Arts, 46, 88, 185
Confederation Players Walking Tours, 110, 185
Confederation Trail, 70, 71, 72, 77–79, 127, 153–54
Connors, Stompin' Tom, 131
Cooper Rebellion, 155
Cornfest Festival, 91, 189
Cornwall, 150
Countryview Golf Club, 64, 199
Cousins Shore, 197
Covehead Harbour, 60
Covehead Wharf, 39
Cow River, 158
Cows, 47
Crafts, 97–103, 192–95
Crapaud, 152
Crapaud Exhibition, 92, 189
Creamer, Bernard, 81
Cruise Manada, 199

Culture Crafts Co-op, 135, 192
Cundall, Henry, 122
Currency exchange, 170–71
Customs duty, 171
Cycling, 68–72, 151, 200–1

Dairy Bar, 102
Dale's Deep-Sea Fishing, 201
Dalton, Charles, 130
Dalvay Beach, 54, 197
Dalvay-by-the-Sea Inn, 175, 179
Dalvay (residence), 137–38
D'Arcy McGee's, 191
Darnley, 39
Darnley Greens Golf & Cottages, 198
Delta Prince Edward, 176, 180, 189
Demonstration woodlot trails, 74
Desable, 151
Details Past and Present, 195
Dewar, Brenda, 167
Dewar, Edgar, 167
Dewhurst, Colleen, 40, 155
Dining, 178–81
    children, 47–48
    lobster suppers, 49–52
Doctor's Inn, 128, 174, 178
Domm, Jeffrey, 61
Doucet House, 141
Duchess of Kent Inn, 176
Dundarave Golf Course, 63, 64, 199
Dundas, 155
Dundas Ploughing Match, 155
Dundee Arms, 176, 191
Dunes Café and Studio Gallery, 99, 140, 179, 193
Dunes Studio Gallery, 195–96
Dunollie Travel Park, 150
Dunrovin Lodge, 151
Dyed in the Wool, 193
Dynasty Restaurant, 166, 181

Eagles Glenn Golf Course, 65, 198
Eagle's View Golf Course & Interpretive Centre, 61, 65, 75, 199
East Point, 60, 79, 157–58
East Point Lighthouse Craft Shop, 99, 194
East Point Lighthouse & Welcome Centre, 105, 112, 186
Eddie May Murder Mystery Dinner Theatre, 190
Eddie May Murder Mystery (Piazza Joe's), 191
Edenhurst Inn, 121, 176
Eliot River Dream Park, 48
Ellen's Creek Gallery, 196
Ellen's Creek Wildlife Management Area, 74
Ellerslie Shellfish Museum, 108, 182
Elmira, 157
Elmira Railway Museum & Miniature Railway, 45, 112, 157, 185–86
Elmwood Heritage Inn, 176
Emerald Junction Irish Festival, 91, 148, 189
Enmore, 133
Eptek Art & Culture Centre, 108, 182, 196
Eptek National Exhibition Centre, 126
Estuary Interpretive Centre and Shops, 159
Evangeline Area Bluegrass & Oldtime Music Festival, 187
Évangéline Tourist Information Centre, 134

Factory Outlet stores, 46
Fairview, 150
Fairy Trails, 76

Fanningbank. *See* Government House
Fantazmagoric Museum of the Strange and Unusual, 44, 183
Farmers' Bank of Rustico Museum, 83, 141, 183
Feast Dinner Theatre (Brothers Two), 190
Feast Dinner Theatre (Rodd Charlottetown), 191
Ferry service, 156, 161, 170
Festival of Lights, 88
Festival Port-La-Joie de Charlottetown, 90, 189
Festival Rendez-vous Rustico Festival, 90, 188
Festivals, and events, 87–92, 187–92
Fête Roma, 91, 190
Fiddlers and Followers Weekend, 91, 188
"Fisherman's Church," 157
Fisherman's Haven, 196
Fisherman's Wharf, 51–52, 142, 179
Fishing, 43, 167, 201
Fitzroy Hall, 176
Folk Art Store, 102
Forest Hills Golf Course, 64, 198
Fort Amherst/Port-La-Joye National Historic Site, 111, 150, 197
Fortune Bay, 40
Fortune Peninsula, 155
Founders' Hall—Canada's Birthplace Pavilion, 110, 185
Foxley River Demonstration Woodlot, 74
Fox Meadow Golf & Country Club, 64, 65, 199
Fox raising, 130
Free Church of Scotland, 151
Freewheeling Adventures, 200
French River Golf Course, 198
Froggies Used Clothing Store, 46, 193
Frosty Treat, 47
Fry, Dana, 63
Fyfe's Landing, 179

Gahan House, 180
Gainsford House, 118–19
Gallery in the Guild, 196
Garden of the Gulf Museum, 111, 166, 186
Gateway Village, 48, 101, 147, 185
Gaudreau Fine Woodworking, 100, 193
Gay & Lesbian Pride Festival, 92, 189
Georgetown, 167–68
Georgetown Packers, 168
Gillis' Drive-In, 166, 181
Glasgow Hills Resort & Golf Club, 64, 198
Glasgow Road Gallery, 196
Glen Afton Golf Course, 64, 199
Glenroy Gallery, 194
Gold Cup and Saucer Race, 92
Golf, 167, 198–99
Goods and Services Tax (GST), 172
Government House, 110–11, 116–17, 185
Graham's Deep-Sea Fishing, 201
Great George, 176
Green Gables Golf Course, 64, 198
Green Gables—Prince Edward Island National Park of Canada, 143–44, 183
Green Park Provincial Park, 56, 196
Green Park Shipbuilding Museum and Historic Yeo House, 108, 127–28, 182
Greenwich, 39, 55, 158–59
Greenwich Beach, 40, 197
Greenwich dunes, 158–59
Greenwich Dunes Trail, 76
Greenwich Interpretation Centre, 186

Greenwich National Park, 159
Griffon Dining Room, 180
Gulf of St. Lawrence, 56, 157–58

Happy Red's Train Station, 102, 193
Harbourfront Jubilee Theatre, 190
Harbour Hippo, 46–47, 185
Harness Racing Entertainment Centre, 185
Harris, Elmer, 155
Harris, William Critchlow, 82, 95, 122, 127
Hedgerow, 95
Hernewood Dining Room, 178
Hertz, car rental, 173
High Bank, 164
Hiking, 73–79, 151, 156, 167
Hillhurst Inn, 123, 176
Hills and Harbours, 161–68, 178, 181, 186–87, 190, 191, 195, 197–98, 199
Hillsborough River Eco-Centre, 160, 186
Historic Site at the Green, 182
History Room, 187
Hogan, Geoff, 61
Holman Homestead, 127
Home Accents, 101, 194
Homestead Trail, 75
Horse shows, 92
Hostel East @ A Place to Stay Inn, 174
Hostels, 174
Hotel Village sur l'Océan, 174, 178
Howards Cove, 132
Howe Bay, 155
Hrabi, Blaine, 81
Hunter River, 149
Hurdzan, Michael, 63

Indian Art and Craft of North America, 103, 192
Indian River Festival, 89–90, 95, 145, 188
Inn at Bay Fortune, 156, 177, 180
Inn at St. Peters, 159, 177, 180
Inn at Spry Point, 155, 177, 180
International Fox Museum and Hall of Fame Inc., 107–8, 127, 182
Irish festivals, 90–91
Irish settlements, 148
Irvings Cape Beach, 197
Island Chocolates, 151, 195
Island Crafts Shop, 101, 194
Island Rally, 91, 188

Jacques Cartier Park Provincial Park, 130, 196
Jansons, Peter, 99, 140
Jazz Air, 170
Jeffrey, Kerras, 103
Joey Gauthier's Deep-Sea Fishing, 201
Johnson Shore Inn, 158, 177
Johnston's beach, 158
Jubilee Theatre, 95

Kayaking. *See* Canoeing and kayaking
Keir Memorial Museum, 107, 183
Kensington Train Station, 107, 183–84
Kindred Spirits, 34
Kingfisher Outdoors Inc., 200
Kings Castle Provincial Park, 198
Kings Playhouse, 191
King's Playhouse, 167
King's Theatre, 167
Kinkora, 148–49
Kinnear's, 168
Koleszar Pottery, 98, 195
Kortgaard, Robert, 95

La Cuisine A Mémé Dinner-Theatre, 190
Lakeview Loyalist Resort, 174, 178–79
Landing Oyster House and Pub, 128, 191
Landmark Café, 94, 180
La Région Evangéline, 103, 134
Larry Gorman Folk Festival, 128, 188
L'Auberge du Village, 134
Launching Peninsula, 154
Leard, Herman, 30
Le Cajun Jacques Restaurant, 178
Lefurgey Cultural Centre, 196
Lennox Island Aboriginal Ecotourism
   Centre, 108–9, 128, 182
L'Étoile de Mer, 134
Le Village de l'Acadie, 134
Lewis, William, 85
L'Exposition Agricole et le Festival
   Acadien, 92, 134, 188
Lighthouses, 45, 104–5, 109, 111, 148
Linkletter Inn and Convention Centre, 174
Linkletter Park Provincial Park, 196
Links at Crowbush Cove, 63, 64, 160, 177,
   199
Little Harbour beach, 157
Little Mermaid, 126
Little Sands, 164
L.M. Montgomery Festival, 34
L.M. Montgomery Institute, 37
Lobsters
   outlets, 52, 168
   suppers, 49–52, 145, 154, 158
Lobster Shanty—Atlantic Resorts
   Restaurant & Lounge, 166, 178
Lobster Shanty Motel & Restaurant, 181
Lodging, 174–78
Log Cabin Arts & Crafts, 98, 194
Long Pond Loop, 39
Longworth Home, 123
Lord Selkirk Provincial Park, 90, 198
Lowden House, 120–21

MacAusland's Woollen Mill, 103, 132–33,
   182
MacDonald, Alexander, 138
Macdonald, Chester Cameron, 31
Macdonald, Ewan, 31, 35
Macdonald, Hugh, 31
Macdonald, John A., 23
MacDonald, Rob, 96
Macdonald, Stuart, 31, 35
MacKinnon's Deep-Sea Fishing, 201
MacLeod, Carol, 98
MacLeod, John, 98
MacLeod's Beach, 198
MacNaught History Centre & Archives,
   107, 187
Macneill, Alexander, 28, 31
Macneill, Clara Woolner, 28–29
Macneill, Lucy Woolner, 28–29
MacNeill's Tuna & Deep-Sea Fishing, 201
Macphail House. See Sir Andrew Macphail
   Homestead
Macphail Woods, 43, 59, 74
MacQueen's Island Tours—Bicycling
   Specialists, 200
Malpeque, 39, 44, 107, 145
Malpeque Bay Sea Kayak Tours, 200
Malpeque Community Centre Ceilidhs, 96
Maplehurst Properties, 178
Marine Adventures Seal Watching, 199
Maritime Union, 22–23, 26
Matthew House Inn, 156, 177
Mavor's Bistro and Bar, 180

McLean House, 81
McLellan, John, 86
McRae, Mary Ann, 29
Meloche, Frans-Xavier, 80
Memories Gift Shop, 100, 193
Merchantman Pub, 180
Mermaid Art Gallery and Framing, 196
Metric system, 172
Midgell Centre, Morell Post Office, 174
Mill River Fun Park, 132, 182
Mill River Provincial Golf Course, 63, 64, 198
Mill River Provincial Park, 63, 132, 196
Millstream Family Restaurant, 179
Milltown Cross, 165
Miminegash Pond, 196
Miminegash, 131
Miscouche, 127
Miss Elly's Genteel Gifts & Stuff, 97, 195
Montague, 40, 51, 98, 111, 162, 166–67
Mont-Carmel, 134
Montgomery, Donald, 29
Montgomery, Hugh John, 28–29
Montgomery, Lucy Maud
   birthplace, 106, 184
   Cavendish Home, 184
   death, 35
   early life, 28–30
   education, 29–30
   Festival, 188
   Heritage Museum, 106, 184
   marriage, 31, 35
   private life, 25–36, 28–31
   scholarly interest in, 35–37
   writings, 30, 31, 32, 33, 35
   See also L.M. Montgomery
Monticello Ceilidhs, 158, 189
Mooney's Pond, 201
Moon Shadow Mementos, 97
Moonsnail Soapworks and Nature Store,
   101, 194
Morell, 160
Mount Pleasant, 133
Mount Stewart, 61, 160
Municipal Marina, 199
Murray Harbour, 164
Murray Islands, 164
Murray River, 92, 164
My Mother's Country Inn, 175
Myron's Restaurant and Pub, 191

Nail Pond, 197
Natural History Society, 61
Naturally Yours, 98, 194
Naufrage, 158
Neil Bennett Autumn Birding Classic, 61
New Glasgow Country Gardens, 51
New Glasgow Lobster Suppers, 51, 179
New Harmony Demonstration Woodlot, 59,
   74
New London, 28, 38, 39
New London lighthouse, 104
New London Wharf Deep-Sea Fishing, 201
Night Life, 190–92
Nordic Ski Trails, 76
North Cape, 60, 124–35, 74–75, 178–79,
   181–83, 187–88, 190, 191, 192–93,
   196–97, 198
North Cape Interpretive Centre, 109
North Cape lighthouse, 109, 131
North Cape Nature and Technology in
   Perfect Harmony, 109, 182
North Lake beach, 158
Northport, 41

Northport Pier Inn, 130, 174, 178
North River, 149–50
North Rustico Beach, 38, 197
North Side, 158
Northumberland Beach Provincial Park, 163, 198
Northumberland Ferries, 170
Northumberland Provincial Fisheries Festival, 52, 92, 189
Northumberland Strait, 56, 158, 163
Northwest Airlines, 170

Off Broadway Café, 180
Official Island Store, 194
Olde Dublin Pub, 191
Old General Store, 97, 164, 195
Old Home Week/PEI Provincial Exhibition, 47, 92, 189
Old Mill Craft Company, 103, 192
O'Leary, 132
Orient Hotel, 151, 176
Orwell Corner Historic Village, 43, 111, 164, 165, 186
Oulton, Robert, 130
Outdoor Pursuits—Canoe Tours, 200
Outside Expeditions, 200
Oyster Festival, 128

Paderno Cookware Factory and Outlet Store, 195
Panmure Island Cultural Grounds, 165–66
Panmure Island Lighthouse, 104–5, 186
Panmure Island Provincial Park, 55, 198
Park Corner, L.M. Montgomery at, 29, 33–34
Passports, 171
Path of Our Forefathers Trails, 76
Paul's Bike Shop, 200
Peake, James, 122
Peake's Quay Restaurant and Bar, 191
Peake's Wharf, 194
Peake's Wharf Boat Tours, 199
PEI Bluegrass & Oldtime Music Festival, 89, 189
PEI Collection, UPEI Robertson Library, 187
PEI/Eastern Canadian Oyster Shucking Championships, 89
PEI/Eastern Chowder Championships, 89
PEI International Shellfish Festival, 86, 91, 189
PEI Kayak Adventures and Rentals, 200
PEI Potato Blossom Festival, 91, 188
PEI Provincial Exhibition, 92
PEI St. Rod Association Show 'N' Shine, 91, 190
PEI T-Shirts, 195
PEI Wine Festival, 189
Penderosa Beach, 39
"Phantom Ship," 150
Pier Restaurant, 179
Pigot Trail, 61, 75
Pilot House, 150
Pinette Provincial Park, 57, 198
Pinette Raceway, 186
Pinette Studios, 196
Plough the Waves Centre, 195
Plover Bike Rentals, 200
Point Prim Chowder House, 181
Point Prim Lighthouse, 85–86, 111, 186
Pooles Corner, 154, 160
Pope, William Henry, 148, 184
Portage, 129
Port-La-Joye-Fort Amherst National

Historic Site of Canada, 185
Prince County Exhibition, 92, 188
Prince Edward Island
    climate, 172–73
    and Confederation, 22–23, 26–27
    economy, 9
    fauna, 17–18
    flora, 15–16
    geography, 12–15
    identity, 22–26
    "Land Question," 8–9, 19–20, 22–23
    medical services, 173
    provincial forests, 79
    settlement, 18–20
    speed limits, 173
    time zone, 172
    visitor guide, 172
Prince Edward Island Marathon, 189
Prince Edward Island Museum and Heritage Foundation, 78, 111
Prince Edward Island National Park of Canada, 39, 53–55, 60, 61, 75–76, 106, 136–39, 184, 197
Prince Edward Island Potato Museum, 109, 132, 182
Prince Edward Island Preserve Co., 51, 179, 193, 195
Prince Edward Island Railway, 153
Prince Edward Island Studio Tour Weekend, 187
Prince of Wales College, 86
Prince William Dining Room, 179
Product Tours and Local Manufacturers, 195
Promenade Acadienne Boardwalk, 135
Province House (legislature), 115–16
Province House National Historic Site of Canada, 46, 110, 115, 185
Provincial Plowing Match and Agricultural Fair, 190
Provincial Sales Tax (PST), 171–72
Public Archives and Records Office, 110, 187
Public transportation, 172
Putnam, Graham, 96

Quality Inn—Garden of the Gulf, 174–75
Quartermaster Marine, 201

Rachael's Restaurant, 179
Rainbow Valley, 44, 142, 184
Rainnie, Matt, 96
Rankin, Allan, 95
Reading Well Bookstore, 101–2, 194
Red Head Harbour, 160
Red Point Provincial Park, 157, 197
Red Sands Golf Course, 64, 198
Red Stone Restaurant, 180-81
Richard's Deep-Sea Fishing, 201
Richmond, 135
Richmond Dairy Bar, 47
Rick's Fish 'N' Chips and Seafood House, 159, 181
Ricky's Bike Rentals, 200–1
Ripley's Believe It Or Not! Museum, 44, 184
Robinsons Island, 54, 197
Rock Barra–Hermanville area, 158
Rocky Point, 150
Rodd Brudenell River Resort, 178, 181, 199
Rodd Charlottetown, 176, 191
Rodd Crowbush Golf & Beach Resort, 160, 177

Rodd Mill River Resort, 56–7, 132, 175, 178
Rodd Resort. *See* Rodd Mill River Resort
Rollo Bay Fiddle Festival, 156, 189
Rollo Bay Greens, 64, 199
Rollo Bay Inn, 177
Rollo Bay scenic lookout, 156
Roma at Three Rivers, 166, 186
Roseneath Bed & Breakfast, 167, 178
Rossignol Estate Winery, 97, 163, 187
Routes for Nature and Health, 74
Royalty Oaks Natural Area, 74
Rubio, Mary, 35, 36
Rum running, 139
Rustico Harbour Fishery Museum and Gift Shop, 112, 142, 184
Rustico region, 140–42
Rustico Resort Golf and Country Club, 62, 64, 198
Rusty Pelican Café, 166, 181

Saga Sailing Adventures, 199
Sailing, 199
Sailor's Hope Bog, 155
St. Andrew's Chapel, 160, 186
St. Ann's Church Lobster Suppers, 51, 179
St. Ann's Sunday Celebrations, 188
St. Augustine's Church, 141
St. Catherine's Cove, 151
St. Catherine's Cove Canoe Rental Inc., 200
St. Felix Golf & Country Club, 64, 198
St. James Gate, 191
St. Malachy's Catholic Church, 148
St. Margarets Lobster Suppers, 158, 181
St. Mary's Church, 82–83, 89–90, 95, 145
St. Nicholas, 135
St. Patrick's Church, 127
St. Peters Bay Courthouse Theatre, 159, 191
St. Peters Bay Craft and Giftware, 159, 194
St. Peters Landing, 186
St. Peters village, 158, 159
St. Peter's Wild Blueberry Festival, 91, 159, 190
St. Raphael, 135
St-Chrysostome, 197
Sally's Beach Provincial Park, 197
Salty Seas Deep-Sea Fishing, 201
Sandhills and River Tours, 199
Sandscript, 193
Sandspit, 44, 184
Sauvé, Eugene, 94
Savage Harbour Beach, 197
Scenic Heritage Roads, 79, 156
Scott, George C., 40
Seacow Head lighthouse, 148
Seacow Pond, 131
Seal Cove, 198
Seal Cove Golf Course, 199
Sea Run Deep-Sea Fishing, 201
Seasway Hammock Shop, 193
Seaview, 39
Seaweed Pie Café & Irish Moss Interpretive Centre, 131, 182
Selkirk Room, 180
Serenity Valley Golf Course, 198
Shaw's Hotel and Cottages, 139, 175, 179
Shining Waters Country Inn and Cottages, 175
Shining Waters Tea Room, 144, 179
Shipbuilding, 139
Shipwright Inn, 177
Shipyard Market, 126, 182
Shopping, 46, 192–96

Shoreline Lobster Pattern Sweaters, 192
Showcase Art Sales and Rentals, 196
Showcase Confederation Centre of the Arts, 194
Silver Fox, Summerside 126, 191–92
Silver Fox Inn, 175
Silver Fox Yacht Club, Summerside, 199
Simple Comforts B&B and Bicycle Hostel, 174
Simpson, Edwin, 30, 31
Sir Andrew Macphail Homestead, 74, 111, 164–65, 181, 187
Sirenella Ristorante, 180
Sloane, Samuel, 122
Smith, Erskine, 95
Smith, Isaac, 86, 111, 116
Smooth Cycle, 201
SMT (Eastern) Ltd, 170
Smuggling. *See* Rum running
Souris, 40, 156
Souris Beach Provincial Park, 197
Souris Causeway, 60
Souris Regatta Festival of the Sea, 91–2, 189–90
South Lake beach, 157
South Rustico Beach, 38
South Side, 157
Spinnakers' Landing, 102, 127, 182, 192
Spit 'N Image, 195
Standard Time, 24–25
Stanfield, Charles E., 152
Stanhope Beach, 39, 54
Stanhope by the Sea Resort & Inn, 175–76
Stanhope Golf and Country Club, 64, 198
Stanhope Lane Beach, 197
Stanley Bridge, 38
Stanley Bridge Country Resort, 176, 179, 190
Stanley Bridge Studios, 100, 193
Stanley Pottery and Weaving Studio and Shop, 102, 149, 194
Stetson, Kent, 96
Stewart, Robert Bruce, 84
Stillwaters Fine Foods & Spirits, 181
Stirling, David, 121
Storytelling, 95
Strathgartney Homestead, 84
Strathgartney Nature Trail, 76
Strathgartney Provincial Park, 151, 197
Studio Gallery, 196
Studio Tour Weekend, 92
Summerfield, 70
Summerside, 126–27
Summerside Golf Club, 64, 198
Summerside Highland Gathering, 90, 187
Summerside Lobster Carnival, 47, 52, 91, 188

Tango (Air Canada), 170
Tanton, Percy, 81
Taxes, 171–72
Taxi service, 170
Tea Hill Beach, 56
Tea Hill Provincial Park, 197
Ten Thousand Villages crafts, 102
Theatre, 93–96
Thirsty's Roadhouse, 192
Tignish, 130–31
Tignish Cultural Centre, 130, 183
Tignish Heritage Inn, 175
Tignish Irish Moss Festival, 188
Tignish Treasures Gift Shop, 103, 192
Toll, Confederation Bridge, 170

Tony's Tuna & Deep-Sea Fishing, 201
Townshend Woodlot, 75, 156
Toy Factory, 100, 143, 149–50, 193
Trailside Inn Café and Adventures, 160, 181, 201
Trout River Pottery, 100, 193
Trout River Trail, 76
Tryon Marsh, 152
Tryon River, 152
Tyne Valley, 40, 128
Tyne Valley Oyster Festival, 52, 91, 188
Tyne Valley Studio, 128

Union Corner, 134
Union Corner Provincial Park, 197
Union Corner School House Museum, 183
University of PEI, 37, 61, 74, 187

Valleyfield Demonstration Woodlot, 59, 74
Venture Out Cycle and Kayak, 201
Victoria, 40
Victoria Beach Provincial Park, 197
Victoria-by-the-Sea, 56, 101, 151–52
Victoria Playhouse, 93–94, 95, 152
Victoria Playhouse Festival, 191
Victoria Provincial Park, 151
Victoria Row, 119–20, 191
Victoria Village Inn & Restaurant, 151, 177, 180
Victoria West, 133
Village Cycling Adventures, 201
Village Emporium, 97
Village Pottery, 100, 193
Vista Bay Golf Course, 199
V'nez Chou Nous Acadian Dinner Theatre, 190

Wade's Deep-Sea Fishing, 201

Wagner's Outdoor Adventure, 200
Walking tour, 114–23
    See also Hiking
Waterston, Elizabeth, 35, 36
Weale, David, 95
Wellington Demonstration Woodlot, 74
Wendell Boyle Celtic Festival, 190
West Point, 60
West Point Lighthouse Craft Shop, 192–93
West Point Lighthouse Festival & Boat Races, 91–92, 188
West Point Lighthouse Inn, Restaurant & Museum, 41, 45, 56, 103, 105, 132, 175, 179, 183
West Prince, 129, 131–32
West Prince Gallery, 128
Whim Inn, 166, 181
White Sands, 164
Widows on the Water Café, 181
Wildlife, 17–18, 45–46
Wind and Reef Restaurant, 131, 179
Windows on the Water Café, 40, 166
Windsurfing, 129
Wine festivals, 91, 189
Wood Islands lighthouse, 111
Wood Islands Provincial Park, 198
Woodlands Trails, 75
Woodleigh Highland Games, 188
Woodleigh Replicas and Gardens, 44, 184
Woods Island Lighthouse & Interpretive Museum, 48, 187
Woolly Wares, 98, 195
Wyatt Centre, 126
Wyatt Heritage Properties, 107, 183

Yacht Club (Charlottetown), 199
Yachting. See Sailing
Yeo House, 82, 108, 127–28

PHOTO CREDITS:

Keith Vaughan is a Halifax-based photographer who has won many prizes and medals at home as well as in national and international competition. His other Formac publications include *Lunenburg: Then and Now*; *The Nova Scotia Colourguide*; and *Maritime Flavours*. All photographs are by Keith Vaughan, except where noted below.

Legend: T=top; M=middle; B=bottom

Julian Beveridge: 2M; 49B; 52M; 55M; 102T; 143M; 150M; 160T. Paul Blacquiere: 112B. Martin Caird: 2B; 12B; 13B; 15B; 17B; 20T; 30T; 31T; 32T; 33T; 36T & M; 37B; 40B; 143T. Central Development Corporation: 140B; 142T. Charlottetown Driving Park: 92T. Confederation Centre of the Arts: 46T (Barrett and MacKay Photography); 93B (Barrett and MacKay Photography); 96. John Davison: 45T. Brenda and Edward Dewar: 90T; 167M&B; 168T & M. Enterprise PEI: 67T (Barrett and MacKay Photography); 45B (Jack LeClair); 51T (Bruce Patton); 48B (John Sylvester); 69B (John Sylvester). Carter Jeffery: 141T & B. Dan Kennedy: 43B; 111B. Kensington/Town of Kensington Staff: 107. Daphne Large/Village Pottery: 100B. Tom LeClair: 111T. Jocelyne Lloyd: 159B. Jim Lorimer: 9T; 38B; 42B; 46B. Kent MacDonald: 10T; 62. Shane MacDougall: 83B. Wendy MacGregor: 2M; 44B. Old Home Week: 87; 97T. Marie Peters: 50B; 52B; 105B; 142M. Reginald Porter: 81T & M. PEI Museum and Heritage Foundation: 108B; 112T. Prince Edward Island National Park/Parks Canada: 28B. Summerside/The City of Summerside Collection: 11B; 47T; 108T; 126. John Sylvester: 4B; 8; 42T; 88M; 90M; 106B; 153T; 157T. Victoria Playhouse: 94B. Len Wagg: 26. John C. Watson: 132M. Debra Wentzell-Hannams: 9B; 27; 109; 110; 114; 115T; 119B; 120T. David Wong: 89T; 93T; 95T.

Maps courtesy of Tourism PEI, except for Charlottetown walking tour: courtesy of Image Works PEI Inc.
Maps edited and altered by Meghan Collins and Peggy McCalla.